MW00979687

LAW OF THE WEB

WEB

A Field Guide to Internet Publishing

2003 Edition

Law of the Web: A Field Guide to Internet Publishing
By Jonathan D. Hart

"Jonathan Hart's *Law of the Web* is a rare blend of scholarship and clarity, invaluable not only to the legal community but to anyone engaged in—or contemplating engaging in—online publishing. *Law of the Web* maps the still-evolving legal landscape of the Internet with information, perspective and wisdom on issues including intellectual property, free speech, privacy and electronic commerce. It is, quite simply, an indispensable resource for the Internet."

— Rich Jaroslovsky, former Managing Editor of *The Wall Street Journal Online* and founding President of the Online News Association.

"The legal system on a national and international scale moves very slowly in contrast to developments of information storage, retrieval and distribution on the Internet which all is on fast forward. Therefore, the *Law of the Web: A Field Guide to Internet Publishing* is a very much needed and timely guide and reference source on the legal issues for publishers and lawyers. The comprehensive text is supported and supplemented with an excellent choice of case summaries that help the reader understand the principles of the law in e-publishing. From the basic copyright issues through to defamation, trademark, jurisdiction through to such key topics as commercial email, data collection, privacy, and commercial code for computer information transactions are all supported by case studies which makes this volume an essential and appropriate resource. It is indeed THE legal guide to Internet publishing."

— Robert E. Baensch
Director, Center for Publishing
School of Continuing and Professional Studies
New York University

"Thorough and thoughtful, the Field Guide captures both settled and emerging legal issues surrounding Internet publishing. Lawyer and layman alike will want it close at hand."

— Andy Merdek, General Counsel, Cox Enterprises, Inc.

"*Law of the Web* is a valuable resource for any journalist attempting to sort through the body of new law developing around news as it is distributed on the Internet instead of through your father's newspaper or television set. Jon Hart guides us ably through case after hazy case with clarifying explanations."

— Doug Feaver, Executive Editor
washingtonpost.com

"Jon Hart has produced a tremendous resource text for anyone interested in knowing what are the important cases and controversies presented by the Internet. This well indexed compendium allows the user to get a handle on the issues that need to be addressed in operating on the web."

— Sandy Baron, Executive Director of the Media Law Resource Center

LAW OF THE WEB

A Field Guide to Internet Publishing

2003 Edition

Jonathan D. Hart

Dow, Lohnes & Albertson, PLLC
1200 New Hampshire Avenue, N.W.
Suite 800
Washington, D.C. 20036-6802
(202) 776-2819
jhart@dowlohnes.com
www.dowlohnes.com

BRADFORD PUBLISHING COMPANY
Denver, Colorado

Library of Congress Cataloging-in-Publication Data

Hart, Jonathan D.
  Law of the Web : a field guide to Internet publishing / by Jonathan D.
Hart.-- 2003 ed.
    p. cm.
  ISBN 1-883726-19-0
  1. Internet--Law and legislation--United States. 2. Web
publishing--United States. 3. Intellectual property--United States. 4.
Freedom of the press--United States. I. Title.

  KF390.5.C6H373 2003
  343.7309'944--dc21

                              2003008179

This book, *Law of the Web: A Field Guide to Internet Publishing, 2003 Edition,* is intended to provide general information with regard to the subject matter covered. It is not meant to provide legal opinions or offer professional advice, nor to serve as a substitute for advice by licensed, legal or other professionals. This book is sold with the understanding that Bradford Publishing Company and the author, by virtue of its publication, are not engaged in rendering legal or other professional services.

Bradford Publishing Company and the author do not warrant that the information herein is complete or accurate, and do not assume and hereby disclaim any liability to any person for any loss or damage caused by errors, inaccuracies or omissions, or usage of this book.

Laws, and interpretations of those laws, change frequently and the subject matter of this book contains important legal consequences. It is the responsibility of the user of this book to know if the information contained in it is applicable to his situation, and if necessary, to consult legal, tax, or other counsel.

Cover design by Brent Beltrone
ISBN: 1-883726-19-0
Published 2003 by Bradford Publishing Company
1743 Wazee Street, Denver, Colorado 80202

Dedication

To Meg, Peter, Molly and Sam, on whose time this book was written.

Acknowledgements

This volume is the work of many: Tracy M. Benjamin, Kathleen E. Fuller, Michael Heath, Todd B. Klessman, Mira J. Koplovsky, Michael Kovaka, Kevin J. Kuzas, Carolyn Wimbly Martin, Jennifer A. Ness, Karen A. Post, Michael D. Rothberg, Prabha R. Rollins, David M. Rudin, Briana E. Thibeau, Heather B. Sachs, and Mitchell H. Stabbe, all lawyers at Dow, Lohnes & Albertson, at one time or another, made substantive contributions. Pat Dawson, my assistant at DL&A, managed the manuscript ably. I am grateful to them all. Any errors are my own. Special thanks to Holly Brady, director of the Stanford Professional Publishing Courses, for inviting me to teach, year after year, in the publishing programs for which this volume was originally prepared, and to Robert Baensch, director of the Center for Publishing at New York University, and Charlene Gaynor, executive director of the Association of Educational Publishers, for persuading me there was a market for it.

Table of Contents

Over the last two decades, the Internet has grown from a novel means of communication among research scientists into a tool of mass communication essential to the daily lives of millions of people. The Internet is now widely used to send and receive correspondence, to access and disseminate information, and to buy and sell goods and services.

A body of law is taking shape. Perhaps most significantly, the United States Supreme Court has made clear that there is "no basis for qualifying the level of First Amendment scrutiny that should be applied to [the Internet]." *Reno v. American Civil Liberties Union*, 521 U.S. 844, 897, 117 S. Ct. 2329, 2344 (1997). In other words, for purposes of applying First Amendment speech protections, speech on the Internet is treated like the printed speech in newspapers, books, and magazines, as opposed to speech broadcast on radio or television, which the government has more latitude to regulate.

Not surprisingly, many of the legal issues that have been addressed to date involve how traditional bodies of law in areas such as trademark, copyright, libel, and privacy apply in this new medium. This volume tracks the case law, legislation, and proposed legislation that have developed around Internet publishing and raises various issues that are likely to become increasingly significant in the coming years.

FREEDOM OF SPEECH

The First Amendment to the Constitution of the United States guarantees that "Congress shall make no law ... abridging the freedom of speech, or of the press; or the right of the people peaceably to assemble, and to petition the government for a redress of grievances."

Although the First Amendment expressly limits Congressional action (that is, it prohibits the enactment of federal laws that improperly limit speech), courts have long applied the protections of the First Amendment to limit state action, as well, through the Due Process Clause of the Fourteenth Amendment. The Fourteenth Amendment prohibits states from depriving anyone of "life, liberty or property" without due process of law. Nearly all the guarantees of the Bill of Rights, including the First Amendment guarantee of freedom of speech, have been found by the Supreme Court to be aspects of "liberty."

First Amendment Basics

Content-based or Content Neutral

In determining whether particular restrictions on speech are permissible despite the First Amendment, the courts have distinguished between restrictions based on the content of the affected speech (which are generally prohibited), and restrictions that are content-neutral (which may, under certain circumstances, be permissible). A restriction on speech is deemed content-based if the restriction is aimed at the communicative impact of the expression. If a restriction is aimed at something other than communicative impact of expression, even if it has the effect of burdening some expression, it is deemed content-neutral.

A content-based regulation is constitutional only if it can be shown to serve a compelling governmental interest and is crafted as narrowly as possible to address that interest. If a restriction is content-neutral, it will generally be found constitutional if it serves an "important or substantial" governmental interest, is crafted as narrowly as possible to address the interest, and leaves alternative channels of communication open to those whose speech the law restricts.

The Supreme Court has also identified categories of speech that it deems generally unprotected by the First Amendment: child pornography; speech that advocates imminent lawless action; speech

3

meeting the constitutional test for obscenity; and certain speech that is shown to be false, defamatory, and uttered, depending on the circumstances, either with knowledge of its falsity, with reckless indifference to its truth or falsity, or negligently. See *Ashcroft v. Free Speech Coalition*, 535 U.S. 234, 245-46 (2002); *New York v. Ferber*, 458 U.S. 747, 765 (1982). Speech not falling into one of these categories is generally deemed protected and restrictions are presumed to be unconstitutional.

Overbreadth

Laws that ban a substantial amount of speech protected by the First Amendment along with speech that may be regulated legitimately may be found unconstitutionally "overbroad." For example, a Massachusetts statute that prohibited adults from posing or exhibiting minors "in a state of nudity" was found overbroad until amended to exempt family photos of nude infants. *See Commonwealth v. Oakes*, 401 Mass. 602, 518 N.E.2d 836 (1988), *overbreadth found moot based on revision of statute*, *Massachusetts v. Oakes*, 491 U.S. 576 (1989).

Vagueness

A law is unconstitutionally vague if the conduct forbidden is defined so unclearly that a reasonable person would have difficulty understanding the difference between legal and illegal conduct. For example, a state law prohibiting public school teachers from engaging in "seditious" utterances was found unconstitutionally vague because it did not distinguish between statements about doctrine and statements intended to incite action in furtherance of that doctrine. *See Keyishian v. Board of Regents*, 385 U.S. 589 (1967).

Print Media Versus Broadcast Media

The Supreme Court has determined that "differences in the characteristics of news media justify differences in the First Amendment standards applied to them." *Red Lion Broadcasting Co. v. FCC*, 395 U.S. 367, 386-87 (1969). In *Red Lion*, the Court ruled that because there are a limited number of broadcast frequencies available, a broadcaster does not have an "unabridgeable First Amendment right to broadcast comparable to the right of every individual to speak, write, or publish." Id. at 388. Accordingly, the Court held that the FCC could require broadcasters to make time available to the public to reply to personal attacks and political editorials. Similarly, in *FCC v. Pacifica Foundation*, 438 U.S. 726 (1978), the Court upheld the FCC's ability to regulate the use of non-obscene "adult language" on the radio, at least in certain circumstances.

By contrast, in *Miami Herald Publishing Co. v. Tornillo*, 418 U.S. 241 (1974), the Supreme Court made clear that the right of a newspaper editor to choose what to publish cannot be circumscribed in the interest of permitting public access to the paper. The Court rejected the notion that a state can require a newspaper to provide free space in the paper for political candidates to reply to personal attacks printed in the paper. The Court justified treating the print media differently from the broadcast media because there is no limit to the number of newspapers that can be published; anyone can publish a newspaper, but there is a finite number of broadcast frequencies available and one must obtain a governmental license to use one.

Speech on the Internet Is Entitled to Full First Amendment Protection

As discussed below, the Supreme Court ruled in *Reno v. ACLU*, 521 U.S. 844 (1997), that speech on the Internet is entitled to the full First Amendment protection afforded to newspapers and other print publications.

The CDA

In *Reno v. ACLU*, 521 U.S. 844 (1997), the U.S. Supreme Court found unconstitutional certain provisions of the Communications Decency Act of 1996 (CDA) that aimed to protect minors from harmful material on the Internet. One such provision, 47 U.S.C. § 223(a)(1)(B)(ii), prohibited transmission of "obscene or indecent" communications to any recipient under 18 years of age, with knowledge that the recipient is a minor. Another provision, 47 U.S.C. § 223(d), prohibited transmission or display to a minor of any message that was "patently offensive" as measured by community standards. The CDA provided for two defenses: one available to persons who used "good faith, reasonable, effective and appropriate actions under the circumstances to restrict or prevent access by minors"; and the other available to persons who restricted access to communications by using a verified credit card or other adult identification number. Violations of either provision were criminally punishable by fines or imprisonment of up to two years, or both.

The Court found that speech on the Internet was entitled to the full First Amendment protection afforded newspapers and other print publications, and held the CDA to be an unconstitutional "content-based blanket restriction on speech." The Court concluded that the CDA lacked the precision required in a statute that regulates the content of speech. To deny minors access to potentially harmful speech, the CDA effectively suppressed speech that adults have a constitutional right to receive and address to one another. The Court first noted that in evaluating the free-speech rights of adults, existing precedent has clearly established that "[s]exual expression which is indecent but not obscene is protected by the First Amendment." The Court then dismissed the government's argument that restricting transmissions to minors would not interfere with adult-to-adult communication.

Critical to the Court's analysis was the district court's finding that at the time of trial there was no technology available to allow senders to avoid sending messages to minors without also restricting access by adults. For the same reason, the Court also rejected the government's argument that the CDA was not overbroad because its prohibition on indecent communications was limited to persons known to be under 18 years of age.

· The Court also found that the CDA's vague definitions of "indecent" or "offensive" communications rendered it problematic under the First Amendment. In particular, the Court found troubling that the two provisions used different terms, neither of which was defined. The use of an indecency standard in one section of the statute, while prohibiting in another section speech that "in context, depicts or describes, in terms patently offensive as measured by contemporary community standards, sexual or excretory activities or organs," resulted in uncertainty among speakers about how the standards related to each other and just what they meant. The Court also found that this inconsistency made it unlikely that the CDA was narrowly tailored to achieve the congressional interest of protecting children from harmful material, and was especially troubling given that violations of the CDA were criminally punishable, creating a further chilling effect on free speech.

Nor did the CDA's affirmative defenses protect the statute from overbreadth. First, with respect to the defense of "good faith, reasonable, effective, and appropriate actions" to prevent transmissions to minors, the Court held that the requirement that the action be effective made the defense "illusory." Although the government suggested that such actions could include "tagging" communications to identify their content, the Court pointed out that such screening software did not then exist and that even if it did, there would be no way to know whether a particular covered communication would actually be blocked so as not to reach a particular underage recipient. The Court found the second affirmative defense, available to sites that require credit card or other forms of adult identification verification, to be an insufficiently narrow burden on noncommercial speech because it would not be economically feasible for most noncommercial speakers to use verification procedures. Finally, the Court rejected the argument that, aside from the interest in protecting children, the government's interest in fostering the growth of the Internet provided sufficient justification for upholding the CDA. The Court found this argument unpersuasive in light of the rapid growth of the Internet and held that the interest in encouraging freedom of expression was greater than any possible benefits from limiting speech.

On December 11, 2001, the National Coalition for Sexual Freedom and photographer Barbara Nitke, who publishes sadomasochistic photos on the Internet, filed suit in the U.S. District Court for the Southern District of New York, seeking to overturn the obscenity-related provisions of the Communications Decency Act that had not already been ruled unconstitutional. The plaintiffs argued that these provisions were unconstitutionally vague. Specifically, the CDA does not provide any definition of "local community standards" as an element of obscenity. *Barbara Nitke, et al. v. Ashcroft*, U.S. Dist. Ct. S.D.N.Y. (2001). The government's motion to dismiss was denied. The plaintiffs' request for a preliminary injunction remained pending as of October 2002

COPA

In October 1998, Congress enacted the Child Online Protection Act, 47 U.S.C. § 231 (COPA, also known as CDA II), an attempt to achieve the CDA's objective of protecting children while addressing the Supreme Court's concerns. COPA is more limited than the CDA in two basic ways. First, COPA prohibits the distribution of material that is "harmful to minors" rather than material that is "obscene or indecent." Second, COPA only applies to communications for commercial purposes. The statute provides that a communication is for a commercial purpose only if the speaker devotes time, labor, and attention to the communication as part of his or her business, and tries to profit from it. COPA also provides a defense for any speaker who has restricted access to material harmful to minors by requiring a credit card or other adult identification number, accepting a digital certificate that verifies age, or through other reasonable means using available technology. The statute restricts the disclosure of information collected while establishing these procedures.

The ACLU filed suit shortly after COPA was enacted. The trial court issued a preliminary injunction prohibiting enforcement of COPA on February 1, 1999, finding that COPA imposed significant burdens on protected speech in violation of the First Amendment. *ACLU v. Reno*, 31 F. Supp. 2d 473 (E.D. Pa. 1999). On June 22, 2000, the United States Court of Appeals for the Third Circuit upheld the lower court's decision, holding that the statute was unconstitutionally broad because, among other things, it affected even non-pornographic websites. *ACLU v. Reno*, 217 F.3d 162 (3d Cir. 2000).

On May 13, 2002, the Supreme Court vacated the judgment and remanded the case to the Third Circuit. The Supreme Court held that the COPA's reliance on community standards to identify what material is harmful to minors does not by itself render the statute substantially overbroad, and therefore unconstitutional, under the First Amendment. The Court remanded the case with instructions to the Third Circuit to evaluate other constitutional challenges to the statute that it had not addressed. The government remains enjoined from enforcing COPA absent further action by the lower courts. *Ashcroft v. ACLU*, 122 S. Ct. 1700 (2002).

CPPA

In 1996, Congress enacted the Child Pornography Protection Act (CPPA), 18 U.S.C. § 2252A, which criminalized the transmission or possession of digital child pornography, whether the pornographic image is computer-generated or an actual photograph. The statute was directed at conduct intrinsically related to the sexual abuse of children.

The constitutionality of the CPPA has been challenged in several federal courts, resulting in conflicting decisions. *United States v. Hilton*, 167 F.3d 61 (1st Cir. 1999), *cert. denied*, 528 U.S. 844 (1999) (CPPA's definition of child pornography comports with the First Amendment); *United States v. Fox*, 248 F.3d 394 (5th Cir. 2001) (CPPA survives strict scrutiny and is neither overbroad nor vague), *vacated by Ashcroft v. Free Speech Coalition*, 122 S. Ct. 1602 (2002); *United States v. Acheson*, 195 F.3d 645 (11th Cir. 1999) (upholding CPPA); *Free Speech Coalition v. Reno*, 198 F.3d 1083 (9th Cir. 1999) (ruling CPPA unconstitutionally vague and overbroad, in part because the definition of child pornography could include otherwise protected speech).

On April 16, 2002, in *Ashcroft v. Free Speech Coalition*, 535 U.S. __, 122 S. Ct. 1389 (2002), the Supreme Court overturned the provisions of CPPA that made it a crime to possess or distribute any sexually explicit image that appears to be, or gives the impression of, a minor engaged in sexual acts. These provisions applied to both depictions of youthful-looking adults and computer-generated images of children. The court held that CPPA "prohibits speech that records no crime and creates no victims by production." Moreover, the statute did not incorporate the community standards test of obscenity or require the artistic merit of a work be judged considering the work as a whole. The government cannot ban protected speech as a means to ban unprotected speech. The court determined that these provisions of the act were overbroad and therefore unconstitutional.

CIPA

In December 2000, Congress enacted the Children's Internet Protection Act (CIPA), Pub. L. No. 106-554, tit. XVII, 114 Stat. 2763A-335 (2000), which required schools and libraries that receive funds under the E-rate program and the Library Service and Technology Act to install "technology protection measures" on all their Internet access terminals, regardless of whether federal programs paid for the terminals or the Internet connections.

On May 31, 2002, in a unanimous decision, a three-judge panel found CIPA invalid under the First Amendment because it requires libraries to use filtering technology that inadvertently blocks access to thousands of legitimate websites while allowing access to some pornographic sites. The panel stated that less restrictive means, such as enforcement of Internet use policies in libraries, would accomplish the underlying purpose while allowing access to websites containing protected speech. On November 12, 2002, the U.S. Supreme Court noted probable jurisdiction to hear the government's appeal. *American Library Ass'n v. United States*, 201 F. Supp. 2d 401 (E.D. Pa. 2002), *prob. juris. noted*, No. 02-361 (U.S., Nov. 12, 2002).

Child Obscenity and Pornography Prevention Act of 2002

New legislation, the Child Obscenity and Pornography Prevention Act of 2002 (H.R. 4623), was approved by the House of Representatives on June 25, 2002, and has been referred to the Senate Committee on the Judiciary, which held hearings on the bill on October 2, 2002 (Senate version is S. 2511). Introduced in response to the Supreme Court's ruling on CPPA in *Ashcroft v. Free Speech Coalition*, discussed above at page 8, the bill would outlaw images, including computer-generated images, of minors engaged in sexually explicit conduct. The bill specifically creates an affirmative defense for alleged violators if they can prove minors were not used for the production of the images. Proponents believe the inclusion of the defense will allow this new legislation to pass Supreme Court scrutiny.

State Laws Restricting Online Content

Despite the Supreme Court's ruling in *Reno v. ACLU* that speech on the Internet is entitled to the highest level of First Amendment protection, states continue to pass Internet censorship laws. Many of these state statutes have been found unconstitutional.

The Commerce Clause of the U.S. Constitution reserves to Congress the regulation of interstate commerce and prevents a state from imposing laws extraterritorially. Because the Internet ignores state boundaries, state attempts to regulate online content often impose restrictions on content providers or users outside a particular state, and are therefore found to be violations of the Commerce Clause as well as the First Amendment.

ACLU of Georgia v. Miller, 977 F. Supp. 1228 (N.D. Ga. 1997).

The plaintiffs filed suit for declaratory and injunctive relief challenging a Georgia statute that criminalized computer communications knowingly made using a false name. The statute also criminalized the knowing transmission on a computer network of a trade name, registered trademark, logo, legal or official seal, or copyrighted symbol in a manner that stated or falsely implied that the speaker was authorized to use the mark when no such permission had been obtained. The court granted a preliminary injunction against the enforcement of the statute and held that the statute was a content-based restriction on speech, subject to strict scrutiny because the identity of a speaker is part of the content of his speech. Although the Georgia legislature's purpose of fraud prevention was compelling, the court found that the statute was not narrowly tailored to achieve this goal. Instead, the statute had an impact on innocent speech as well as fraudulent speech, because several terms of the statute were not well defined. The court also held that the plaintiffs were likely to succeed on claims of overbreadth and unconstitutional vagueness.

American Library Ass'n v. Pataki, 969 F. Supp. 160 (S.D.N.Y. 1997).

New York made it a crime for an individual intentionally to use a computer to initiate or engage in communication with a minor, knowing that the communication depicted nudity, sexual conduct, or sadomasochistic abuse and would be harmful to minors. N.Y. Penal Law § 235.21. The statute defined "harmful to minors" as any representation or description of nudity, sexual conduct or excitement, or sadomasochistic abuse when it (1) considered as a whole, appealed to the prurient interest in sex of minors; (2) was patently offensive according to prevailing standards in the adult community regarding suitable material for minors; and (3) considered as a whole, lacked serious literary, artistic, political, and scientific value for minors. N.Y. Penal Law § 235.20(6).

Several individuals and organizations filed suit to prevent the state from enforcing the statute, claiming that it violated the Commerce Clause and the First Amendment. The U.S. District Court granted a preliminary injunction because the plaintiffs had shown a likelihood of success on the merits of the Commerce Clause claim. The court found that the statute clearly involved interstate commerce because the legislative history demonstrated the intent to reach citizens of other states, and because the nature of the Internet makes it impossible to determine where communications are coming from. The Commerce Clause, the court noted, applies even to activities that are not motivated by profit. Direct state regulation of interstate commerce is a per se violation of the Commerce Clause. The court also found that the burden on interstate commerce outweighed any local benefit of the law. While the objective of protecting children from sexual exploitation was valuable, the law would only have limited effect. For example, it would not reach any communications from outside the United States. The burden, however, would be great, as it would chill communications nationwide or even worldwide. Finally, the court found that this law subjected Internet communication to inconsistent regulations, since each state could develop its own laws; the Internet, the court noted, is in even more need for consistency than traditional industries. The court did not consider the First Amendment claim because the Commerce Clause claim supported the preliminary injunction.

Mainstream Loudoun v. Board of Trustees of the Loudoun County Library, 24 F. Supp. 2d 552 (E.D. Va. 1998).

A library board of trustees passed a policy restricting Internet access at public libraries in a Virginia county. Under this policy, libraries were required to install software to block child pornography and other obscene websites, and other material deemed harmful to juveniles. The court held that the policy was subject to strict scrutiny because it was a content-based regulation of speech and the libraries were limited public forums. The court found that the asserted state interest in minimizing access to illegal pornography and avoiding the creation of a sexually hostile environment was compelling. However, the court found insufficient evidence to demonstrate that such a policy was necessary and determined that other less restrictive means were available to serve the compelling interest without infringing the rights of adult patrons. The court also held that the policy was a prior restraint on speech in violation of the First Amendment because it blocked material without a prior judicial decision on whether the material was constitutionally protected and because it did not include adequate procedural safeguards.

This case is discussed further in Chapter 4, at page 140.

ACLU v. Johnson, 194 F.3d 1149 (10th Cir. 1999).

In 1998, New Mexico enacted a statute that prohibited dissemination by computer of material harmful to minors. A person would be guilty of a misdemeanor if he or she "knowingly and intentionally" initiated or engaged in computer communication with a minor when the communication depicted nudity or any sexual conduct. N.M. Stat. 30-37-3.2(a). The statute also provided for defenses where the speaker took certain steps to restrict access to indecent material. The ACLU and other organizations filed suit to prevent enforcement of the statute. The district court granted a preliminary injunction. The Court of Appeals for the Tenth Circuit affirmed, relying heavily on the Supreme Court's reasoning in *ACLU v. Reno*, 521 U.S. 844, discussed above at page 5. The court found that the statute was an unconstitutional burden on adult speech. The statute's restriction to knowing and intentional conduct did not effectively limit the burden because the definition of "knowing" only required general knowledge, reason to know, or belief that necessitated inquiry into the age of the minor. Therefore, given the lack of age verification mechanism on the Internet and the size of the audience, almost all communication would be subject to the statute. The court observed that the Internet should be subject to national regulation, rather than inconsistent state laws.

Cyberspace Communications, Inc. v. Engler, 55 F. Supp. 2d 737 (E.D. Mich. 1999), *aff'd and remanded*, 238 F.3d 420 (6th Cir. 2000).

In 1999, the Michigan legislature amended a statute that prohibited the distribution of obscene materials to children to add Internet communications to the prohibition, and to change the language of the statute so that it prohibited dissemination of sexually explicit, rather than obscene, materials. Mich. Comp. Laws § 722.675 (1999).

The district court entered a preliminary injunction on First Amendment and Commerce Clause grounds. Although the Supreme Court had held in *Ginsberg v. New York*, 390 U.S. 629 (1968), that states could prohibit the dissemination of sexually explicit materials to minors, even where the materials would not be obscene as to an adult, the court found that this analysis did not apply based on the unique nature of the Internet. Because a speaker on the Internet cannot reliably know to whom he or she is speaking (or whether the recipient is a minor), such a prohibition would require that all speakers use language suitable for children. In analyzing the content-based restriction, the court acknowledged that the state's interest in protecting children was compelling, but found that the statute was not necessary to further that interest and, in fact, could stifle important discussion about issues such as public health. The court also found that the statute was not narrowly tailored, and identified other measures that would accomplish the same goal, such as blocking software and parental supervision.

The court also found a likelihood of success as to the Commerce Clause claim. Because the Internet does not recognize geographical boundaries, the impact of the statute could not realistically be limited to Michigan and the burdens on interstate commerce (chilled speech and inconsistent regulation) would exceed any local benefits from the statute.

The Court of Appeals for the Sixth Circuit affirmed the preliminary injunction, but remanded the case for further proceedings before the trial court after deciding that the district court's final conclusions were premature and inappropriate at this stage of the proceedings. *Cyberspace Communications, Inc. v. Engler*, 238 F.3d 420 (6th Cir. 2000).

People v. Wheelock, No. 990875-7 (Cal. Super. Ct. Jan. 3, 2000).

The Contra Costa County California Superior Court found unconstitutional a California statute that made it illegal to transmit sexual material over the Internet knowing that the recipient is a minor (California Penal Code § 288.2(b)). The court held that the statute was overbroad in violation of the First and Fourteenth Amendments and the Commerce Clause. The supreme court of California declined to review this decision. *People v. Wheelock*, Case No. 01-10-2001, 2001 Cal. LEXIS 62 (Cal. Jan 10, 2001).

People v. Foley, 709 N.Y.S.2d 467 (N.Y. 2000), cert. denied, 531 U.S. 875 (2000).

The defendant was convicted under a New York statute that barred the invitation or inducement of a minor to engage in sexual activity through the knowing transmission of indecent materials (defined as materials that are harmful to a minor) to a minor by computer (New York Penal Code § 235.22). The defendant asserted that the statute was unconstitutionally overbroad and vague, and a content-based restriction inconsistent with the First Amendment.

The court held that the statute did not violate the First Amendment because it was precisely drawn to serve a compelling state interest, and was neither overbroad nor vague; the statute would not chill adult speech because it requires intent to lure a minor to engage in sexual conduct for the sender's benefit. Additionally, the court noted that, unlike the CDA, the New York statute clearly defined the "harmful to minors" standard.

The court also held that the statute did not violate the Commerce Clause because the effects on commerce would be small compared to the benefit of protecting children. The statute was not designed to regulate commerce and was narrow enough (due to the requirement that the person invite or induce a minor to engage in sexual activity) to limit any potential burden on commerce.

People v. Hsu, 99 Cal. Rptr. 2d 184 (Cal. Ct. App. 2000).

In August 2000, a California court of appeal upheld a conviction under the same statute found unconstitutional by a trial court in *People v. Wheelock*, discussed above (§ 2882.2(b) of the California Penal Code). The statute makes it illegal to transmit sexual material over the Internet knowing that the recipient is a minor, with intent to appeal to the sexual desires of the minor and with intent to seduce the minor.

The court found that the statute targeted speech based on its content and was therefore subject to strict judicial scrutiny. But the court concluded that the statute was narrowly tailored and represented the least restrictive means available to achieve the state's compelling interest. To violate the statute, the sender must have knowledge that the recipient is a minor, must know that he or she is sending harmful material, must intend to excite the sexual desires of the minor, and must intend to seduce the minor. The double-intent requirement, the court reasoned, distinguishes the California statute from the CDA and the similar Michigan statute struck down in *Cyberspace Communications, Inc. v. Engler*.

The court also stated that the statute did not suffer from the overbreadth problems associated with COPA, noting that the definition of "harmful matter" includes a reference to contemporary statewide community standards (as discussed in *Miller v. California*, 413 U.S. 15 (1973)). The statute's built-in affirmative defenses also narrow its scope.

In response to the defendant's Commerce Clause challenge, the court simply stated that the proscription against use of the Internet for the statute's specifically defined purposes (knowing and intentional arousal and seduction of minors) does not burden interstate commerce. The court reasoned that the knowledge and intent requirements distinguished this statute from the New York statute struck down in *American Library*

Ass'n v. Pataki. Additionally, the court noted that when harmonized with the rest of the California Penal Code, the statute does not have the effect of regulating activity outside of the state; California only prosecutes criminal acts occurring within the state. The California state supreme court declined to review the decision. *People v. Hsu,* No. S091535, 2000 Cal. LEXIS 9303 (Cal. Nov. 29, 2000).

PSINet, Inc. v. Chapman, 167 F. Supp. 2d 878 (W.D. Va. 2001).

Virginia enacted a law prohibiting the knowing display, for commercial purposes, of images harmful to minors in a place where children may be able to access the material. In 1999, the statute was amended to include electronic media. Va. Code Ann. § 18.2-391 (1999). In addition to requiring newsstands, for example, to obscure the covers of pornographic magazines displayed on their shelves, the statute specifically applied to electronic files and messages.

In *PSINet,* the court permanently prohibited the defendants from enforcing the statute to the extent it barred the "sale, rental, loan, or display of an 'electronic file or message containing an image' or an 'electronic file or message containing words' that is harmful to minors." The court agreed that the Virginia statute sought to achieve a compelling state interest (*i.e.,* protecting the Commonwealth's minors from exposure to indecent and harmful materials); however, the statute failed because of its overly broad scope. The statute, as it applied to electronic files and messages, was likely to result in an undue burden on commercial websites, as well as on the rights of adults seeking to access electronic materials that fall within the reach of the statute. Citing the indefinite language of the statute and the lack of defenses available to potential violators (*e.g.,* legitimate steps taken to screen consumers, such as requiring credit cards or personal identification numbers for access to electronic files), the court indicated that compliance with the statute would be overly difficult and that the statute imposed significant burdens on electronic bulletin boards, newsgroups, and websites that feature material that is not harmful to minors. Finally, the court commented that even if the statute were upheld, it would not be effective in protecting minors because current technology cannot prevent content originating abroad from being accessed in the U.S. Therefore, because the statute could not effectively support the compelling state interest, the court found its burden on protected speech to be unconstitutional.

⚖ *Am. Booksellers Foundation for Freedom of Expression v. Dean*, 202 F. Supp. 2d 300 (D. Vt. 2002).

The plaintiffs challenged a Vermont statute that criminalized the distribution to minors of any image or written material in an electronic format that is sexually explicit and found to be "harmful to minors." The court invalidated the statute because it restricted constitutionally protected adult speech in an effort to protect minors. The court also took issue with the fact that the definition of a violation "forces every speaker on the Internet in every state or community in the United States to abide by Vermont's standards, even if the online speech would not be found 'harmful to minors' in any other location." *Id.* The statute also lacked practical safe harbors or exceptions for Web publishers.

⚖ *Bookfriends, Inc. et al. v. Taft*, No. C-3-02-210 (S.D. Ohio, filed May 6, 2002).

Bookstores, publishers, and video software dealers have had some success challenging Ohio's newly revised "harmful-to-juveniles" law, which expanded the definition of prohibited material to include any kind of electronic images and computer equipment, including the Internet. On August 2, 2002, the U.S. District Court issued a temporary restraining order to block enforcement of the statute, which went into effect on August 5, 2002. The court, which plans to issue a preliminary injunction at a later date, indicated that the law is too broad and appears to violate First Amendment rights of free speech.

Obscenity and "Community Standards" Online

Part of the legal test for obscenity, established by the Supreme Court in *Miller v. California*, 413 U.S. 15 (1973), asks whether "the average person applying contemporary community standards would find that the work, taken as a whole, appeals to the prurient interest." *Miller* established as a general principle that in cases involving interstate transportation of obscene material, juries are properly instructed to apply the community standards of the geographic area where the materials are sent. *Miller*, 413 U.S. at 30-34. Because the legal definition of obscenity is determined with reference to the community standards of a particular community, courts must figure out where obscene materials are "sent" on the Internet to determine which community's standards apply.

U.S. v. Thomas, 74 F.3d 701 (6th Cir. 1996), *cert. denied*, 519 U.S. 820 (1996).

A couple in California operated a computer bulletin board system (BBS). They purchased sexually explicit magazines and scanned the images onto a computer for downloading by BBS members. The couple was convicted of knowingly transporting obscene files in interstate commerce under a federal obscenity statute, 18 U.S.C. § 1465. The appellate court affirmed that "the venue for federal obscenity prosecutions lies in any district from, through, or into which the allegedly obscene material moves." *Id.* at 709 (quoting federal jurisdictional statute 18 U.S.C. § 3237). Because the BBS user who complained was in the Western District of Tennessee, venue there was proper.

The court found that because the images in question had been purposely sent to Tennessee, the community standards of Tennessee were properly applied. *Id.* at 711. The court refused to consider a new definition of "community," under which offenses allegedly committed online would be measured against the standards of the online community, in part because the BBS operators in the case had a mechanism for tailoring content offerings to varying community standards depending on the location of users. The court specifically found that, through its membership process, the BBS operators had knowledge of and control over the jurisdictions from which their materials were being accessed. *Id.* at 711-12.

Use of Zoning Law to Restrict Access to Internet Content

The government attempted to defend the CDA by analogizing it to zoning law. In *Reno v. ACLU*, 521 U.S. 844 (1997), discussed above at page 5, Justice Stevens, writing for the majority, rejected the government's "cyberzoning" analogy, which compared the CDA to ordinances such as those that bar adult theatres from residential neighborhoods (upheld in *Renton v. Playtime Theatres*, 475 U.S. 41 (1986)). Justice Stevens instead characterized the CDA as an invalid content-based restriction, rather than a permissible content-neutral restriction such as a zoning ordinance. However, in a concurring opinion, Justice O'Connor disagreed, saying she would have upheld the CDA by analogy to zoning law if adults had been able to obtain access to the regulated speech. Justice O'Connor noted that online speakers have already begun to "zone" cyberspace through the use of technology that requires users to enter information about themselves before they can access certain areas, much like a bouncer checks a person's driver's license before he admits him or her into a nightclub in the physical world. Despite what Justice O'Connor characterized as the promising prospects for the eventual zoning of the Internet, she agreed with the court that, as of 1997, technology was not yet advanced enough to allow zoning-like content restrictions on the Internet.

Voyeur Dorm L.C. v. City of Tampa, 265 F.3d 1232 (11th Cir. Fla. 2001), *cert. denied*, 122 S. Ct. 1172 (2002).

The City of Tampa alleged that Voyeur Dorm was violating a local zoning ordinance by operating its voyeurdorm.com website from a Tampa residence. The zoning ordinance prohibits property owners in residential areas from "offer[ing] [] adult entertainment to members of the public." *See* Tampa, Fla., Code § 27-523. Voyeur Dorm's website provides subscribers with a 24-hour-a-day video transmission portraying the lives of young single women living together in a Tampa home. Subscribers pay a monthly fee for access to the website and opportunities to "chat" with the women living in the house. The women in the house are employees of Voyeur Dorm and are compensated for their entertainment services. The house from which the images are filmed is located in a residential neighborhood within a restricted zoning area. The trial court upheld application of the zoning restrictions, finding that the residential house was a "premises on which is offered to members of the public for consideration entertainment featuring specified sexual activities within the plain meaning of the City Code." *Voyeur Dorm v. Tampa*, 121 F. Supp. 2d 1373 (M.D. Fla. 2000).

The court of appeals reversed because it agreed with Voyeur Dorm that the Tampa zoning ordinance applies to locations at which adult entertainment is actually available to the public. Voyeur Dorm's entertainment exists wholly on the Internet. The public cannot physically visit the Voyeur Dorm house to observe the adult entertainment: "The offering occurs when the videotaped images are dispersed over the internet and into the public eye for consumption. The City Code cannot be applied to a location that does not, itself, offer adult entertainment to the public." *Voyeur Dorm*, 265 F.3d at 1236. Therefore, the court held that the Voyeur Dorm house was not subject to regulation as an adult entertainment establishment under Tampa's zoning ordinance.

The U.S. Supreme Court declined to review the appellate court's decision.

Dot-Kids Implementation and Efficiency Act of 2002

On December 4, 2002, President Bush signed legislation (Pub. L. 107-317) creating a new second-level Internet domain that is intended to be a safe haven for online material for children and families. The new domain, ".kids," will be within the U.S. country code domain; domain names will appear as "www.website.kids.us." Internet sites using .kids in their addresses will not be permitted to link to other websites and may not offer chat or instant messaging features. All content must be suitable for children under the age of 13.

The law defines two standards for allowable content: not harmful to minors and suitable for minors. Mirroring the three-prong test for obscenity established by the Supreme Court in *Miller v. California*, discussed above at page 16, "harmful to minors" is defined as material (1) that the average person, applying contemporary community standards, would find, taking the material as a whole and with respect to minors, is designed to appeal to, or is designed to pander to, the prurient interest; (2) that depicts, describes, or represents, in a manner patently offensive with respect to minors, an actual or simulated sexual act or sexual contact, an actual or simulated normal or perverted sexual act, or a lewd exhibition of the genitals or post-pubescent female breast; and (3) that taken as a whole, the material lacks serious, literary, artistic, political, or scientific value for minors. "Suitable for minors" means material that is not psychologically or intellectually inappropriate for minors and that serves the educational, informational, intellectual, social, emotional, entertainment, or cognitive needs of minors. The bill states that the domain-name registry of the ".kids.us" domain would provide written content standards and would promulgate rules and procedures for enforcement and oversight that "minimize the possibility" that the new domain would provide access to content that is inconsistent with these standards. The registry would also create a process for removing content that violates the articulated standards, as well as a process for resolving disputes over the exclusion of particular material.

For discussion of .kids in the context of trademarks, *see* Chapter 2, page 37.

Liability of Public Libraries for Providing Unrestricted Internet Access

In addition to various attempts by Congress to regulate online speech deemed harmful to children, at least one lawsuit has attempted (unsuccessfully) to hold a public library accountable for providing children access to unsuitable online speech.

➤ *Kathleen R. v. City of Livermore*, 87 Cal. App. 4th 684 (Cal. Ct. App. 2001).

Several individuals and organizations, led by a mother of a 12-year-old boy who was able to download pornography at a library in Livermore, California, brought a suit that included causes of action for waste of public funds, nuisance, premises liability, and denial of due process. A California court of appeal held that libraries cannot be sued for damages for providing unfettered access to the Internet, even if it means that children might be able to view pornography on library computers. The court specifically found that as long as the library is simply providing computer access and is not assisting children in viewing particular material, it cannot be held liable for failing to police the content available over the Internet.

The court of appeal affirmed the trial court's dismissal of the suit and held that the state government has no "constitutional duty" to protect minors from harmful materials available over the Internet. The library's alleged awareness that minors were being exposed at library computers to obscenity and harmful matter from the Internet was insufficient to establish liability.

Discovery of the Identities of Anonymous Internet Users

Online message boards have provided a forum for Internet users to speak out on issues, companies, and individuals, often cloaked in apparent anonymity. The targets of disparaging comments have sometimes responded by filing lawsuits against various unidentified "John Doe" defendants claiming, among other things, libel, breach of confidentiality agreement, or violation of securities laws. In these lawsuits, subpoenas are issued to the message board hosts in an effort to obtain identifying information about the authors. The courts have varied in their treatment of these subpoenas. *See generally* J. Hart and M. Rothberg, "Anonymous Internet Postings Pit Free Speech Against Accountability," WSJ.com (March 6, 2002), *available at* http://online.wsj.com/public/resources/documents/SB101526197251036720, 00,html.

Columbia Insurance Co. v. Seescandy.com, 185 F.R.D. 573 (N.D. Cal. 1999).

The plaintiff attempted to sue anonymous defendants for registering the plaintiff's trademark as the defendants' domain name. The court would not issue a temporary restraining order against the defendants until the complaint was properly served upon the defendants. Balancing the public interest in providing injured parties with a forum to seek redress for grievances against the legitimate and valuable right to participate in online forums anonymously, the court formulated a four-part test for deciding when to permit discovery to uncover the identity of an anonymous defendant before a complaint has been served:

The plaintiff (1) must identify the missing party with sufficient specificity to allow the court to determine that the defendant is a real person or entity that could be sued in federal court; (2) must identify all previous steps taken to locate the elusive defendant; (3) must establish to the court's satisfaction that the plaintiff's suit against the defendant has sufficient merit to withstand a motion to dismiss; and (4) must file a request for discovery with the court, along with a statement of reasons justifying the specific discovery requested, as well as identification of a limited number of persons or entities on whom the discovery process might lead to identifying information that would make service of process possible. *Columbia Insurance Co.*, 185 F.R.D. at 578-580.

 In re Subpoena Duces Tecum to America Online, Inc., 52 Va. Cir. 26 (Va. Cir. Ct. 2000).

An anonymous plaintiff company filed suit in Indiana alleging that five John Doe defendants published in Internet chat rooms defamatory material, misrepresentations, and confidential inside information concerning the plaintiff. Four of the defendants were AOL subscribers and, upon a motion by the plaintiff, the Virginia trial court was asked by the Indiana trial court to issue a subpoena ordering AOL to produce documentation from which the identity of the four AOL subscriber defendants could be ascertained. AOL moved to quash the subpoena.

The plaintiff argued that AOL lacked standing to quash the subpoena and that the John Does were the proper persons to seek such relief. The court held that AOL had standing because (1) if AOL does not keep confidential the identities of its subscribers, subscribers would look to AOL's competitors for anonymity, and thus the subpoena would have an oppressive effect on AOL; (2) the John Does may not have actual notice of the proceedings; and (3) forcing the John Does to respond would nullify the anonymity that the motion to quash was seeking to protect.

The trial court held that it will "only order a non-party Internet Service Provider to provide information concerning the identity of a subscriber (1) when the court is satisfied by the pleadings or evidence supplied to that court that the party requesting the subpoena has a legitimate, good faith basis to contend that it may be the victim of conduct actionable in the jurisdiction where suit was filed; and (2) the subpoenaed identity information is centrally needed to advance that claim." *Id.* at 37. The court denied AOL's motion to quash the subpoena.

The Virginia Court of Appeals overturned the trial court's order, stating that the anonymous plaintiff company had to reveal its identity if it wished to proceed further with the case, including to subpoena AOL documents. For more discussion, *see AOL Inc. v. Anonymous Publicly Traded Co.*, 542 S.E.2d 377 (Va. 2001), discussed in Chapter 4, at page 145.

Doe a/k/a Aquacool_2000 v. Yahoo!, Inc., Case No. CV 00-04993 WMB (RZx) (C.D. Cal. filed May 11, 2000).

On May 11, 2000, a complaint was filed in the U.S. District Court for the Central District of California alleging that Yahoo! Inc. violated the right to privacy guaranteed by the California constitution and its contract with its message-board users by turning over to a company bringing a defamation action identifying information about a user posting messages critical of the company. This case was settled on June 1, 2001, pursuant to a confidentiality agreement.

Irwin Toy Ltd. v. Doe, 99 A.C.W.S. (3d) 399, 2000 CarswellOnt 3164 (Ont. Super. Ct. Sept. 8, 2000).

The plaintiffs, a corporation and its president, applied to the court for an order forcing an ISP to provide the identity of a subscriber who sent e-mails containing allegedly defamatory material. The Ontario Superior Court of Justice ordered the ISP to reveal the information, holding that when a plaintiff has established a *prima facie* case against the anonymous defendant, as was the case here, the ISP must release the identity of the maker of the allegedly defamatory statements.

Doe v. 2TheMart.com, 140 F. Supp. 2d 1088 (W.D. Wash. 2001).

An anonymous plaintiff moved to quash 2TheMart.com's subpoena requesting disclosure of the identity of 23 anonymous speakers who participated on Internet message boards. The court granted the plaintiff's motion and established a four-part test for evaluating a civil subpoena that seeks the identity of an anonymous Internet user who is not a party to the underlying litigation. The court said it would consider (1) whether the subpoena seeking the information was issued in good faith and not for any improper purpose; (2) whether the information sought relates to a core claim or defense; (3) whether the identifying information is directly and materially relevant to that claim or defense; and (4) whether the information sought to establish or to disprove the claim or defense is unavailable from any other source. The court held that 2TheMart.com had not demonstrated that the identity of the anonymous Internet message posters was directly and materially relevant to the core defense in its underlying securities litigation.

 Dendrite International Inc. v. Doe, 775 A.2d 756 (N.J. Super. Ct. App. Div. 2001).

The plaintiff, Dendrite, a publicly traded New Jersey corporation, filed suit against numerous anonymous individuals alleging that postings made by one of the defendants, John Doe No. 3, on a Yahoo! Internet message board were libelous. Yahoo! maintains a message board for every publicly traded company, including Dendrite, on which Internet users post comments related to the company's stock performance. These messages are usually posted anonymously, but Yahoo! requires all users to provide identifying information before using its message boards. Yahoo! guarantees in its privacy policy that such user information will remain confidential unless Yahoo! believes that disclosure "is necessary to identify, contact or bring legal action against someone who may be violating Yahoo!'s Terms of Service or may be causing injury to ... anyone ... that could be harmed by such activities." *Dendrite*, at 762. Dendrite sought discovery of the identities of all the defendants, including John Doe No. 3, whose postings included accusations that Dendrite inflated earnings by changing the way it recognized revenue and that the president wanted to sell the company but was finding no takers.

The trial court granted Dendrite's motion to conduct limited discovery to ascertain the identities of John Doe defendants Nos. 1 and 2, but denied the motion as to John Doe defendants Nos. 3 and 4. Dendrite appealed only as to John Doe No. 3, and the appellate court affirmed the trial court's decision denying discovery of John Doe No. 3's identity. The court outlined four requirements that it stated must be met before a plaintiff can compel discovery of the identity of an anonymous Internet poster: (1) the plaintiff must attempt to notify the anonymous poster, by posting a notice in the forum where the offending comment was made, that a disclosure of his or her identity is being sought; (2) the plaintiff must identify the specific statements that are allegedly actionable; (3) the plaintiff must make a *prima facie* showing of the cause of action, providing evidence supporting each element; and (4) the court must balance the anonymous poster's First Amendment right of anonymous free speech against the strength of the plaintiff's case and the necessity of the disclosure to allow plaintiff to proceed. *See id.* at 767-768.

In affirming the trial court's denial of discovery of the identity of John Doe 3, the appellate court, while acknowledging that Dendrite had stated a defamation claim sufficient to survive under a traditional motion-to-dismiss standard, focused on the third requirement and stated that a higher level of scrutiny is required when a case involves the right to anonymous speech. The court reasoned that this more exacting test can be satisfied by showing a nexus between the anonymous speaker's comments and the harm alleged by the plaintiff. However, the court found that Dendrite had failed to establish that it was harmed by John Doe No. 3's statements because the company's stock value had not fluctuated.

Immunomedics, Inc. v. Doe, 775 A.2d 773 (N.J. Super. Ct. App. Div. 2001).

A publicly held New Jersey corporation brought a breach of contract action against an anonymous Internet poster who had posted information that the company alleged was confidential and proprietary. The court reiterated the four-part test it set forth in *Dendrite* and held that disclosure of the defendant's identity was warranted because there was evidence that defendant was an employee or former employee bound by the company's confidentiality agreement, and the content of the Internet postings provided evidence of breach of the agreement. The court distinguished this case from *Dendrite*, a libel action where the plaintiff failed to demonstrate that it suffered damages, because Immunomedics established a *prima facie* cause of action for breach of confidentiality agreement.

America Online, Inc. v. Nam Tai Electronics, Inc., 571 S.E.2d 128 (Va. 2002).

Nam Tai Electronics filed a libel and unfair business practice suit in California against 51 anonymous bulletin-board posters who criticized the company and its directors on a Yahoo! message board. One of the anonymous posters accessed the Internet through AOL. Nam Tai subpoenaed Virginia-based AOL to identify the anonymous poster. AOL moved to quash the subpoena, citing the poster's First Amendment right to speak anonymously; the California court denied AOL's motion. AOL then asked a Virginia court to quash the subpoena, again arguing the poster's right to speak anonymously. Nam Tai argued that the Virginia court should not revisit issues that had already been decided by the California court. The Virginia trial court agreed with Nam Tai, and the Supreme Court of Virginia affirmed: principles of "comity" prevented the Virginia court from quashing a subpoena already reviewed by the California court under substantially the same standard Virginia would have applied.

Penalties for Posting Personal Information of Others

In addition to the cases described above addressing anonymous speech on the Internet, recent cases have considered whether posting material that discloses *others'* personal information without their consent is protected by the First Amendment.

 Planned Parenthood of the Columbia/Willamette, Inc. v. Am. Coalition of Life Activists, 290 F.3d 1058, 2002 U.S. App. LEXIS 9314 (9th Cir. en banc, May 16, 2002).

The defendant, American Coalition of Life Activists, created "wanted-style" posters containing the names and addresses of, and other personal information about, several abortion providers. (Doctors have been murdered in the past after being the subject of similar posters.) The distribution of the posters, both in paper form and electronically on an anti-abortion website called the Nuremberg Files, was found to meet the definition of a "threat of force" under the Freedom of Access to Clinics Entrances Act (FACE), 18 U.S.C. § 248. Despite the fact that the speech could be characterized as being political and taking place in a public forum, the court declared it unprotected by the First Amendment.

 Mitchell v. Trummel, No. 01-2-04698-5 (Wash. Ct. App. 2001), *petition for review granted*, 53 P.3d 1007 (Wash. 2002).

Paul Trummel, a resident of Council House, a federally subsidized retirement home in Seattle, spent 3½ months in jail for refusing to comply with an anti-harassment order prohibiting him from contacting, or listing on his website, the addresses and phone numbers of any past, present, or future residents or managers at Council House. Trummel accused staff and residents of bigotry, violations of housing laws, and conspiring to keep him awake at night. Trummel was released from jail only after agreeing to remove the information from his website.

Anti-Teacher Speech in Cyberspace

Harm resulting from allegedly defamatory speech on the Internet may be redressed through criminal and civil litigation. When the source of the online speech is a student and the target a school official or a member of the school community, the student may also be subject to discipline by the school.

Schools maintain some control over speech and displays on school property, but many schools attempt to assert disciplinary jurisdiction over Internet speech that originates and is accessed wholly off campus. Some courts have held that a school may discipline a student for off-campus activities where the activities substantially interfere with the education process.

➤ *In re I.M.L., a minor v. State of Utah*, No. 20010159, 2002 Utah LEXIS 171, *1 (Utah Nov. 15, 2002).

On his home computer, a 16-year-old student at Utah's Milford High School created a website displaying disparaging comments about his school, his teachers, the principal, and other students, including a list of classmates with descriptions of their sexual histories. The website did not contain any violent content or threats of any kind. The student was charged with criminal libel. He moved to dismiss the charges, asserting that Utah's criminal libel statute was unconstitutional because it unfairly burdened his freedom of speech. The juvenile court denied the motion, but the state supreme court reversed the ruling, dismissed the case, and declared the statute unconstitutional because it would have permitted conviction without the constitutionally required showing that the defendant knew the statements he published were false, and that he had published them with reckless disregard for whether they were true. The statute is also constitutionally overbroad because it did not provide for truth as an absolute defense. In January 2003, the juvenile court dismissed all remaining charges at the request of the county attorney. The student was not sued civilly for defamation of those he featured on his website.

➤ *J.S. v. Bethlehem Area Sch. Dist.*, 757 A.2d 412 (Pa. Commw. Ct. 2000), *aff'd*, No. 33 MAP 2001 (Pa. Sept. 25, 2002).

A Pennsylvania middle school student created a website containing derogatory statements about, and pictures of, his teachers and school principal. On his "Teacher Sux" website, created at home on his personal computer, the student depicted his teacher's likeness morphing into an image of Adolph Hitler, called his teacher a "fat bitch," displayed a picture of her severed head dripping with blood, accused the school principal of having an extramarital affair, and solicited donations for hiring a hit man to kill his teacher. The teacher and principal pursued civil remedies against the student. The school permanently expelled him.

The student and his family filed suit against the school for violating his constitutional rights of free expression, privacy, and equal protection. The Pennsylvania court held in favor of the defendant school, stating that the website hindered the educational process sufficiently to warrant a school disciplinary response. The court reasoned that the website's effect on the teacher's ability to continue educating, as well as its effect on the school community in general, led to material interference with the educational process outside the scope of constitutional protection.

In affirming the trial court's decision, the Pennsylvania Supreme Court indicated that the website included "on-campus" speech because the site was accessed at school and was aimed at the specific audience of people affiliated with the school. The school was therefore permitted to discipline the student for his speech without infringing his First Amendment rights.

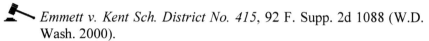 *Emmett v. Kent Sch. District No. 415,* 92 F. Supp. 2d 1088 (W.D. Wash. 2000).

Nick Emmett, an 18-year-old high school student in Kent, Washington, created from his home the "Unofficial Kentlake High Home Page," a website; he did not use any school resources, time, or materials. The website included disclaimers indicating that the school was not affiliated with the site and that it was for entertainment purposes only. The site included satire about the school, its faculty, and students. One feature of Emmett's website drew particular attention from the school: mock obituaries of Emmett's fellow students. The website was accessible over the Internet for four days. Though no one reported feeling threatened or intimidated by the obituary parodies, the school expelled Emmett for, among other things, intimidation, harassment, and disruption to the educational process. Emmett's expulsion was reduced to a five-day suspension.

Emmett successfully secured an injunction to prevent the school from enforcing its suspension. The court found that Emmett was likely to succeed in showing that it is not within the school's purview to limit speech that is wholly outside school supervision and control, particularly where there is no evidence that the site intended to, or did, threaten anyone.

Emmett's case eventually settled out of court.

U.S. First Amendment Protections in the International Context of the Internet

As reflected above, one of the most complex issues raised by online speech is that the Internet does not recognize geographic boundaries. This worldwide reach not only raises complicated jurisdictional questions, discussed in more detail in Chapter 8, pages 264-271, but also raises significant questions as to how other countries will deal with the unique speech protections provided under the First Amendment to the U.S. Constitution.

Yahoo!, Inc. v. La Ligue Contre Le Racisme et L'Antisemitisme, 169 F. Supp. 2d 1181 (N.D. Cal. 2001).

In November 2000, a French court held Yahoo! auctions in violation of a French law prohibiting exhibition for sale of Nazi propaganda and artifacts. The French court ordered Yahoo! to eliminate French citizens' access to the prohibited material. Yahoo! France barred the sale of Nazi memorabilia, but a French user could still access Yahoo.com, where such items were listed for sale. Yahoo! contended that banning Nazi-related material from Yahoo.com would infringe impermissibly on its rights under the First Amendment. Accordingly, Yahoo! asked a U.S. court for a declaratory judgment that the French court's order was not enforceable.

A federal court in California framed the issue as "whether it is consistent with the Constitution and laws of the United States for another nation to regulate speech by a United States resident within the United States on the basis that such speech can be accessed by Internet users in that nation." *Id.* at 1186. "Although France has the sovereign right to regulate what speech is permissible in France, this Court may not enforce a foreign order that violates the protections of the United States Constitution by chilling protected speech that occurs simultaneously within our borders." *Id.* at 1192. Summary judgment was granted for Yahoo!. The case is currently on appeal.

Despite the ruling of the U.S. court, a French criminal court said it will try Yahoo! and its former CEO, Timothy Koogle, for allegedly condoning war crimes by allowing the sale of Nazi memorabilia. The criminal hearing is set for January 2003.

For discussion of this case in the context of enforcement of foreign judgments, *see* Chapter 8, page 271. For a discussion of international forum shopping in libel cases, *see* pages 148-151.

TRADEMARK ISSUES

Trademark Basics

Trademark law has played a significant role in the development of the Internet. Most disputes (whether between parties with competing trademark rights or between a trademark owner and a "cybersquatter") center on the desire of trademark owners to ensure or establish online brand recognition and loyalty through the use of domain names. Trademarks and domain names, however, are not one and the same. This chapter examines both traditional trademark law as it applies to the Internet, as well as laws and policies designed specifically to protect trademark rights online.

Definition of a Trademark

A "trademark" is a designation that is used to identify the source of goods and to distinguish that source from other sources. A "service mark" is a designation that is used to identify the source of services and to distinguish that source from other sources. A mark (whether a trademark or service mark) can consist of a word or words, a stylized rendition of a word or words, a number or numbers, a design, a color, a sound, or any combination of these elements. *See* 15 U.S.C. § 1127. The term "trademark" is frequently used to encompass both trademarks and service marks, and the law applicable to each is essentially the same.

Policy Reasons for Trademark Protection

Protection of marks serves the interests of both trademark owners and consumers. Trademark owners do not want others to use marks that would be confusingly similar to their marks for two reasons. First, they do not want to lose to competitors sales they would otherwise make to consumers who mistakenly believe they are purchasing goods or services from the trademark owner. Second, trademark owners do not want consumers to mistakenly believe that inferior goods or services sold under a mark identical or similar to the trademark owner's mark are associated with the trademark owner's goods or services. And, when they make purchasing decisions, consumers want to be able to rely on marks as an indication of the source of a product or service.

Indication of Origin

Not all designations qualify as protectable marks. To create trademark rights, a designation must identify the source of a product and distinguish it from other sources. If a designation does not serve as an indication of origin (for example, because the designation is merely descriptive of or generic for the goods or services), the law does not protect it.

Obtaining Trademark Rights

Common Law. Common-law rights in a trademark are established by a history of exclusive use in connection with a particular product. The protection extended to the owner of a common law mark is limited to the geographical area in which the mark is used. *See, e.g., Union Nat'l Bank v. Union Nat'l Bank*, 909 F.2d 839 (5th Cir. 1990).

Registered. A trademark owner can register a trademark with the U.S. Patent and Trademark Office. Federal registration of a mark provides the owner with benefits not extended to owners of common law marks, such as presumed validity and presumed exclusive nationwide rights in the mark. *See* 15 U.S.C. § 1057(b) (2001).

Famous. Under § 43(c) of the Lanham Act and many state statutes, the owner of a "famous" mark is entitled to protection from dilution. Whether a mark qualifies as "famous" depends on numerous factors, including degree of recognizability, extent and duration of use, advertising of the mark, and geographical scope of use. *See Lexington Management Corp. v. Lexington Capital Partners*, 10 F. Supp. 2d 271, 288 (S.D.N.Y. 1998).

Trademark Ownership Actions and Remedies

Infringement and Unfair Competition

Registered Marks. A registered trademark is infringed when a person uses "in commerce any reproduction, counterfeit, copy, or colorable imitation of a registered mark in connection with the sale ... or advertising of any goods or services on or in connection with which such use is likely to cause confusion, or to cause mistake, or to deceive." Lanham Act § 32(1)(a), 15 U.S.C. § 1114(1)(a).

Common Law Marks. Section 43(a) of the Lanham Act prohibits the use of "any word, term, name, symbol, or device, or any combination thereof ... which is likely to cause confusion, or to cause mistake, or to deceive as to the affiliation, connection, or association of such person with another person, or as to the origin, sponsorship, or approval of his or her goods, services, or commercial activities by another person." 15 U.S.C. § 1125. Many states have parallel statutes or recognize similar claims under common law.

Prevailing Test. Once a plaintiff has demonstrated ownership of a mark, the ultimate test under a claim of trademark infringement is likelihood of consumer confusion (such as confusion as to sponsorship, origin, or endorsement).

Dilution

Trademark dilution is actionable under 15 U.S.C. § 1125(c), and many state laws as well. Under the federal statute, dilution is defined as the "lessening of the capacity of a famous mark to identify and distinguish goods or services, regardless of the presence or absence" of competition between the parties or likelihood of confusion. 15 U.S.C. § 1127. Dilution can occur as a result of "blurring" (when customers see the mark used to identify goods or services not produced by the trademark owner) or as a result of "tarnishment" (unauthorized trademark use that taints or degrades the owner's mark). *See Intermatic Inc. v. Toeppen*, 947 F. Supp. 1227 (N.D. Ill. 1996); *Hasbro, Inc. v Internet Entertainment Group, Ltd.*, 40 U.S.P.Q.2d (BNA) 1479, No. C96-130WD, 1996 U.S. Dist. LEXIS 11626 (W.D. Wash. February 9, 1996); *Kraft Foods Holdings, Inc. v. Helm*, 2002 U.S. Dist. LEXIS 10258 (N.D. Ill. June 7, 2002) (finding that the defendant's use of "King VelVeeda" on website containing pornographic material diluted Kraft's famous "Velveeta" mark).

Difference between Dilution and Infringement

In contrast to the plaintiff in a trademark infringement action, the plaintiff in a dilution action does not need to prove likelihood of confusion to prevail. Instead, a dilution plaintiff must show that its mark is famous and that the defendant is engaged in a commercial use that will cause "dilution" of the trademark by blurring its distinctiveness or tarnishing or disparaging it. A trademark not famous to the general public may still qualify as "famous" where "both the plaintiff and defendant are operating in the same or related markets, so long as the plaintiff's mark possesses a high degree of fame in its niche market." *See Times Mirror Magazines, Inc. v. Las Vegas Sports News, L.L.C.*, 212 F.3d 157 (3d Cir. 2000) (holding that "The Sporting News" mark was entitled to protection from dilution because it was famous in the sports periodicals market).

Statutory Remedies

Trademark Infringement. The remedies a plaintiff may obtain for trademark infringement include injunctive relief, damages (including the defendant's profits, damages sustained by the plaintiff, and the costs of the action), and, in some cases, attorney fees. 15 U.S.C. §§ 1116, 1117. Injunctive relief is an important remedy in trademark infringement cases because the nature of the injury makes it difficult to assess money damages. In relatively rare cases, the court may also order impoundment and destruction of the infringing goods. 15 U.S.C. § 1118.

Dilution. A plaintiff may obtain injunctive relief barring any conduct that "dilutes" a "famous" trademark. In exceptional cases in which willful intent is proved, the owner of a famous mark may also be entitled to the infringement remedies set forth above. 15 U.S.C. § 1125.

Domain-Name Disputes

General

Is a Domain Name a Trademark?

A registered domain name is not automatically entitled to trademark protection. Simply registering the name does not constitute "use" or establish priority in the mark under federal trademark law. *See Brookfield Communications, Inc. v. West Coast Entertainment Corp.*, 174 F.3d 1036 (9th Cir. 1999). A domain name is protectable as a trademark only if the domain name is also used to brand the website located at that address (*e.g.*, amazon.com, washingtonpost.com, AutoTrader.com). *See* U.S.P.T.O., *Marks Composed, in Whole or Part, of Domain Names* (September 29, 1999) available at http://www.uspto.gov/web/offices/tac/notices/guide299.htm. Trademark registration will not be granted where the domain name is merely being used as an address for the applicant's website. *Id.* Simply registering a domain name can, however, constitute trademark infringement if it creates a likelihood of confusion. *See Panavision International, L.P. v. Toeppen*, 141 F.3d 1316 (9th Cir. 1998).

Restricted Scope of Trademark Licenses

A trademark licensee with distribution and marketing rights to a protected trade name does not necessarily obtain the right to use the trade name in connection with its online business. In *Creative Gifts, Inc. v. UFO*, 235 F.3d 540 (10th Cir. 2000), the defendant purchased and distributed anti-gravity "Levitron" tops manufactured by the plaintiff. Although the parties had no written licensing agreement, the court recognized that the defendant had a license to use the plaintiff's trademark in conjunction with its advertising to the extent that it promoted the Levitron tops with the knowledge and approval of the plaintiff. However, it rejected the defendant's assertion that the right to use the domain name Levitron.com was within the scope of that license. The court also found that it would be inequitable to allow the defendant to assert a "naked licensing" defense, which is essentially a claim of trademark abandonment, because the defendant had continued to recognize the validity of the plaintiff's trademark by securing a license. *See also SARL Alifax v. Sony Corp.*, Cours d'Appel de Versailles, September 14, 2000.

Extra-Statutory Relief in Domain Name Cases

The most common remedy in trademark infringement cases and dilution cases is the issuance of an injunction prohibiting future infringement of the mark. But an injunction does little to help the owner of a trademark secure a domain name containing its trademark where that domain name has been registered to another. Courts have gone beyond traditional injunctive relief—ordering the transfer of a domain name from the domain name owner to the trademark owner. *See, e.g., ActMedia, Inc. v. Active Media Int'l*, No. 96C3448, 1996 WL 466527, 1996 U.S. Dist. LEXIS 20814 (N.D. Ill. July 17, 1996); *Intermatic Inc. v. Toeppen*, 947 F. Supp. 1227 (N.D. Ill. 1996); *PACCAR, Inc. v. TeleScan Techs, LLC*, 115 F. Supp. 2d 772 (E.D. Mich. 2000); *Trans Union LLC v. Credit Research, Inc.*, 142 F. Supp. 2d 1029 (N.D. Ill. 2001).

Domain-Name Registration

Background

Until 1998, the Department of Commerce exercised exclusive control over the domain name system, and it contracted with a private company, Network Solutions, Inc., to be the exclusive registrar of second-level domain names (*e.g.,* the "amazon" in amazon.com, the "npr" in npr.org) in the top-level ".com," ".org," ".net," and ".edu" domains (TLD). Network Solutions was therefore the focal point of early disputes over these names. However, in 1998, the Department of Commerce decided to move the non-competitive, government-funded, domain-name registration system into the private sector. In November 1998, the Department of Commerce entered into a Memorandum of Understanding with the nonprofit Internet Corporation for Assigned Names and Numbers (ICANN), under which ICANN assumed responsibility for management of much of the domain name system. Since then, ICANN has approved and accredited almost 200 companies, including Network Solutions, to offer domain-name registrations in seven of the active TLDs (".com," ".net," ".org," ".aero," .biz, ".info," and ".name"). One hundred sixty-eight of these companies were operational as of October 2002. ICANN does not accredit registrars for TLDs that are restricted to specific entities and purposes. These TLDs include ".edu" (educational institutions), ".gov" (U.S. government entities), and ".mil" (U.S. military sites).

New Top-Level Domain Names

On November 16, 2000, ICANN announced seven new top-level domain names. Four of the new domain names are "unsponsored" names for use by broad segments of the Internet community: ".biz" (for use by businesses), ".info" (unrestricted use), ".name" (for use by individuals), and ".pro" (for use by accountants, lawyers, physicians, and other professionals). The other three approved TLDs are "sponsored" TLDs, which are defined as specialized TLDs, each of which has a sponsoring organization representing the narrower community most affected by the TLD. These three are: ".aero" (air transport industry), ".coop" (cooperatives), and ".museum" (museums).

An agreement was reached in May 2001 to allow any company currently accredited by ICANN as a domain-name registrar to begin registering ".biz" and ".info" domain names upon completion of the required registry documents, and a similar agreement was reached in July 2001 for the ".name" domain. Distribution of the ".biz," ".info," and ".name" domain names will give some form of preferential treatment to existing trademark holders.

1. *Status of the ".biz" Domain*. ".biz" domain names became available for registration beginning November 7, 2001. NeuLevel is the overseeing registry. Registration information for the ".biz" domain can be obtained at http://www.neulevel.com. NeuLevel has been attacked for allegedly running an illegal lottery. In *Smiley v. ICANN*, No. BC-254659 (Cal. Super. Ct. filed July 23, 2001), the plaintiffs filed a class-action suit against ICANN, NeuLevel, and several agents, alleging that NeuLevel's practice of selling applications that provided the chance to win the right to register a domain name constituted an illegal lottery under California law. On October 11, 2001, a California state court ordered a temporary injunction, finding that NeuLevel's decision to charge a $2.00 fee for processing certain ".biz" domain name applications might violate California's lottery law. However, that injunction was dissolved on October 23, 2001, when the plaintiffs failed to post the appropriate bond. On

December 13, 2002, the trial court approved the public release of a proposed settlement. Under the proposed settlement, those who applied for a ".biz" domain name before September 25, 2001 may be eligible for a refund of the $2.00 fee and may be able to retain their domain names. The court scheduled a hearing to consider approval of the proposed settlement on March 17, 2003.

2. *Status of the ".info" Domain*. ".info" domain names became available for registration on a first-come, first-served basis beginning October 1, 2001. The overseeing registry for ".info" is a consortium of domain-name registrants called Afilias. Registration information for the ".info" domain can be obtained at http://www.afilias.com/.

3. *Status of the ".name" Domain*. ".name" domain names "went live" on January 15, 2002. The overseeing registry is a privately held company called Global Name Registry. Registration information for the ".name" domain can be obtained at http://www.nic.name.

4. According to a study by Ben Edelman at Harvard's Berkman Center For Internet & Society, thousands of registrations for ".name" domain names apparently violate ICANN regulations, either by not adhering to the prescribed format "firstname.lastname.name" or by not being a person's real name (or a name by which the person is commonly known). In May 2002, an arbitration panel ordered that two such domain names, "aim5.instantmessenger.name" and "instant.messenger.name," be cancelled for failure to comply with these requirements. *America Online, Inc. v. AD 2000 D.Com*, Claim No. FA0203000108377 (NAF May 6, 2002).

5. *Status of the ".pro" Domain*. ".pro" domain names were scheduled to begin registration in late 2002. The overseeing registry is RegistryPro. Registration information for the ".pro" domain can be found at http://www.registrypro.com.

6. *Restrictions on Pre-registration*. No organization is authorized to "pre-register" domain names in the new TLDs. Domain names may only be assigned pursuant to the procedures authorized by ICANN for each TLD. Persons who attempt to pre-register do so at their own risk and with no assurance from ICANN that they will receive the pre-registered names once the TLDs become operational.

New ".us" Domain

The U.S. Department of Commerce has entered into an agreement with NeuStar to commercialize and administer the ".us" TLD. (NeuStar is the parent of NeuLevel, the company that is the registry for the ".biz" top-level domain.) The ".us" TLD is being marketed as "America's Internet Address."

Applications for ".us" domain names can be submitted through any U.S.-accredited registrar. As was the case with the ".info" top-level domain names, there will first be a Sunrise period for ".us" top-level domain names. On April 24, 2002, registrations became available to owners of marks that were the subject of U.S. registrations or applications for registration on file with the Patent and Trademark Office as of July 27, 2001. The ".us" domain names will be assigned on a random basis. A challenge to a ".us" domain-name registration is made through the "usTLD DRP," similar to the UDRP. The usTLD DRP was approved by the Department of Commerce on February 21, 2002, and is available online at http://www.nic.us/policies/docs/usdrp.pdf.

Only American citizens, residents, people who are domiciled in the U.S., entities incorporated under United States law, and entities that have a bona fide presence in the USA may secure ".us" domain names.

Country Code Top-Level Domain Names

ccTLDs are two-letter combinations that are obtained by host countries, or dependent areas not directly bordering their parent countries, from the Internet Assigned Numbers Authority (IANA). The actual code formulations are determined by the ISO 3166 Maintenance Agency. These domain names can only be procured in accordance with IANA rules and procedures. The IANA provides a database of assigned ccTLDs, as well as the procedures and restrictions for obtaining secondary domain names for each, at http://www.iana.org/cctld/cctld-whois.htm.

Some countries have entered into agreements under which they license the right to use ccTLDs for purposes other than to suggest an affiliation with the host country. Under an agreement with the Laotian government, for example, a Los Angeles-based company, dotLA, has purchased the right to market ".la" domain names to companies and organizations in Los Angeles, Latin America, and Louisiana. Another company, dotTV, has made a similar agreement to market ".tv" domain names for purposes unrelated to the nation of Tuvalu, the country that owns the right to that TLD. ICANN has yet to take a position on the propriety of such arrangements, but its former president and CEO,

Michael Roberts, asserted that it is legal for a country to license the control of its top-level domain to a private company. *See* Todd R. Weiss, "Laos Licenses .la for Corporate Sites," *Computerworld*, December 18, 2000, at 24.

Top-Level Domain Names and the First Amendment

While future top-level domain names may be sufficiently expressive to receive First Amendment protection, restrictions limiting the current availability of top-level domain names do not violate the First Amendment. They have been found to be reasonable "time, place, and manner" restrictions on speech. *Name.space, Inc. v. Network Solutions, Inc.*, 202 F.3d 573 (2d Cir. 2000). For a discussion of constitutional limitations on restrictions on freedom of speech generally, *see* Chapter 1.

Unauthorized Top-Level Domain Names

Some Internet companies have attempted to circumvent ICANN by setting up unsanctioned TLDs ranging from ".kids" to ".xxx." The companies that run these TLDs would make websites in these domains accessible to the public by entering into agreements with individual ISPs to make such sites available to their subscribers. This approach has created concern that in the future, multiple registrars may register duplicative names. This development also may serve to limit the TLDs that could ultimately be made available through ICANN, or alternatively, to force ICANN to either accept these pre-registered names or take away existing domain names from website operators as it establishes new official TLDs.

Domain-Name Legislation

There has been a recent push in Congress to create legislation dealing with certain perceived problems relating to domain names and domain-name registration. These bills include:

Dot-Kids Implementation and Efficiency Act of 2002 (H.R. 3833). In March 2002, a bill was introduced to create a new second-level Internet domain within the United States country code domain to be used as a haven for material that promotes positive experiences for children and families and helps to prevent children from being exposed to harmful material on the Internet. This bill was passed by the House of Representatives on May 22, 2002. The Senate Committee on Commerce, Science, and Transportation held hearings on this bill and the Senate's companion bill (S. 2537) on September 12, 2002.

For a discussion of this legislation in the context of freedom of speech, *see* Chapter 1, page 19.

Truth in Domain Names Act (H.R. 4658). In May 2002, legislation was introduced in the 107th Congress that would prohibit knowingly using a misleading domain name with the intent to attract a minor into viewing a visual depiction of sexually explicit conduct on the Internet. This bill is currently being reviewed by the House of Representatives' Judiciary Committee, and Subcommittee on Crime, Terrorism, and Homeland Security.

Criminalizing False Registration Information (H.R. 4640). Also in May 2002, separate legislation was introduced that would impose criminal penalties, including a maximum of five years' imprisonment, on anyone who knowingly provides "material and misleading false contact information" when registering a domain name. This bill is also currently under review by the House Judiciary Committee's Subcommittee on Crime, Terrorism, and Homeland Security.

Cases Where Domain Name is Used in Competition with Trademark Owner

Domain-name disputes in which the operator of a website uses a domain name that is identical to a competitor's trade name are analyzed under the usual principles of trademark infringement and dilution. Cases illustrating that analysis follow.

Brookfield Communications, Inc. v. West Coast Entertainment Corp., 174 F.3d 1036 (9th Cir. 1999).

Brookfield Communications, a movie industry vendor and operator of moviebuffonline.com, filed suit against video rental chain West Coast Entertainment Corp. to prevent its planned launch of moviebuff.com. Even though West Coast had registered the domain name almost two years before Brookfield used the Moviebuff name on the Internet, the Court of Appeals for the Ninth Circuit held that West Coast's registration of the domain name did not by itself constitute "use" for purposes of trademark priority, and that Brookfield's use of the mark in commerce since 1993 qualified it as the senior user. The court further stated that the senior user of a mark is the legitimate owner of the mark, and enjoined the defendant from using the "moviebuff" trademark either in a domain name or in metatags. (For discussion of this case in the context of metatags, *see* page 82, below.)

In reaching its conclusion, the court recognized "initial interest confusion" (the possibility of customers inadvertently finding a site and becoming interested in the services offered there instead of the services they were initially looking for) as sufficient to constitute the confusing similarity necessary to support a trademark infringement claim. While not explicitly stated in *Brookfield*, a number of courts have required a showing that defendant designed the site in bad faith to create initial interest confusion. *See Interstellar Starship Servs., Ltd. v. Epix, Inc.*, 125 F. Supp. 2d 1269 (D. Or. 2001); *Bigstar Entertainment Group, Inc. v. Next Big Star, L.L.C.*, 105 F. Supp. 2d 185 (S.D.N.Y. 2000).

Washington Speakers Bureau, Inc. v. Leading Authorities, Inc., 33 F. Supp. 2d 488 (E.D. Va. 1999), *aff'd*, Nos. 99-1440 and 99-1442, 2000 U.S. App. LEXIS 14669 (4th Cir. June 27, 2000).

In March 1998, Leading Authorities registered the domain names washingtonspeakers.com, washingtonspeakers.net, washington-speakers.com, and washington-speakers.net, along with other names incorporating the word "speakers." The Washington Speakers Bureau, which has represented many well-known speakers for nearly two decades, sued its rival for infringement and dilution of its common law mark. The court found a likelihood that consumers would be confused by the defendant's use of a "colorable imitation" of the mark and that Leading Authorities had registered the domain names in a bad-faith effort to attract its competitor's business. Leading Authorities was directed to relinquish rights to those names.

PACCAR, Inc. v. TeleScan Techs, LLC, 115 F. Supp. 2d 772 (E.D. Mich. 2000).

PACCAR, a manufacturer of heavy trucks and truck parts under the "Peterbilt" and "Kenworth" trademarks, filed suit against TeleScan Technologies, the operator of several websites that allow consumers to locate new and used heavy truck dealers. TeleScan had registered domain names that incorporated PACCAR's trademarks (peterbilttrucks.com, kenworthtrucks.com, peterbiltnewtrucks.com, kenworthdealers.com, and others).

The court applied traditional analysis to PACCAR's claims of trademark infringement and dilution under the Lanham Act. The court rejected TeleScan's argument that its use of the PACCAR marks in its domain names was akin to the use of a manufacturer's marks to identify a vehicle in a classified ad or to identify merchandise for the purpose of stocking, displaying, or reselling. In the court's words, "a classified advertisement communicates information as to the source of the truck, not information as to the seller of the truck. Words in domain names, however, do communicate information as to the nature of the entity sponsoring the website." Because the domain names identified the websites, not the trucks that TeleScan advertised via those websites, the court found trademark infringement and dilution. The court did note that some authority exists for the proposition that use of a trademark in the post-domain path of a URL could be acceptable (*e.g.*, www.telescan.com/peterbilt). *See Patmont Motor Werks, Inc. v. Gateway Marine, Inc.*, 1997 U.S. Dist. LEXIS 20877, *4 n.6 (N.D. Cal. Dec. 18, 1997).

The court issued a preliminary injunction, ordered TeleScan to transfer registration of the offending domain names to PACCAR, and enjoined TeleScan from using any PACCAR mark or colorable imitation of any such mark in any domain name, metatag, or portion of a Web page (such as "wallpaper") if such use would cause consumers to associate the Peterbilt or Kenworth mark with TeleScan. TeleScan was also ordered to post the court's order on its website.

For discussion of this case in the context of metatags, *see* page 83, below.

Cases in Which Two Trademark Owners Have Competing Claims to a Domain Name

Courts have also applied traditional trademark analysis to cases involving competing trademark interests in domain names. The following cases are examples of that analysis.

Gateway 2000, Inc. v. Gateway.com, Inc., 1997 U.S. Dist. LEXIS 2144 (E.D.N.C. Feb. 6, 1997).

The plaintiff, a manufacturer and distributor of personal computer products, sought a preliminary injunction against the defendant, the operator of a computer consulting company and owner of the domain name gateway.com, based on claims of dilution and trademark infringement. The plaintiff alleged that it used both its full name, "Gateway 2000, Inc.," and the shortened version, "Gateway," to promote its products; however, only the former trademark was registered, and the plaintiff relied on the shortened version to support its claims. The court noted that the defendant was not a cybersquatter, but instead had operated a legitimate business using the gateway.com domain name. The court refused to grant a preliminary injunction because the plaintiff did not demonstrate that it used the shortened "Gateway" name to promote its products before the defendant used the name in its website domain name.

▲ *Hasbro, Inc. v. Clue Computing, Inc.*, 66 F. Supp. 2d 117 (D. Mass. 1999), *aff'd*, 232 F.3d 1 (1st Cir. 2000).

The plaintiff, the manufacturer of the Clue detective board game, brought suit against the defendant, claiming that the defendant's registration of the clue.com domain name infringed the plaintiff's registered trademark and diluted its famous mark. The defendant offered computer consulting services. The plaintiff produced no evidence demonstrating that the defendant chose its company name to create consumer confusion. On the trademark infringement claim, the court granted summary judgment for the defendant because the plaintiff failed to demonstrate that there was a likelihood that consumers would confuse the game with the defendant's services. A significant factor was the finding that numerous businesses use "Clue" as part of their trade names in the U.S. As part of its analysis, the court specifically found that the confusion that would result from a consumer typing in clue.com, realizing he or she was at the wrong site, and searching for the right site is "not substantial enough to be legally significant." On the dilution claim, the court held that the plaintiff failed to establish that its mark was famous, and was therefore not entitled to protection from dilution. Nevertheless, the court proceeded with the dilution analysis, and found neither tarnishment nor blurring of the plaintiff's mark. The court noted "while use of a trademark as a domain name to extort money from the markholder or to prevent that markholder from using the domain name may be per se dilution, a legitimate competing use of the domain name is not." The court awarded judgment for the defendant on the dilution claims.

▲ *Network Network v. CBS, Inc.*, 2000 U.S. Dist. LEXIS 4751 (C.D. Cal. January 19, 2000).

The plaintiff, The Network Network (Network), an information technology consulting group, brought suit seeking a declaratory judgment that its use of the TNN.com domain name did not infringe on trademark of defendant, The Nashville Network (Nashville), a cable television network broadcasting country music and related programming.

The court rejected the "initial interest confusion" analysis relied on in *Brookfield Communications* noting that Network and Nashville offer goods and services that are unrelated: "though both companies use the internet as a marketing device, the types of confusion potentially created by such a situation are not present where the goods and services offered are wholly distinct."

The court also placed significant weight on the facts that Network registered tnn.com six years before Nashville complained and that Network's domain name was based on Network's use of the initials "TNN" in commerce since 1989.

Virtual Works, Inc. v. Network Solutions, Inc., 106 F. Supp. 2d 845 (E.D. Va. 2000), *aff'd sub nom. Virtual Works, Inc. v. Volkswagen of Am., Inc.*, 238 F.3d 264 (4th Cir. 2001)..

The defendant, Virtual Works, an Internet Service Provider, registered the domain name vw.net in 1996. In 1999, Volkswagen requested that Network Solutions, Inc. (NSI) place the domain name on hold pursuant to its dispute resolution policy. In response, Virtual Works filed suit against NSI and Volkswagen claiming that Volkswagen's attempts to claim vw.net amounted to tortious interference. Volkswagen counterclaimed for trademark infringement, dilution, and cybersquatting. Both parties moved for summary judgment; the court denied Virtual Works' motion and granted Volkswagen's motion.

With respect to the cybersquatting claim, the court retroactively applied the Anticybersquatting Consumer Protection Act (discussed at page 49, below) and found that Virtual Works "attempted to profit from the trafficking of a domain name of a previously trademarked name." The court based its finding on the fact that Virtual Works did not have any rights in, and had never conducted business using, the initials "VW." It found that Volkswagen is the only entity with any intellectual property rights in the VW mark, that use of vw.net had already caused confusion, that Volkswagen's VW mark is famous, and that Virtual Works had attempted to sell the domain name for financial gain.

The court also found that Virtual Works infringed and diluted Volkswagen's trademark. It noted that "the holder of a domain name should give up that domain name when it is 'an intuitive domain name' that belongs to another" and that VW is the intuitive domain name of Volkswagen. The court discounted the fact that the companies offered different products because both used the same channel of commerce, the Internet.

Nissan Motor Co. v. Nissan Computer Corp., 204 F.R.D. 460 (C.D. Cal. 2001).

The plaintiff, Nissan Motor, has held several U.S. registered trademarks including the word mark "Nissan" since 1959. The defendant, Nissan Computer Corp., was founded in 1991 by Uzi Nissan, who had used his name in connection with several businesses since 1980.

In the mid-1990s, Nissan Computer registered its logo as a trademark in North Carolina and registered its domain names nissan.com and nissan.net, which were associated with Nissan Computer's website. Nissan Motor "purchased" the search terms "nissan" and "nissan.com" from various search engine operators to ensure that users searching for such terms would be directed to its website rather than the website of Nissan Computer. Because Nissan Motor had a "valid, protectable trademark interest in the 'Nissan' mark," Nissan Motor could not be held liable for purchasing these search terms even though Nissan Computer held the rights to the nissan.com and nissan.net domain names.

 Jay D. Sallen d/b/a J.D.S. Enterprises v. Corinthians Licenciamentos LTDA, 273 F.3d 14 (1st Cir. 2001).

The defendants asserted that they had rights in Brazil to the name "Corinthiao," which is the name of a popular soccer team in Brazil and the Portuguese equivalent of "Corinthians." Sallen was the initial registrant of the corinthian.com domain name. A WIPO panel originally ordered the domain name transferred to the soccer team. Sallen appealed to federal court. The district court declined to rule on the case, saying that there was no actual controversy because the defendants never claimed that Sallen had violated the ACPA. The Court of Appeals for the First Circuit overturned the decision on December 5, 2001, finding that a registrant who has lost a domain name under the UDRP has a right to sue in court for an injunction ordering return of the domain name if the registrant can show that the registration and use of the domain name was not unlawful under the ACPA. The case has been sent back to the district court.

 *WWF Worldwide Fund for Nature (Formerly World Wildlife Fund), World Wildlife Fund Inc. v. World Wrestling Federation Entertainment, Inc.*, Neutral Citation No.: [2002] EWCA Civ 196, available at http://www.courtservice.gov.uk/judgmentsfiles/j1056/civil_wwf.htm.

A United Kingdom appeals court decided on February 27, 2002, that the World Wrestling Federation must give up its WWF.com address and curtail use of the WWF logo outside of the U.S. A lawsuit brought by the World Wildlife Fund in Switzerland ended in a 1994 agreement in which the wrestling federation, which holds U.S. trademarks containing the initials "WWF," would cancel pending applications for additional WWF trademarks and curtail use of the letters in broadcasting and print outside of the U.S. The court found that the website was more than a technical infringement of that agreement. In May 2002, the wrestling organization agreed to change its name to World Wrestling Entertainment to end the dispute.

⚖ *Entrepreneur Media Inc. v. Smith d/b/a EntrepreneurPR*, 279 F.3d 1135 (9th Cir. 2002).

The plaintiff, Entrepreneur Media Inc., had published Entrepreneur Magazine since 1978, and operated a website available at the domain names entrepreneur.com and entrepreneurmag.com.

In 1987, the company had registered the trademark "Entrepreneur" for magazines, books, publishing reports, and computer programs. Since 1995, the defendant had operated a public relations company using the name Icon Publications. In 1997, the defendant changed the name of the company to EntrepreneurPR and changed the name of a periodical that he published to Entrepreneur Illustrated. At that time, he registered the domain name EntrepreneurPR.com.

The court held that a domain name does not infringe a descriptive trademark when the domain name is not exactly the same as the mark. In this case, the small difference in the letters "pr" between the mark Entrepreneur and the domain name entrepreneurpr.com precluded a finding that the domain name was infringing. The court said that, because of the need for economy of language in domain names, "very small differences matter."

⚖ *Nike, Inc. v. Crystal International*, Case No. D2002-0352 (WIPO July 4, 2002).

A WIPO panel refused to order the transfer of Nike-related domain names, including nikepark.com, nikeshops.com, nikegolf.net, and nikemen.com. Nike, Inc. owns numerous trademarks in its name and related names. Although the registrant of the domain names did not file a response to Nike's complaint, the panel found no evidence of bad faith on the part of the registrant, and no evidence that Nike made an effort to resolve the matter directly with the registrant prior to filing its complaint with WIPO. Accordingly, the panel denied Nike's request to order the names transferred.

⚖ *Instellar Starship Services, Ltd. v. Epix, Inc.*, No. 01-35155 (9th Cir. Sept. 20, 2002).

The defendant, Epix, Inc., held the trademark EPIX, which it used to identify its hardware and software products related to imaging. The plaintiff registered the domain name epix.com to establish a website featuring personal photographs and promoting video imaging hardware and software design services. The plaintiff brought suit seeking declaratory judgment that its epix.com domain name did not infringe on Epix's trademark. The defendant counterclaimed under federal and state trademark law. The court of appeals upheld the trial court's ruling that the plaintiff's use infringed Epix's mark, but only to the extent the website promoted similar products and services. Instellar was permitted to retain the domain name and continue to use if for non-infringing purposes.

▟ *Visa International Service Ass'n v. JSL Corp.*, No. CV-S-01-0294 (D. Nev. Oct. 24, 2002).

A federal court in Nevada enjoined a company that operated language schools in Japan from using the domain name evisa.com because it diluted the famous Visa credit card company's trademark. Although the court acknowledged that the word "visa" has ordinary meaning beyond the credit card company's commercial use, it said that trademark dilution was likely because use of the evisa.com domain name increases the possibility of customer confusion when searching for the Visa credit card company website. The court granted Visa International's motion for summary judgment with respect to the trademark infringement claim. However, the court did not decide Visa International's cybersquatting claim, finding that factual questions remained concerning whether the language school acted in bad faith in registering the domain name.

Cases in Which Domain Name is Used for a Harmful Purpose

Domain-name disputes in which the domain name has allegedly been used for a harmful purpose are analyzed under the usual principles of trademark infringement and dilution. Trademark dilution by tarnishment is often claimed in domain-name disputes when a website sponsor offers; for example, pornographic material through a domain name that is the same as or similar to a trademark held by a business. Trademark dilution by blurring is often alleged when a website operator's use of a domain name that is the same as or similar to a business's trademark lessens the capacity of the business' mark to identify and distinguish the business's goods.

Cases In Which Domain Name is Identical to Another's Trademark

➤ *Hasbro, Inc. v. Internet Entertainment Group, Ltd.*, 1996 U.S. Dist. LEXIS 11626 (W.D. Wash. February 9, 1996).

Internet Entertainment Group (IEG) registered candyland.com for its adult entertainment site. Hasbro, Inc., the makers of the trademarked game "Candy Land," sought a preliminary injunction claiming that IEG's use created a negative image in connection with the Candy Land trademark. The U.S. District Court for the Western District of Washington found that the defendant's use of candyland.com had been "diluting the value of Hasbro's Candy Land mark" in violation of both the Washington State anti-dilution law and the Federal Dilution Act.

➤ *Planned Parenthood Federation of America, Inc. v. Bucci*, 1997 U.S. Dist. LEXIS 3338 (S.D.N.Y. March 24, 1997).

The court enjoined use of plannedparenthood.com for an anti-abortion site because of the likelihood of confusion with the "Planned Parenthood" trademark. The court provided relief even though the domain-name registrant was using the site for the legitimate exercise of a First Amendment right and had not registered the domain name, unlike many "cybersquatters," with the intent of selling the name to the trademark owner.

Cases In Which Domain Name is Similar, But Not Identical, to Another's Trademark

➤ *Toys "R" Us, Inc. v. Akkaoui*, 40 U.S.P.Q.2d 1836, 1996 U.S. Dist. LEXIS 17090 (N.D. Cal. Oct. 29, 1996).

Akkaoui registered adultsrus.com used it to sell "a variety of sexual devices and clothing" over the Internet. The court issued a preliminary injunction, finding that "'Adults R Us' tarnishe[d] the 'R Us' family of marks by associating them with a line of sexual products that are inconsistent with the image Toys 'R' Us has striven to maintain for itself."

➤ *Peterson Publishing Co. v. Blue Gravity Communications*, 2000 U.S. Dist. LEXIS 6959 (D.N.J. Feb. 22, 2000).

The owner of *Teen Magazine* obtained a temporary restraining order against the operator of teenmagazine.com. The defendants operated a pornographic site. The temporary restraining order enjoined the defendants from using or transferring teenmagazine.com and required the defendants to turn over the domain name to the plaintiff pending the preliminary injunction hearing.

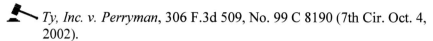 *Ty, Inc. v. Perryman*, 306 F.3d 509, No. 99 C 8190 (7th Cir. Oct. 4, 2002).

Ty, Inc., manufacturers of the well-known beanbag animals "Beanie Babies" and holder of the "Beanie Babies" trademark, sued Perryman, the owner of a second-hand beanbag animal retailer operating under the domain name bargainbeanies.com. The suit alleged trademark infringement under the Lanham Act. The district court granted Ty, Inc.'s request for an injunction, but the Court of Appeals for the Seventh Circuit reversed the injunction, with one minor exception. Because the defendant, Perryman, was in the business of selling the very product to which the trademark attached, it would be illogical to prohibit her from using the mark: it would be like "forbidding a used car dealer who specializes in selling Chevrolets to mention the name in his advertising." *Ty, Inc. v. Perryman*, 306 F.3d at 509. The court allowed Perryman to continue using the domain name, operating her website, and referring to "Beanies," except when referring to beanbag plush toys that were not manufactured by Ty, Inc.

Case in Which Domain Name was Unlawfully Appropriated

Not surprisingly, a court found liability where defendant fraudulently transferred a domain name and then used the name to operate a profitable website.

 Kremen v. Cohen, No. C-98-20718 JW, 2000 WL 1811403 (N.D. Cal. November 27, 2000), *dismissed in part by* Nos. 01-15886, 01-5899, 01-17034, 2002 WL 2017073 (9th Cir. Aug. 30, 2002).

The plaintiff, Kremen, registered sex.com with Network Solutions (NSI) on May 9, 1994, in the name of a fictitious business, Online Classified, Inc. (OCI). In October 1995, the defendant, Cohen, forged a letter to NSI in the name of Kremen's housemate, Sharon Dimmick, that asserted that she was president of OCI and that she wished to transfer the domain name to Cohen. NSI transferred the name, and the defendant began operating a pornographic site at sex.com. The court found that the defendant, whose sex.com website generated substantial revenue, had used fraud to obtain the name from Network Solutions. Therefore, the court granted summary judgment for the plaintiff, holding that a domain name is a form of intangible property and thus the transfer was invalid under the property rule that a "forged document is void *ab initio* and constitutes a nullity." The court ordered the domain name to be returned immediately to its rightful owner and froze $25 million in the defendant's assets.

On appeal, the Court of Appeals for the Ninth Circuit will consider whether NSI can be held liable for its role in transferring the domain name to Cohen based on his fraudulent letter. The district court found that because the domain name is intangible property, the registrar could not successfully be sued. On January 3, 2003, the Ninth Circuit "certified" to the California Supreme Court the question of whether, as a matter of California law, an Internet domain name is within the scope of property subject to the tort of conversion. In tort law, conversion is wrongfully possessing or disposing of another's personal property as if it were one's own.

Cybersquatting and Typosquatting

The term "cybersquatting" describes the act of obtaining a trademark-associated domain name with the aim of selling it to the trademark owner or otherwise benefiting from the association with the mark. "Typosquatting" is the registration of a domain name that is similar to another's for the purpose of capitalizing on typos that may lead the user to the squatter's website rather than the site the user intends to locate. Cybersquatter and typosquatter motivations may include a desire to market a competing or entirely different product or service or to sell the domain name back to the trademark owner for a profit.

Development of the Law

Prior to the 1999 enactment of the Anticybersquatting Consumer Protection Act (ACPA), discussed at page 49 below, cybersquatting and typosquatting cases were analyzed under the traditional principles of trademark infringement and dilution.

Intermatic Inc. v. Toeppen, 947 F. Supp. 1227 (N.D. Ill. 1996).

Dennis Toeppen reserved the domain name intermatic.com, based on the plaintiff's well-known Intermatic trademark for electrical and electronic products. The court found that the Intermatic mark was "famous" and that Toeppen's registration of the intermatic.com domain for the purpose of selling it to Intermatic was "sufficient to meet the 'commercial use' requirement of the Federal Dilution Act." The court found that Toeppen had lessened the capacity of Intermatic to identify and distinguish its goods and services by means of the Internet, and had diluted the Intermatic mark.

Panavision International, L.P. v. Toeppen, 141 F.3d 1316 (9th Cir. 1998).

Toeppen registered the domain name Panavision.com, used it to display an aerial view of Pana, Ill., and offered to release it to the owner of the Panavision trademark for $13,000. The Court of Appeals for the Ninth Circuit affirmed the entry of summary judgment against Toeppen, finding that his actions violated California and federal trademark dilution laws and that his use of Panavision on the website diluted the distinctive quality of the trademark.

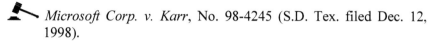 *Microsoft Corp. v. Karr*, No. 98-4245 (S.D. Tex. filed Dec. 12, 1998).

Microsoft filed suit against two Texans, Kurtis Karr and Kenny Brewer, who had registered microsoftwindows.com and nine other domain names, allegedly with the intent to sell them to Microsoft. Microsoft alleged trademark infringement and misleading the public. The court ordered the domain names to be relinquished to Microsoft.

PaineWebber v. Fortuny, No. 99-0456-A, 1999 U.S. Dist. LEXIS 6552 (E.D. Va. April 9, 1999).

The court issued a preliminary injunction against a Miami man who allegedly linked the address wwwpainewebber.com to a pornographic website. The defendant allegedly sought to capitalize on typographical errors and lure people to his pornographic sites. The court held that, "Paine Webber is a famous mark that will be diluted ... by being linked with pornography." Network Solutions was ordered to put the domain name on "hold."

The Anticybersquatting Consumer Protection Act

Enactment of ACPA. The Anticybersquatting Consumer Protection Act (ACPA) became effective on November 29, 1999, as an addition to the federal Lanham Act. The ACPA was enacted to address perceived deficiencies under traditional law that limited the ability of trademark owners to stop others from registering and using domain names that were intended to trade off the goodwill developed in their marks. For example, a claim of trademark infringement or dilution under the Lanham Act requires "use" of a mark. Courts have generally found "use" to exist where the defendant had an active website or offered to sell the registration for the domain name to the trademark owner. Where the cybersquatter simply registered the domain name and did nothing more, the courts could not find "use" and therefore there was no remedy for the trademark owner. *See Juno Online Services L.P. v. Juno Lighting, Inc.,*

979 F. Supp. 684, 691-92 (N.D. Ill. 1997) (no remedy under the Lanham Act for "warehousing" a domain name). In addition, if the cybersquatter used the domain name for a website but not for one in a field similar to that of the trademark owner, there might not be a likelihood of consumer confusion as required for a finding of trademark infringement. In such, the only remedy might lie in dilution of a famous mark. The new law was written to overcome such problems.

Liability for Bad-Faith Use or Registration of Domain Names. The ACPA imposes liability on a person who registers, traffics in, or uses a domain name that is identical or confusingly similar to a distinctive mark or dilutes a famous mark, and has a bad-faith intent to profit from the domain name.

The ACPA outlines nine factors that a court may consider in determining whether bad faith exists: (1) the intellectual property rights that the defendant has in the domain name; (2) the extent to which the domain name is the same as the defendant's name or nickname; (3) the defendant's prior lawful use of the domain name in making an offer of goods or services; (4) the defendant's noncommercial or fair use of the mark in the website; (5) the defendant's intent to divert customers to a website that could harm the goodwill of the mark; (6) whether the defendant has offered to assign the domain name for monetary gain without use or whether the defendant intended to use the name; (7) whether the defendant provided false contact information when applying for the domain name; (8) whether the defendant registered multiple domain names that are confusingly similar to distinctive marks or dilute famous marks; and (9) whether the mark is famous or distinctive.

Remedies. The owner of the mark may seek actual or statutory damages (from $1,000 to $100,000 per domain name) and a court order requiring the forfeiture, cancellation, or transfer of the domain name.

In rem Action. The ACPA allows the owner of a mark to bring an action against the domain name itself, rather than the domain-name registrant, if the registrant cannot be located. (An action brought against personal, real, or intellectual property is referred to as *in rem*, as distinguished from an action brought against a person or other entity, which is referred to as *in personam*). The relevant provision of the ACPA states that the owner of a mark may maintain an *in rem* action against an infringing domain name if (1) the action is brought in the jurisdiction where the registrar or registry of the infringing domain name is located; and (2) if *in personam* jurisdiction over the registrant does not exist.

Although the element of bad faith is discussed solely in the *in personam* section of the ACPA, some courts have held that bad faith is a substantive element of *in rem* ACPA actions, as well. *See Hartog & Co., AS v. SWIX.com*, 136 F. Supp. 2d 531 (E.D. Va. 2001); *Harrods Ltd. v. Sixty Internet Domain Names*, 110 F. Supp. 2d 420 (E.D. Va. 2000); and a related case, *Harrods Ltd. v. Sixty Internet Domain Names*, 157 F. Supp. 2d 658 (E.D. Va. 2001), *aff'd in part, rev'd in part, remanded by* 302 F.3d 214, No. 00-2414 (4th Cir. Aug. 23, 2002); *BroadBridge Media, LLC v. Hypercd.com*, 106 F. Supp. 2d 505 (S.D.N.Y. 2000). However, in a more recent decision, the United States District Court for the Eastern District of Virginia clarified that while bad faith may be a substantive element of an ACPA cause of action, it is not a jurisdictional element of the ACPA's *in rem* provisions. *See Cable News Network v. Cnnews.com*, 162 F. Supp. 2d 484 (E.D. Va. 2001). That court explained:

"[The plaintiff] mistakenly relies on [*Harrods* and *BroadBridge Media*] in support of the proposition that bad faith is a jurisdictional element of an ACPA *in rem* action. Neither case stands for this proposition. Although the court in *Harrods* did hold that bad faith indeed was an element of an *in rem* action, it *did not* hold that it was a jurisdictional element of such an action ... . Similarly, *BroadBridge Media* neither considers nor decides that bad faith is a jurisdictional requirement of an ACPA action."

Cable News Network, 162 F. Supp. 2d at 493 n.24. *See also* page 59, below, for a further discussion of this case.

A plaintiff may not proceed simultaneously *in personam* and *in rem*, but may amend or re-file if unable to sustain the claim initially pled. *See Alitalia-Linee Aeree Italiane S.p.A. v. CASINOALITALIA.COM*, 128 F. Supp. 2d 340 (E.D. Va. 2001); *V'soske, Inc. v. vsoske.com*, No. 00-CIV-6099 (DC), 2001 WL 546567 (S.D.N.Y. May 23, 2001) (granting plaintiff leave to amend its complaint to include an *in rem* action against defendant domain name). However, *in rem* actions may only be filed "in the judicial district in which the domain name registry, registrar, or other domain name authority is located." *See Fleetboston Financial Corp. v. Fleetbostonfinancial.com*, 138 F. Supp. 2d 121 (2001).

The *in rem* provisions of the ACPA have been found Constitutional by the U.S. Court of Appeals for the Fourth Circuit. The court concluded that domain names are property; by registering the domains within a state's jurisdiction, a registrant exposes the domain names to the state's jurisdiction—at least for the purpose of determining proper ownership. *See Porsche Cars N. Amer., Inc. v. Porsche.net*, 302 F.3d 248, No. 01-

2703 (4th Cir. Aug. 23, 2002); *Harrods Ltd. v. Sixty Internet Domain Names*, 302 F.3d 214, No. 00-2414 (4th Cir. Aug. 23, 2002).

The United States Court of Appeals for the Second Circuit ruled in November 2002 that *in rem* jurisdiction over a domain name in an ACPA case is appropriate only in the judicial district in which the domain-name registrar or "a similar authority" is located. Because none of the domain names in dispute was within the judicial district, the trial court lacked *in rem* jurisdiction over them. *See Mattel, Inc. v. Barbie-Club.com*, 310 F.2d 293 (2d Cir. 2002).

Cybersquatting Cases under the ACPA

For the most part, courts have found violations of the ACPA in situations where a similar domain name was registered for purposes of sale, or where the defendant was a competitor of the trademark owner or was aware of the trademark owner's prior rights in the mark. The ACPA may not apply, however, to Internet sites specializing in auctioning domain names.

Sporty's Farm LLC v. Sportsman's Market, Inc., 202 F.3d 489 (2d Cir.), cert. denied, 530 U.S. 1262 (2000).

The ACPA was enacted while this case was on appeal. The U.S. Court of Appeals for the Second Circuit used the new act to affirm an award of injunctive relief. The trial court had decided the case based on the Federal Trademark Dilution Act. Sportsman's Market, Inc., a catalog company known for selling aviation products, had been using the logo "sporty" to identify its products since the 1960s. Omega Engineering, Inc., a mail-order catalog company that primarily sold scientific process instruments, formed a subsidiary, Pilot's Depot, LLC, in late 1994 or early 1995 to sell aviation-related products by mail order. Omega then registered the domain name sportys.com. Nine months later, Omega formed another subsidiary, Sporty's Farm, to sell Christmas trees, and transferred the rights to the domain name. The Second Circuit found that "sporty's" was a distinctive mark owned by Sportsman's Market, and that sportys.com was confusingly similar to the mark. The court also found "more than enough evidence" to find bad faith. First, neither Sporty's Farm nor Omega had any intellectual property rights in sportys.com when Omega registered the domain name. Second, the domain name was not the legal name of the party that registered it. Third, Sporty's Farm did not use the website until after the lawsuit had been filed. Fourth, Omega planned to enter into direct competition with Sportsman's Market, Inc. and Omega's owners were fully aware of

Sportsman's Market's rights in the "sporty's" mark. Finally, no credible explanation was given for Omega's registration of sportys.com.

⚖ *E-Stamp Corp. v. Lahoti*, No. 00-9287 (C.D. Cal. July 31, 2000).

E-Stamp Corporation filed suit against Dave Lahoti who had registered estamps.com and estampsnow.com and offered to sell them to E-Stamp Corp., holder of the "E-Stamp" mark. E-Stamp prevailed on its trademark infringement claim, federal and state dilution claims, and its ACPA claim. In making its determination on the ACPA claim, the court found that Lahoti acted with a bad-faith intent to profit from the sale of infringing domain names to the plaintiff and others. The court also stated that the inclusion of the letter "e" in the mark did not render it generic, and that Lahoti did not have a fair-use defense because "E-Stamp" was not descriptive and Lahoti had used the mark in bad faith. Accordingly, the court issued a permanent injunction in favor of E-Stamp. The court also awarded E-Stamp over $300,000 in attorney fees based on a finding that Lahoti's "attack" on E-Stamp's mark qualified the case as exceptional under § 35(a) of the Lanham Act. The defendant has filed a notice of appeal with the Court of Appeals for the Ninth Circuit.

⚖ *Northern Light Tech., Inc. v. Northern Lights Club*, 97 F. Supp. 2d 96 (D. Mass. 2000), *aff'd*, 236 F.3d 57 (1st Cir. 2001), *cert. denied*, 121 S. Ct. 2263 (2001).

Northern Light Technology, Inc., owner of northernlight.com, brought suit against the owner of northernlights.com alleging trademark infringement and violation of the ACPA. The defendant used the northernlights.com domain to run a website for the Northern Lights Club, a club with no actual members, and allegedly had offered to sell the domain name to Northern Light Technology. The court found that the defendant demonstrated bad faith by registering the domain name in question, as well as other domain names of known trademarks (*e.g.*, yankees1.com, rollingstones.com, evinrude.com), by disregarding numerous cease-and-desist letters and by its willingness to sell the northernlights.com domain name. The court also compared the ACPA's "confusingly similar" standard to the traditional trademark infringement "likelihood of confusion" test and stated, "for purposes of [the ACPA], Congress intended simply a comparison of the mark and the allegedly offensive domain name." Therefore, the court concluded that the plaintiff was likely to succeed on its ACPA claim, and issued a preliminary injunction accordingly.

But see Mattel, Inc. v. Internet Dimensions, Inc., 2000 U.S. Dist LEXIS 9747 (S.D.N.Y. July 13, 2000) (finding defendant had acted in bad faith in registering barbiesplaypen.com and noting that the ACPA's "confusingly similar" standard is different from the "likelihood of confusion" standard for trademark infringement).

⚖ *E.&J. Gallo Winery v. Spider Webs Ltd.*, 129 F. Supp. 2d 1033 (S.D. Tex. 2001), *aff'd*, 286 F.3d 270 (5th Cir. 2002).

Spider Webs registered nearly 2,000 domain names, based on the names of famous places, people, and companies, including the domain name ErnestandJulioGallo.com. The company spent an average of $70 per domain name, but offered the domain names for sale on eBay.com and on its own website for a substantially higher price, seeking millions of dollars for some. The defendant admitted that it intended to sell the Gallo domain name. The lower court rejected the defendant's claims that the ACPA was unconstitutional as overbroad or as an unconstitutional taking, explaining that the law is not retroactive in application, even though it had been enacted after the defendant had registered the Gallo name, because cybersquatting is a continuing wrong. The defendant was enjoined from using the domain name as well as from registering any domain name containing the name "Gallo" or a combination of the names "Ernest" and "Julio."

On April 3, 2002, the Court of Appeals for the Fifth Circuit held that holding on to a domain-name registration with plans to sell it should the federal anticybersquatting statute be declared unconstitutional was a basis for a finding of bad-faith use of the domain name.

⚖ *Eurotech, Inc. v. Cosmos European Travels*, Civ. No. 01-1689-A (E.D. Va. July 23, 2002).

Bad faith can also be evidenced by a failure to conduct a trademark search before establishing a domain name. The plaintiff, Eurotech, registered the domain name cosmos.com with the apparent intent to sell space on the site to the trademark holder, Cosmos. A WIPO proceeding led to an order to transfer the domain name to the trademark holder. Eurotech brought suit in federal court under the ACPA seeking a declaration legitimizing the domain name and preventing the transfer. The court concluded that Eurotech was not an ongoing business and it did not have a legitimate purpose in securing the domain name. The court therefore refused to declare that Eurotech had a legitimate right to the domain name.

Victoria's Cyber Secret v. Victoria's Secret Catalogue, Inc., 161 F. Supp. 2d 1339 (S.D. Fla. 2001).

The defendant, the well-known lingerie manufacturer and retailer Victoria's Secret, had filed an administrative action under the UDRP in January 2001 contesting plaintiff's right to own victoriassexsecret.com, victoriassexysecret.com, victoriasexsecret.com, and victoriasexysecret.com. The domain names were not associated with any websites, but the plaintiff asserted that its domain names were going to be used for websites devoted to former Playboy Playmate of the Year Victoria Silvstedt. An arbitrator ordered the domain names transferred to the defendant, and the plaintiff then brought this action requesting a declaratory ruling that it could retain ownership of the names. The defendant counterclaimed, alleging trademark infringement and dilution, unfair competition, and cybersquatting.

The court granted the defendant's motion for summary judgment on all of its counterclaims. As regards the ACPA claim, the court held that the plaintiff's registration and use of the domain names constituted a violation of the ACPA because the plaintiff had no valid trademark rights in the Victoria's Secret mark and none of the plaintiff's domain names bore a relation to the adult entertainment websites that the plaintiff proposed to create. Further, the plaintiff had previously agreed to transfer the domain names to the defendant but rescinded its promise. Therefore, the court concluded that the plaintiff registered the names with a bad-faith intent to trade upon the fame of the Victoria's Secret mark.

The court dismissed the plaintiff's complaint and issued a permanent injunction against the plaintiff, enjoining it from using the Victoria's Secret trademarks and registering domain names incorporating a mark similar or identical to Victoria's Secret's marks. The court ordered the domain names transferred to the defendant, and awarded the defendant treble damages calculated on the basis of $10,000 in statutory damages for each bad-faith domain-name registration. The court also found that the circumstances of this case were "exceptional" such that the defendant was entitled to reasonable attorney fees and costs under the ACPA.

 Ford Motor Co. v. Greatdomains.com, E.D. Mich., No. 00-CV-71544-DT (December 20, 2001).

Greatdomains.com operates a website that specializes in auctioning Internet domain names. Ford filed suit against Greatdomains and several individual defendants, claiming that numerous domain names registered by individual defendants and offered for sale on the Greatdomains website infringed Ford trademarks. The allegedly infringing domain names included, among others, fordtrucks.com, jaguarcenter.com, and lincolntrucks.com. The court held that the ACPA only prohibits directly transferring or receiving a property interest in a domain name and therefore an Internet auction site cannot be held liable for violation of the ACPA.

For discussion of third-party liability for trademark infringement generally, *see below* at pages 85-86.

➤ *Caterpillar Inc. v. Telescan Technologies LLC*, Civil Action No. 00-1111 (C.D. Ill. February 13, 2002).

The plaintiff, Caterpillar, Inc., a manufacturer of heavy equipment, brought suit against Telescan Technologies, LLC, charging trademark infringement, trademark dilution, and cybersquatting. Telescan had registered at least six domain names incorporating Caterpillar's marks, such as caterpillarusedequip.com, caterpillarequipment.com, and caterpillardealers .com.

The court found that Telescan's use of the mark was likely to cause confusion under 15 U.S.C. §§ 1114 and 1116 and that adding words to the marks, such as "dealers," did not lower the risk that Internet users would assume that the sites were sponsored by Caterpillar. Moreover, Telescan's listing of Telescan's affiliated heavy-equipment dealers increased the likelihood of confusion. These facts led to a determination that the defendant's site was designed to direct traffic to Telescan's own dealers, who were in the same market as the plaintiff. The court held that Telescan's use of the mark diluted Caterpillar's marks and that Telescan's registration of the domain names was in violation of the ACPA.

See also Saturn Corp. v. Saturn Service, Inc., No. 01-6939 (S.D. Fla. Sept. 13, 2001) (finding that defendant violated the ACPA by using the "Saturn" trademark in its domain name, www.saturnusedparts.com where defendant was in no way affiliated with Saturn, and was not authorized to use the Saturn name or marks in association with its businesses. Accordingly, the court issued a permanent injunction against defendant and ordered the infringing domain name transferred to Saturn.).

Typosquatting Cases Under the ACPA

As discussed above at page 48, typosquatting is the registration of a domain name that differs from another domain name by only one or a few characters in the hope that users looking for the other website will mis-type the domain name and arrive accidentally at the typosquatter's site. While the ACPA does not address the practice of typosquatting specifically, courts have generally held that typosquatting is actionable as a form of cybersquatting under the ACPA.

 *Bargain Bid v. Ubid & Belcher*, 2000 U.S. Dist. LEXIS 3021 (E.D.N.Y. Jan. 3, 2000).

The plaintiff operated an online auction site at bargainbid.com. The defendant, Belcher, registered a misspelling, barginbid.com, and operated a site at that address that provided users with a link to an online auction site called "Ubid," a competitor of Bargain Bid. Belcher was a Ubid affiliate and received a fee for providing the link to the Ubid site. The court granted the plaintiff's request for a preliminarily injunction under the ACPA enjoining the defendants from using the marks and names Bargain Bid and Barginbid, and from indicating sponsorship or affiliation with the plaintiff.

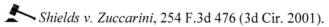 *Spear, Leeds & Kellogg v. Rosado*, 122 F. Supp. 2d 403 (S.D.N.Y. 2000).

The plaintiff, a securities brokerage firm and owner of a federal registration for the "Redi" mark and common-law trademark rights in the "Redibook" mark, brought claims against the defendant for trademark infringement, false designation of origin, and cybersquatting based on the defendant's registration and use of numerous domain names containing the plaintiff's marks. The defendant used the domain name redibook.com for an online stock-trading website that featured links to the plaintiff's competitors. The court found for the plaintiff on all claims. In its ACPA analysis, the court noted that the defendant lacked intellectual property rights in the Redi or Redibook marks and had registered numerous domain names containing the marks of other third parties besides the plaintiff. Finding that the defendant acted in bad faith, the court ordered the defendant to transfer all disputed domain names to the plaintiff and permanently enjoined the defendant from using any of the plaintiff's marks or any confusingly similar marks.

Shields v. Zuccarini, 254 F.3d 476 (3d Cir. 2001).

The plaintiff owned the trademark "Joe Cartoon" and used the name professionally for several years to identify his cartoons and related products. He also registered and used the domain name joecartoon.com. In 1999, the defendant registered the domain names joescartoon.com, joecarton.com, joescartons.com, joescartoons.com, and cartoonjoe.com. The plaintiff filed suit under the ACPA alleging that the defendant had registered the domain names in bad faith.

The court found that the registration of purposeful misspellings of a trademark, or "typosquatting," does fall within the scope of the ACPA. The court stated that the plain meaning and the purpose of the ACPA encompass registering misspellings to increase website traffic. The court also rejected the defendant's fair-use argument because the defendant had added text to the sites criticizing the plaintiff's cartoons only after this suit was filed. Therefore, the court upheld the district court order granting a permanent injunction, statutory damages of $10,000 for each of the five domain names, and attorney fees.

The Federal Trade Commission recently won a $1.9 million judgment against Zuccarini for his cybersquatting and typosquatting practices, as well as an order barring Zuccarini from diverting or obstructing consumers on the Internet and from launching new Web pages that belong to unrelated third parties. *Federal Trade Commission v. Zuccarini*, No. 01CV4854 (E.D. Pa. April 9, 2002); *see also Electronic Boutiques Holdings Corp. v. Zuccarini*, 2000 U.S. Dist. LEXIS 15719 (E.D. Pa. Oct. 30, 2000) (imposing a total of $500,000 in damages for other violations of ACPA).

Toronto-Dominion Bank v. Karpachev, 188 F. Supp. 2d 110 (D. Mass. 2002).

The plaintiff brought suit against Boris Karpachev, a disgruntled former customer of the online brokerage services of TD Waterhouse Group, Inc., a subsidiary of the Toronto-Dominion Bank, under the ACPA. Karpachev had registered 16 domain names that incorporated misspellings and alternative spellings of TD Waterhouse's domain name. The domain names linked to a site featuring criticism and disparaging remarks about TD Waterhouse. The court held that the intentional use of confusingly similar domain names to draw customers to a critical website was a bad-faith act under the federal anticybersquatting statute.

Minarik Elec. Co. v. Electro Sales Co., No. 2001-12352-RBC (D. Mass. Sept. 26, 2002).

The ACPA's reach is retroactive. A prior judgment under trademark law does not bar a later claim of infringement and cybersquatting. The plaintiff, Minarik Electric, had failed in its 1996 trademark infringement suit against the defendant, Electro Sales, complaining that Electro Sales had improperly registered and used the domain name minarik.com. At the time of the original suit, Electro was an authorized distributor of Minarik's products. A federal court in California granted the defendant's motion for summary judgment because the use of Minarik's mark was in furtherance of the distribution contract. The contractual arrangement expired in 1997. In December 2001, Minarik brought suit again, complaining of Electro's continued use of the MINARIK trademark. Due to the change in the business relationship between the parties and the enactment of the ACPA, the U.S. District Court for the District of Massachusetts held that the 1996 suit did not bar the 2001 action.

Foreign Nationals Under the ACPA

Courts in the United States have generally found that the ACPA applies equally to foreign nationals and extends to foreign websites that have sufficient contacts within the United States. (For discussion of international jursidictional issues that apply to websites generally, *see* Chapter 8, pages 264-271.)

 Barcelona.com, Inc. v. Excelentisimo Ayuntamiento de Barcelona, 189 F. Supp. 2d 367 (E.D. Va. 2002), *on appeal,* No. 02-1396 (4th Cir. filed Apr. 16, 2002).

An arbitration panel ordered the transfer of Barcelona.com to the City of Barcelona, concluding that the confusion people would experience upon visiting the site and expecting the official homepage of Barcelona constituted sufficient bad faith to warrant such a transfer. *Excelentisimo Ayuntamiento de Barcelona v. Barcelona.com, Inc.,* Case No. D2000-0505 (WIPO August 4, 2000) (discussed below at page 73).

In a controversial decision, the Chief Judge of the U.S. District Court for the Eastern District of Virginia ruled that under the ACPA, as well as the trademark law of Spain, the Internet address should be awarded to the city. The court wrote that the ACPA makes "no distinction between U.S. and foreign [trademark] even though trademark law has historically been governed and regulated on a national level." The decision is on appeal to the U.S. Court of Appeals for the Fourth Circuit. Oral argument was scheduled for February 28, 2003. The court has said that the case will turn on whether the district court properly considered the city's Spanish trademark rights in relation to a registrant's rights to an identical domain name.

 Cable News Network v. Cnnews.com, No. 00-2022-A (E.D. Va. 2002).

The plaintiff, Cable News Network, filed suit against an English-language site, based in Hong Kong, over the use of the cnnews.com domain name. The court ruled that use of the domain name in connection with the Hong Kong-based website was a use in commerce within the ACPA, and that the U.S. court had jurisdiction over the Chinese registrar in asking for the transfer of the domain name. The court found that the defendant had acted in bad faith in registering the domain name. Transfer of the domain name is pending appeal.

Schmeidheiny v. Weber, No. 01-377 (E.D. Pa. February 14, 2002).

Schmeidheiny, a Swiss national, filed suit against Steven Weber, who had registered Schmeidheiny.com, on February 28, 1999. The court found that the ACPA extended standing to foreign nationals to sue in the United States over violations of the provisions of the ACPA that protect surnames. The court's opinion is among the first to consider whether the ACPA's reach as to protection of family names, 15 U.S.C. § 1129, extends to domain names initially registered prior to the effective date of the statute. The court held that Congress did not intend to make anticybersquatting protections for surnames retroactive, while it just as clearly extended retroactive protection for registered or famous trademarks under § 1129(d). The court held that the ACPA does not cover the defendant's initial registration and subsequent re-registration of the Schmeidheiny.com domain name because these actions predated the statute.

Domain-Name Dispute Resolution

In addition to remedies under the ACPA and trademark law, a party who wishes to obtain the transfer of a domain name may choose to initiate an arbitration proceeding. Domain-name registrants are required to submit to these arbitration proceedings under the terms of their agreements with their registrars.

Former Policy: The NSI Policy

The NSI dispute resolution policy allowed the owner of a federally registered trademark or a foreign trademark owner to register a complaint with NSI if its trademark was registered as a domain name by someone else. If the owner of the mark was able to demonstrate that it had a prior registration, NSI would place the domain name "on hold."

NSI's dispute resolution policy provided no relief to the owner of a trademark that was substantially similar, but not identical, to the disputed domain name, or to owners of common law trademarks or state-registered trademarks. The policy also did not address concurrent uses of the same trademark in different lines of commerce, or conflicts between U.S. and foreign trademarks. *See Roadrunner Computer Systems, Inc. v. Network Solutions, Inc.*, No. 96-413-A (E.D. Va. June 21, 1996) (NSI refused to allow plaintiff to keep roadrunner.com, despite receipt of foreign trademark registration, after Warner Brothers, Inc., owner of "Road Runner" trademark in the United States, complained to NSI).

The Current Domain-Name Dispute Policy: Uniform Dispute Resolution Policy (UDRP)

Effective January 3, 2000, the Uniform Dispute Resolution Policy (UDRP), adopted by ICANN, governs disputes concerning all ".com," ".net," ".org," ".aero," ".biz," ".coop," ".info," ".museum," and ".name" domain names in existence or subsequently registered. The registrars for a number of country-code top-level domains (*e.g.*, ".nv" (Niue), ".tv" (Tuvalu), ".ws" (Western Samoa), ".ac" (Ascencion Island), ".gt" (Guatemala), ".sh" (St. Helena), and ".tt" (Trinidad and Tobago)) have also agreed to be bound by the UDRP.

Under the current policy, a complainant can challenge a domain-name assignment by bringing a complaint before an authorized administrative dispute resolution service provider. Domain-name holders are not allowed to transfer the name to a new holder or change registrars during administrative proceedings, or for 15 days after a proceeding is concluded. There are currently three authorized dispute resolution service providers:

- World Intellectual Property Organization (WIPO) (which, as of October 25, 2002, is the sole dispute resolution service for ".edu" domain names. These cases are available at http://www.wipo.int/search/en/. Enter the case number in the search field and click the "Search" button. The relevant case should be the first listed result of the search.

- National Arbitration Forum (NAF). These cases are available at http://www.arb-forum.com/domains/decisions.asp. Enter the case number in the "Case No." field and click the "Search Cases" button. The relevant case summary will appear. For the full text of the case, click on the link in the "Status" column.

- CPR Institute for Dispute Resolution. These cases are available at http://www.cpradr.org/ICANN_Cases.htm.

To prevail, a complainant must establish three elements at an administrative proceeding:

1. that the domain name is identical or confusingly similar to a trademark or service mark in which the complainant has rights;

2. that the domain-name registrant has no rights or legitimate interests with respect to the name; and

3. that the domain name was registered and is being used in bad faith. The UDRP sets forth four nonexclusive factors that, if

found, will be evidence of bad faith: (i) whether the domain name was registered primarily for the purpose of selling it for profit to a trademark owner or its competitors; (ii) whether the name was registered to prevent the trademark owner from using the mark in its domain name, provided the registrant has engaged in a pattern of this behavior; (iii) whether the registration was intended primarily to disrupt the business of a competitor; or (iv) whether the registrant used the domain name in an intentional attempt to attract users to a site, for commercial gain, by creating a likelihood of confusion as to the source of the site or a product on the site.

Unlike the NSI policy, the UDRP provides for cancellation of the domain name or transfer to the complainant. Decisions are stayed for ten days to allow a losing party to file a complaint in court. If such a complaint is filed, the administrative decision is stayed.

Over 7,800 complaints involving over 12,900 domain names had been filed under the UDRP as of January 31, 2003. Of the cases decided as of that date, the trademark owner or complainant prevailed in 5,137 out of 6,530 cases. An additional 43 decisions had split results, with some of those decisions leading to the transfer of additional domain names. Over 8,800 domain names have been transferred or cancelled as a result of UDRP proceedings. The most recent statistics can be found at http://www.icann.org/udrp/proceedings-stat.htm.

The UDRP was recently challenged in a case brought against the Department of Commerce for promulgating the UDRP. In *Bord v. Banco de Chile*, Civ. Action No. 01-1360A (E.D. Va. May 15, 2002), a plaintiff who had a domain name transferred under the URDP attempted to argue that the Department of Commerce had unlawfully delegated policymaking authority to ICANN and that the UDRP is void because it is unconscionable. However, the court rejected the claim on the ground that the plaintiff was not able to show that he had standing to sue the Department of Commerce.

UDRP Decisions

As discussed above, a complainant in a UDRP proceeding must prove that the registered domain is identical or confusingly similar to the protected trademark, that the registrant has no legitimate rights or interest in the domain name, and that the domain name has been registered and used in bad faith. If the complainant fails to prove one of these elements, the contested domain name will remain with the current registrant. The determination of these three issues is often extremely fact-specific, which makes generalizing from these decisions difficult.

Domain Name is Identical or Confusingly Similar to Trademark in Which Complainant Has Rights

Generally, any domain name that includes the trademark, or a "confusingly similar approximation" will be considered identical or confusingly similar to the trademark. *See e.g., The Rival Co. v. DVO Enterprises*, Case No. D2002-0265 (WIPO Aug. 2, 2002) (ordering transfer of crockpotrecipes.net domain name to the owner of Crock-Pot trademark); *Wal-Mart Stores, Inc. v. Richard MacLeod*, Case No. D2000-0662 (WIPO Sept. 19, 2000) (finding walmartsucks.com confusingly similar to "Wal-Mart"); *see also Dell Computer Corp. v. Farmi Phull*, Case No. D20001-0285 (WIPO April 11, 2001) (finding dellonline.net and dellonline.org confusingly similar to "Dell"); *Adaptive Molecular Technologies, Inc., v. Woodward*, Case No. D2000-0006 (WIPO Feb. 28, 2000) (finding militec.com confusingly similar to trademarks "MILITEC (& design)" and "MILITEC-1"); *Ingersoll-Rand Co. v. Gully*, Case No. D2000-0021 (WIPO March 9, 2000) (finding ingersoll-rand.net, ingersoll-rand.org, and ingersollrand.org identical or confusingly similar to "Ingersoll Rand").

In at least one decision, however, the inclusion of a registered trademark in a domain name was not sufficient to make the domain name confusingly similar to that trademark. The domain names foxfashion.com, foxfashion.net, foxforfun.com, foxdownload.com, and tcfhv.com were deemed not to be confusingly similar to the "Fox" trademark, because they were not suggestive of segments of the entertainment industry in which Fox participates. *Twentieth Century Fox Film Corp. v. Risser*, Case No. FA 0002000093761 (NAF May 18, 2000). However, as discussed below at page 69, the panel found that other domain names registered by the respondent, including foxnewsnetwork.com, foxvideos.com, and foxflicks.com, were confusingly similar to the "Fox" mark and ordered their transfer.

The tribunal's decision on this first UDRP factor, confusing similarity, may turn on the rights of the complainant in the trademark:

Bryant v. Yerke, AF-0315 (eResolution October 15, 2000).

The complainant had registered AS SEEN ON THE INTERNET with the U.S. Patent and Trademark Office in conjunction with his Internet advertising company. The respondent registered the name Asseenontheinternet.com, but had not posted a website at that address and was allegedly attempting to sell the domain name. Despite these allegations of cybersquatting, the arbitrator declined to order transfer of the domain name, holding that the complainant had not established a trademark interest in the phrase despite the formal registration. This phrase was deemed to be merely descriptive and not to have acquired the distinctiveness in the marketplace as a source identifier required to justify trademark protection.

Lack of a Legitimate Right or Interest in the Domain Name

There is no uniform definition of what constitutes a legitimate right or interest in a domain name for purposes of evaluating the registrant's rights in a trademark used as a domain name. Because the complainant has the burden of proving that the registrant of the domain name does not have a legitimate right in the name (as opposed to the registrant being required to prove that it has a legitimate right in the name), UDRP panels will find either that respondent has no legitimate right or interest in the disputed name, or that the complainant has failed to prove that the respondent lacks a legitimate interest.

For example, speculation in domain names has been determined not to be a legitimate right or interest. *See J.Crew Int'l, Inc. v. crew.com*, Case No. D2000-0054 (WIPO Apr. 20, 2000) ("Speculation is not recognized by the Policy as a legitimate interest in a name, and the Policy should not be interpreted to hold that mere speculation in domain names is a legitimate interest."). This case is also discussed at page 68.There is also no legitimate right to use a domain name to "damage" the trademark owner. *Reg Vardy PLC v. Wilkinson*, Case No. D2001-0593 (WIPO July 3, 2001). This case is also discussed at page 70.

Decisions concluding that the complainant failed to prove that the registrant lacked a legitimate interest in the domain name include a situation in which the registrant had operated a business for five years under a name similar to the trademark and had registered domain names incorporating that business name. *Digitronics Inventioneering Corp. v. @Six.Net Registered*, Case No. D2000-0008 (WIPO March 1, 2000) (finding that the complainant could not prove that the respondent did not have a right or legitimate interest in sixnet.com and six.net, even though the complainant owned trademark "Sixnet"). Other examples include:

Adaptive Molecular Technologies, Inc. v. Woodward, Case No. D2000-0006 (WIPO Feb. 28, 2000).

The complainant has trademarks in "Militec (& design)" and "Militec-1." The respondent had registered the domain name militec.com for a website that sold the complainant's Militec-1 product. The arbitration panel found that although there was "confusing similarity," questions as to whether the complainant acquiesced in use of domain name or whether use and registration of domain name constituted fair use, precluded a finding that the respondent had no "rights or legitimate interests" in the domain name.

Pearson v. Byers Choice, File No. FA92015 (NAF March 9, 2000).

The respondent, Byers Choice, registered the domain names byerschoice.com and buyerschoice.com with the intention of linking the names to the Byers Choice website. The respondent registered buyerschoice.com to ensure that customers who misspelled the Byers Choice name would nevertheless be able to locate the respondent's website. The complainant, who operated a real estate business under the trademark Buyers Choice, contested the respondent's right to own the buyerchoice.com domain name. The arbitration panel found that the complainant had failed to prove that (1) the respondent did not have a legitimate interest in the domain name and (2) the respondent had registered the domain name in bad faith.

Pfizer, Inc. v. Deep Soni and Ashok Soni, Case No. D2000-0782 (WIPO August 29, 2000).

The respondents claimed they registered pfizerindia.com for a "charitable foundation for Jeffrey Pfizer and his family, German benefactors who helped displaced Indians during the partition of India in 1948" but had not yet begun operating such a site. The arbitrator indicated that the respondents had produced no evidence in support of their position and questioned why they would choose the ".com" domain to run a charitable site. The domain name was transferred to Pfizer, Inc.

Miller Brewing Company v. The Miller Family, File No. FA0201000104177 (NAF April 15, 2002).

A UDRP panel ordered the domain name "Millertime.com" to be transferred to Miller Brewing Company. The name had been in use by the Miller family of San Mateo, California, who used the website to post family photos and also to offer educational services and sell computer software. The panel found that there was no evidence that the family was ever commonly known by the domain name "millertime," and that the fact that the site was used for commercial purposes precluded a finding of noncommercial fair use. There are reports that the Miller family planned to file suit against Miller Brewing Co. in a U.S. District Court. *See* Lisa M. Bowman, "Family Names Flop in Domain Name Disputes," c/net news.com, May 1, 2002, *available at* http://news.com.com/2100-1023-896561.html?tag=fd_top.

⚖ *Amazon.com, Inc. v. Amazonpic*, Case No. D2002-0330 (WIPO July 22, 2002).

A Korean company operated under the name amazonpic.com, and holds the trademark in the name in Korea. Amazonpic.com sold DVD's via its website at the domain name. Amazon.com, the U.S. based e-tailer, filed a complaint with WIPO to compel transfer of the name. A divided panel transferred the domain name despite the Korean trademark registration and evidence that Amazon.com is not well-known in Korea. The dissenters cautioned that this decision might preclude anyone from registering a domain name that includes "Amazon" because of Amazon.com's trademark.

The Domain Name Was Registered and Is Being Used in Bad Faith

There is no uniform definition of what constitutes bad-faith registration or use. Among the important factors are the registrant's conduct and intention in securing the domain name. *Hearst Magazines Property, Inc. v. David Spencer*, Case No. FA0093763 (NAF Feb. 13, 2000) (finding that although the registrant had registered esquire.com before cybersquatting became a public issue, the fact that it had registered other names confusingly similar to well-known marks was indicative of bad faith).

If a party does not respond to allegations of bad-faith registration or use, that silence will be taken as evidence of bad faith. *Cigna Corp. v. JIT Consulting*, AF-00174 (eResolution June 6, 2000) (finding failure to dispute allegations supports a conclusion of bad-faith registration); *Alcoholics Anonymous World Services, Inc. v. Lauren Raymond*, Case No. D2000-0007 (WIPO March 6, 2000) (fact that the respondent did not contest the allegations of the complaint allows an inference that evidence would not have been favorable to the respondent, which, in turn, allows an inference of bad faith).

Decisions are split regarding whether failure to use a domain name can be considered a bad-faith use. At least two UDRP decisions have found that passive holding of a domain name, in light of evidence of bad-faith registration, may constitute bad-faith use.

⚖ *University of Iowa v. Juraj Vyletelka*, Case No. D2002-0349 (WIPO May 31, 2002).

The complainant university had used the trademark "Virtual Hospital" for nearly ten years before it brought the action, and had owned a federal registration in the mark since 1997. The respondent registered virtualhospital.com, but the corresponding website remained "under construction." The respondent indicated that he planned to conduct business activities using the domain. In a letter to the complainant, he requested $10,000 in lost revenue from the planned business activities in exchange for transferring the domain name. The panel found that the respondent's passive holding of the website, coupled with his demand for $10,000, constituted bad faith and ordered the domain name transferred to the complainant.

 Telstra Corp. Ltd. v. Nuclear Marshmallows, Case No. D2000-0003 (WIPO Feb. 18, 2000).

Telstra owns the trademark "Telstra" and is the registrant of various domain names that include that mark. The respondent, who could not be identified, registered telstra.org, which did not resolve to a website or any other online presence. The arbitration panel concluded that the passive holding of the domain name by the respondent amounted to bad faith because Telstra's trademark has a strong reputation and is widely known, the respondent provided no evidence of any actual or contemplated good-faith use of the domain name, and the respondent took steps to conceal its identity. Given these factors, the panel concluded that there could be no active use of the domain name by the registrant that would be legitimate.

At least one panel, however, has concluded that passive holding alone does not constitute bad-faith use. *Ingram Micro, Inc. v. Ingredients Among Modern Microwaves*, Case No. D2002-0301 (WIPO May 15, 2002) (finding that the complainant failed to establish bad-faith use where the registrant had not made an effort to sell the contested domain name, the registrant did not prevent the mark owner from owning a corresponding domain name, the registrant did not attempt to disrupt business of mark owner and made no attempt to attract users to the site for commercial gain).

The following decisions are examples of situations in which the arbitration panel found evidence of bad-faith use.

 FaceTime Communications, Inc. v. Live Pearson, Inc., Case No. FA0092048 (NAF Feb. 18, 2000).

Both the complainant and respondent were involved in the business of offering customer-service solutions to companies with websites. The complainant was aware of misdirected e-mails sent to the disputed domain that had not been forwarded by the respondent. The arbitration panel found that the respondent had demonstrated a pattern of conduct that interfered with the complainant's right to conduct business, which showed use and registration in bad faith.

⚖ *Bennett Coleman & Co. v. Lalwani; Bennett Coleman & Co. v. Long Distance Telephone Co.*, Case No. D2000-0014 and D2000-0015 (WIPO March 11, 2000).

The respondent's domain names theeconomictimes.com and thetimesofindia.com differ from the complainant's only by incorporation of the definite article "the," and visitors who attempt to access the complainant's sites, but include the article, are redirected to respondent's websites. The similarity in domain names makes it inevitable that visitors would go to respondent's site because of complainant's reputation. The arbitration panel found that use and registration were in bad faith; they established an intentional attempt to attract users by creating a "likelihood of confusion."

⚖ *J.Crew International, Inc. v. crew.com*, Case No. D2000-0054 (WIPO April 20, 2000).

The respondent had registered the domain name crew.com. The arbitration panel found that the fact that the registration prevented the trademark holder from having a domain name that corresponded to its registered mark, when coupled with constructive notice, was sufficient evidence of bad faith. *See also Valspar Sourcing, Inc. v. TIGRE*, Case No. FA0204000112596 (NAF June 4, 2002) (finding respondent's registration of disputed domain name while on notice of Complainant's rights in "PAINT.BIZ" is evidence of bad faith).

⚖ *Home Interiors & Gifts, Inc. v. Home Interiors*, Case No. D2000-0010 (WIPO March 7, 2000).

The respondent registered the domain names homeinterioursandgifts.com and homeinteriors.net and posted advertisements for competitors of complainant and links to commercial websites hosted by competitors of the complainant. The arbitration panel found bad faith due to its conclusions that the "counter" on the website, which reflected the number of visits to the site, amounted to an advertisement for sale and that registration of the domain names within one week of each other suggested that the respondent was aware of the complainant's marks.

Sankyo Co., Ltd. v. Zhu Jia Jun, Case No. D2000-1791 (WIPO March 23, 2001).

The complainant owns the trademark "Sankyo," which is represented by a Chinese character identical to the character corresponding to the respondent's domain name. This case involves a Multilingual Domain Name (MDN), which serves as a method for entering non-English language characters in certain gTLDs. The panel concluded that the respondent registered its address in bad faith for the purpose of selling the domain name to the complainant. This is the first case finding that an MDN infringes upon an existing trademark.

 Dell Computer Corporation v. Parmi Phull, Case No. D2001-0285 (WIPO April 11, 2001).

The respondent, a resident of Spain, registered the domain names dellonline.net and dellonline.org, which linked to his personal website where they were listed for sale among other names he has acquired. In finding bad faith, the panel held that advertising to the public at large that the domain name is for sale is evidence of bad faith and is properly regarded as an offer to sell the domain name to the complainant or a competitor.

See also Twentieth Century Fox Film Corp. v. Risser, Case No. FA 0002000093761 (NAF May 18, 2000) (finding that 16 domain names that were variations on the "Fox" trademark, including foxnewsnetwork.com, foxvideos.com, and foxflicks.com, were obtained in bad faith with the intent to sell them to Fox). This case is also discussed at page 63, above.

 America Online, Inc. v. John Deep Buddy USA, Inc., Case No. FA0103000096795 (NAF May 14, 2001).

The respondent operates a messaging and file-swapping site called "Aimster," located at aimster.com, which has functions similar to Napster and AIM (AOL Instant Messaging). The respondent registered misspelled variations of aimster.com that would direct users to the Aimster site. There is a disclaimer on the Aimster site stating that "Aimster is in no way affiliated with America Online." A divided arbitration panel ordered the transfer of all the domain names to AOL, holding that the domain names infringed on AOL's AIM trademark. The dissenting panelist argued that the UDRP proceeding should be reserved for more egregious violations and that use of AIM was likely fair as it has developed a generic descriptive identity similar to "kleenex" or "scotch tape." In June 2001, Aimster filed suit against AOL, seeking to have a judge overturn the panel's decision, and AOL filed suit against Aimster alleging trademark infringement. Both suits were filed with the United States District Court for the Eastern District of Virginia. Aimster has since been rebranded as Madster.com.

✦ *Reg Vardy PLC v. Wilkinson*, Case No. D2001-0593 (WIPO July 3, 2001).

The complainant, Reg Vardy PLC, operates car dealerships in England and Scotland and operates a website at regvardy.com. The respondent, David Wilkinson, was involved in a dispute with Reg Vardy regarding the purchase of a van, and he registered the domain names reg-vardy.com, reg-vardy.net, and reg-vardy.org in order to associate them with a website containing disparaging remarks about Reg Vardy. The arbitrator found that Wilkinson's expressed intent to "disrupt [Reg Vardy's] business" was a valid basis for finding bad faith, even though Wilkinson was not a competitor of Reg Vardy.

The decisions that follow include findings by arbitration panels that bad-faith registration or use had not been proved by the complainant, and the registrants of the domain names at issue were allowed to retain possession of the domain names:

✦ *Union des Associations Europeennes de Football v. Hallam*, Case No. D2001-0717 (WIPO July 10, 2001).

The respondent's use of a domain name that was confusingly similar to a trademark of European soccer's governing body was not considered a bad-faith use because the uefa2004.com domain name was registered more than eight months before the complainant registered its UEFA EURO 2004 trademark, and the respondent had sufficient explanations for why his 2004 European soccer championship chat site was not yet constructed. The complainant also failed to show that the respondent had no rights or legitimate interests in the domain name.

✦ *Gloria-Werke H. Schulte-Frankenfeld GmbH & Co. v. Internet Development Corp. and Gloria MacKenzie*, Case No. D2002-0056 (WIPO April 26, 2002).

The respondent registered gloria.com, which is identical to the complainant's registered mark. The panel declined to find bad-faith registration or use, however, because the complainant's mark was not well-known in the United States at the time of registration of the domain name. The panel also noted that the respondent was a dealer in domain names, which might ordinarily create an inference that the respondent was aware of Gloria-Werke's mark; however, this inference was unpersuasive because the name "Gloria" is also a common name for women, and as such "a commodity greatly to be desired by those dealing in domain names," even those having no desire to exploit the marks of others.

PwC Business Trust v. Ultimate Search, Case No. D2002-0087 (WIPO May 22, 2002).

The respondent's use of pwc.com was not found to be a bad-faith registration or use of PwC's trademark "PWC" (held in trust for PricewaterhouseCoopers) because the three letters are inherently indistinctive and are not uniquely associated with the complainant. The panel also considered the effect that a previously lapsed registration of the domain name has on a finding of bad faith and determined that, while in certain cases it may be evidence of a lack of bad faith, it should not be considered compelling as a matter of course.

Personal and Geographic Names

In addition to policing the misleading use of trademarks in domain names, UDRP arbitration panels have begun to expand protection to other intellectual property rights, such as trade and personal names and geographic regions (*e.g.*, Bordeaux for wine).

Julia Fiona Roberts v. Russell Boyd, Case No. D2000-0210 (WIPO May 29, 2000).

The arbitration panel ruled that an accused cybersquatter who registered www.juliaroberts.com had no legitimate interest in the domain name and used it in bad faith. In finding bad-faith intent, the panel cited evidence that the defendant, Russell Boyd, had registered names of several famous movie and sports figures, and even tried to auction juliaroberts.com on eBay. *But see Gordon Sumner, p/k/a Sting v. Michael Urvan*, Case No. D2000-0596 (WIPO July 19, 2000) (finding inadequate evidence of bad faith and noting that, unlike "Julia Roberts," "sting" is a common word as well as a name); *Bruce Springsteen v. Jeff Burgar; Bruce Springsteen Club*, Case No. D2000-1532 (WIPO Jan. 25, 2001) (finding that the registrant has some legitimate right to the domain name and that Springsteen failed to establish bad faith).

Kathleen Kennedy Townsend v. B. G. Birt, Case No. D2002-0030 (WIPO April 11, 2002).

A WIPO panel has issued a decision involving several domains using the name of Kathleen Kennedy Townsend, the former Lieutenant Governor of Maryland and the eldest daughter of the late Robert F.

Kennedy. The panel declined to transfer the domains to Townsend, noting that the second WIPO report on the domain name process issued in the fall of 2001 indicated that the UDRP should be limited to personal names that had been commercially exploited. Townsend again failed to win transfer of the domain names from the same respondent in July 2002, when a group called Friends of Kathleen Kennedy Townsend brought the complaint instead of Townsend personally. This strategy sought to emphasize the commercial/political nature of Townsend's name. WIPO again denied the request to order transfer. *Friends of Kathleen Kennedy Townsend v. B. G. Birt*, Case No. D2002-0451 (WIPO July 31, 2002).

Peter Frampton v. Frampton Enterprises, Inc., Case No. D2002-0141 (WIPO April 17, 2002).

A WIPO panelist ordered the transfer of peterframpton.com from L. Peter Frampton to Peter Frampton, the singer. The panelist concluded that the use of the "Peter Frampton" trademark, in conjunction with the sale of goods and services similar to those offered by the singer, was an attempt by the registrant to benefit commercially from the inevitable confusion regarding ownership of the domain name.

Kevin Spacey v. Alberta Hot Rods, Claim No. FA0205000114437 (NAF Aug. 1, 2002).

After several failed attempts to compel the transfer of kevinspacey.com to him via the U.S. court system, the well-known actor succeeded in a UDRP action. The respondent's "persistent behavior" in registering celebrity names indicated his bad- faith intent in registering kevinspacey.com.

Kur-und Verkehrsverein St. Moritz v. StMoritz.com, Case No. D2000-0617 (WIPO August 17, 2000).

The official organization representing the resort community of St. Moritz was unsuccessful in obtaining the rights to StMoritz.com from a company in the United Arab Emirates. The company runs a website at StMoritz.com about St. Moritz hotels and restaurants. The same company also owns rostock.com, malaga.com, majorca.com, et cetera, at which it runs websites providing similar information about those locations.

But see Excelentisimo Ayuntamiento de Barcelona v. Barcelona.com, Inc., Case No. D2000-0505 (WIPO August 4, 2000), ordering the transfer of Barcelona.com to the City of Barcelona on the ground that the confusion people would experience upon visiting the site and expecting the official website of Barcelona constituted sufficient bad faith to warrant such a transfer. (This case is also discussed above at page 59, in the context of a later ACPA proceeding upholding the panel's decision.)

◤ *City of Potsdam v. Transglobal Networx, Inc.*, Case No. D2002-0856 (WIPO Nov. 5, 2002).

The ancient city of Potsdam, Germany, a tourist attraction well known as the site of the castle "Sanssouci," successfully obtained the rights to four domain names that incorporated the city's name: potsdam.com, potsdam.net, potsdam.org, and potsdam.info. These domain names corresponded to the website of a company providing IT services. The city contended that the city name trademark and the domain names are identical; that the registrant had no right or legitimate interest in the domain names; and that the registrant used the domain names in bad faith to mislead consumers. The respondent did not file a response to the complaint, and, the panel said, had no obvious connection to the domain names. Because an Internet user seeking information about the city of Potsdam would likely seek such information at the respondent's domain names and would find only the company in four major TLD's, the city had demonstrated sufficient bad faith on the part of the registrant to warrant transfer of the domain names.

Reverse Domain Name Hijacking

If a panel determines that a UDRP complaint was brought in bad faith and was an abuse of the administrative proceeding, the panel will make a declaratory finding of reverse domain name hijacking. A complainant need not "knowingly" file an insupportable claim but need only be reckless as to whether the complaint is supportable or not. One panel found that this recklessness standard was met in the initiation of a UDRP proceeding by a trademark holder of a generic name where the respondent was preparing to run a legitimate site. *See Smart Design LLC v. Carolyn Hughes*, Case No. D2000-0993 (WIPO October 18, 2000). A win by the respondent is not sufficient, by itself, to support a finding of reverse domain name hijacking. The complainant must actually be found to have brought the complaint in bad faith. *EasyJet Airline Co. v. Holt*, Case No D2000-0465 (WIPO August 24, 2000) (declining to make a finding of reverse domain name hijacking).

The reverse domain name hijacking concept also applies under the .biz Start-Up Trademark Opposition Policy (STOP), adopted by ICANN in May, 2001. STOP is a policy exclusive to the .biz TLD to resolve disputes over domain names that were registered during the .biz start up period, from June 25 to September 21, 2001. The owner of intellectual property rights in a trade name was notified that an application for a domain name incorporating the mark had been submitted. The owner had an opportunity to dispute the application. All other .biz domain-name disputes are required to go through the UDRP.

A WIPO decision found that complainant Zuckerman brought a STOP action in bad faith when he failed to assert a trademark right in the name shoes.biz, and failed to establish that the respondent did not have rights to the name. *Zuckerman v. Peeris*, Case No. DBIZ2002-00245 (WIPO Aug. 12, 2002).

First Amendment Issues in Trademark Disputes

Use of Trademarks as Communicative Speech

Trademark owners have sometimes attempted to apply trademark law to prevent the communication of unflattering messages about the trademark owner or its products. However, trademark law recognizes a "fair use" defense if the trademark is used only "to describe the goods or services of [a] party, or their geographic origin." 15 U.S.C. § 1115(b)(4). The First Amendment is also a potential bar to such claims.

 *Intel Trade Secret Dispute.*

Robert Collins created a website entitled "The Intel Secrets' Home Page." He stated that the purpose of the page was to provide information about the Intel architecture processors. Intel complained that Collins's use of the Intel Secrets logo infringed Intel's trademark. Collins claimed that his use of the Intel Secrets logo was a parody that did not cause confusion and therefore did not infringe Intel's trademark. He modified the site to make the parody unmistakable and continued to publish.

Playboy Enters., Inc. v. Terri Welles, Inc., 7 F. Supp. 2d 1098 (S.D. Cal.), *aff'd*, 162 F.3d 1169 (9th Cir. 1998), *summary judgment granted by* 78 F. Supp. 2d 1066 (S.D. Cal. 1999), *aff'd*, 279 F.3d 796 (9th Cir. February 1, 2002).

Playboy sued former playboy playmate Terri Welles for her use of the terms "playmate" and "playboy" on her website and in metatags. (For discussion of use of trademarks in metatags generally, *see* pages 81-84.) In April 1998, a federal court held that Welles' use of the terms was a descriptive or nominative fair use of the marks to describe her career, which could not be accomplished without the use of Playboy's marks. Playboy's request for a preliminary injunction was denied.

In December 1999, the district court granted summary judgment for the defendant on all trademark, dilution, and unfair competition counts, finding that she made descriptive and fair uses of Playboy's marks and did not act in bad faith.

On February 1, 2002, the U.S. Court of Appeals for the Ninth Circuit ruled that the use of the trademarks "Playboy," "Playmate," and "Playmate of the Year 1981," was permissible "nominative fair use" of the marks: "There is simply no descriptive substitute for the trademarks used in Welles' metatags. Precluding their use would have the unwanted effect of hindering the free flow of information on the internet, something which is certainly not a goal of the trademark law." The court, however, remanded to the district court the issue of whether the repeated use of the phrase "PMOY'81" as online wallpaper was entitled to trademark protection because it failed the first test for nominative fair use of a trademark as set out in *New Kids on the Block v. New America Publishing Inc.*, 971 F.2d 302 (9th Cir. 1992).

Parody and Criticism

Courts ordinarily will allow the use of a trademark in a parody website or a "gripe site" so long as there is no confusion as to whether the site is conveying parody or criticism or as to the origin or sponsorship of the website itself.

Gripe Sites

 Bally Total Fitness Holding Corp. v. Faber, 29 F. Supp. 2d 1161 (C.D. Cal. 1998).

The use of "Bally Sucks" on a website criticizing the health clubs was not found to constitute dilution because the "Bally" trademark was being used for noncommercial expression and was therefore not being "used in commerce" as required for a dilution claim. Furthermore, the use of the trademark was protected by the First Amendment, as it was crucial to identifying the goods that were the subject of constitutionally protected speech.

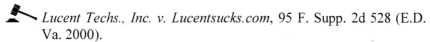 *Lucent Techs., Inc. v. Lucentsucks.com*, 95 F. Supp. 2d 528 (E.D. Va. 2000).

The court acknowledged that consumers would be unlikely to confuse lucentsucks.com with an official website of Lucent Technologies. The court also recognized that a so-called "cybergriping" or "sucks" site, if able to demonstrate effective parody or critical commentary, could counter a trademark holder's claim of bad-faith intent in registration. Bad faith is a necessary element of a cybersquatting claim under the ACPA. Lucentsucks.com was allowed to retain its domain name based on Lucent Technologies' failure to comply with the jurisdictional requirements of an *in rem* action under the ACPA.

Ford Motor Co. v. 2600 Enterprises, 177 F. Supp. 2d 661 (E.D. Mich. 2001).

The defendant had registered the domain name fuckgeneralmotors.com and linked it to the Ford Motor Company website. Ford sought an injunction requiring the defendant to remove the link. On December 20, 2001, the U.S. District Court for the Eastern District of Michigan denied Ford's motion. The court ruled that the programmatic link was not a commercial use or a use in connection with goods or services within the meaning of the Lanham Act and that there was therefore no trademark infringement. The court distinguished and criticized two of the earlier cases on the Lanham Act's application to domain names used in connection with sites that disparage the marks owners. *Planned Parenthood Federation of America, Inc. v. Bucci*, No. 97 Civ. 06 29 (KMW) (S.D.N.Y. March 27, 1997), and *Jews for Jesus v. Brodsky*, 993 F. Supp. 282 (D.N.J. 1998).

Parody Sites

People for the Ethical Treatment of Animals v. Doughney, 113 F. Supp. 2d 915 (E.D. Va. 2000), *aff'd*, No. 00-1918 (L) (CA 99-1336-A) (4th Cir. Sept. 18, 2001).

The plaintiffs brought an action for trademark infringement, dilution, and cybersquatting against the defendant, who used the domain name peta.org for his website "People Eating Tasty Animals." The plaintiffs own the registered service mark for PETA, People for the Ethical Treatment of Animals. The defendant claimed that the suit constituted an attempt to infringe his political speech and that his site was a parody. The district court found the use of the identical mark prevented the defendant's site from protection as a parody because Web users would not realize they were being taken to a parody of PETA until after they had used PETA's mark to access the website. The district court granted summary judgment in favor of PETA, and the domain name was transferred. The Court of Appeals for the Fourth Circuit affirmed the district court's ruling, agreeing that the defendant was liable for trademark infringement, unfair competition, and violation of the ACPA.

🔨 *OBH, Inc. v. Spotlight Magazine, Inc.*, 86 F. Supp. 2d 176 (W.D.N.Y. 2000).

The defendant operated a "parody" site criticizing The Buffalo News at www.thebuffalonews.com. The court found that the parody defense required a lack of confusion and that confusion was likely because users would only realize they were visiting a parody site after they arrived. The defendant's use of a disclaimer on the site could not overcome this confusion. The court inferred from the circumstances that the defendant used the Buffalo News trademark knowingly and intentionally to trick some Internet users into receiving his message instead of The Buffalo News.

Treatment of Cybergripe and Parody Web Sites in UDRP Proceedings

In UDRP proceedings, a website operator that has established a legitimate consumer gripe site may be able to defend its use of the site's associated domain name on the ground that it has a protectable First Amendment interest in criticizing the company. Most of the proceedings brought under the UDRP involving [company name]sucks.com have led to a transfer of the domain name, particularly where they have involved cybersquatters who acquired the domain name with the commercial purpose to sell the domain name to the trademark owner. *See, e.g., Wal-Mart Stores, Inc. v. Walsucks*, Case No. D2000-0477 (WIPO July 20, 2000); *Vivendi Universal v. Jay D. Sallen*, Case No. D2001-1121 (WIPO Nov. 7, 2001) (finding that many non-English speakers may associate [trademark]sucks sites with the trademark owner, and that Sallen's free speech claim was concocted after receiving a cease-and-desist letter).

However, where the website operator has established a legitimate consumer gripe or parody site, the operator may be able to defend use of the domain name on the ground that it has a protectable First Amendment interest in criticizing the company. *See McLane Co. v. Craig*, Case No. D2000-1455 (WIPO January 11, 2001) (refusing to cancel or transfer mclanenortheast.com and mclanenortheastsucks.com)

🔨 *Falwell v. Cohn*, Case No. D2002-0184 (WIPO June 3, 2002).

A UDRP panel refused to transfer jerryfalwell.com and jerryfallwell.com to noted televangelist Jerry Falwell. The panel based its refusal to transfer on the ground that Falwell had failed to prove he had common law trademark rights in his name, but the panel also found that the respondent's use of the domain names to provide parody, satire, and criticism of Jerry Falwell was a legitimate noncommercial or fair use. In late June 2002, Falwell filed suit in a federal court in Virginia to force a transfer of the domain names. See "Falwell Files Suit Against Site Owner," The News & Advance (June 20, 2002).

First Amendment Claims Brought Against NSI

Suits have been brought against Network Solutions, Inc. (NSI) and the National Science Foundation (NSF) on First Amendment grounds based on NSI's policy of refusing to register second-level domain names that contain seven words widely regarded as indecent, and, in the most recent case, based on NSI's policy of allowing trademark holders to contest domain-name registrations. *See Dluhos v. Strasberg*, No. 00-3163 (D.N.J. Aug. 31, 2001) (the plaintiff alleged that it was a violation of the First Amendment to "allow trademark law to trump free expression"); *National A-1 Advertising, Inc. v. Network Solutions, Inc.*, 121 F. Supp. 2d 156 (D.N.H. 2000); *Island Online, Inc. v. Network Solutions, Inc.*, 119 F. Supp. 2d 289 (E.D.N.Y. 2000). However, because NSI developed its policies independently of the NSF, the courts have held that NSI is not a state actor. Accordingly, they have rejected the assertion that there is a First Amendment right to domain names.

The courts have also noted that speech via domain names is not absolutely protected because NSF is not a public forum; NSI's failure to register the names does not serve as a prior restraint on speech because a domain-name owner could still have the words in its URL by placing the desired words in a subdirectory (the court explained that it saw no meaningful difference between www.photos.com/feelmytits and www.feelmytits.photos.com). *See Dluhos*, No. 00-3163 (holding that NSI is not a state or federal actor capable of violating the First, Fourth, Fifth, or Fourteenth Amendments in its administration of domain-name registration and dispute resolution policy); *National A-1 Advertising, Inc.*, 121 F. Supp. 2d at 168 (holding that NSI is not a state actor capable of violating First Amendment free-speech rights in its denial of certain domain names); *Island Online, Inc.*, 119 F. Supp. 2d at 307 (holding that despite its Cooperative Agreement with NSF, NSI is not a state or federal actor under the close nexus, public function, and symbiotic relationship tests).

Linking and Framing

Linking

Linking to external Web pages sometimes raises intellectual property questions. A hyperlink alone is not generally understood to imply sponsorship or endorsement of the linking site by the linked-to site.

However, it is possible to imagine circumstances where the use of a word or design mark associated with the linked site could create confusion regarding origin, affiliation, endorsement, or sponsorship in violation of the Lanham Act or state laws regulating unfair competition.

For discussion of linking in the context of copyright infringement, *see* Chapter 3, pages 97-100.

Linking Cases

 Ticketmaster Corp. v. Microsoft Corp., No. 97-3055 (C.D. Cal. filed Apr. 28, 1997).

Microsoft deep-linked from its "Seattle sidewalk" website, where events were described to the pages on the Ticketmaster site on which tickets to those events could be purchased, bypassing the Ticketmaster home page and the various pages users would otherwise have to click through before reaching a page on which tickets could be purchased. Ticketmaster objected, claiming that the deep-linking infringed Ticketmaster's trademark, diluted the mark's value, and violated state and federal laws prohibiting unfair competition. This lawsuit was settled in February 1999 and resulted in no substantive rulings.

 Ticketmaster Corp. v. Tickets.Com, Inc., 2000 U.S. Dist. LEXIS 4553, 54 U.S.P.Q.2d (BNA) 1344 (C.D. Cal. March 27, 2000), *preliminary injunction denied*, 2000 U.S. Dist. LEXIS 12987 (C.D. Cal. August 10, 2000).

Ticketmaster sued Tickets.com, alleging that it had provided false and misleading information and illegally linked into the Ticketmaster website. Among other claims, Ticketmaster accused Tickets.com of "deep linking" by offering an unauthorized connection from the Tickets.com site to a location several pages within the Ticketmaster site. On the defendant's motion, the court dismissed several of the plaintiff's claims. Although the court did not dismiss the copyright infringement, passing-off, reverse passing-off, or false advertising claims, the court concluded that "hyperlinking does not itself involve a violation of the Copyright Act" and that "deep linking by itself (*i.e.*, without confusion of source) does not necessarily involve unfair competition." On August 10, 2000, the court denied Ticketmaster's request for a preliminary injunction, taking into account, but not specifically relying on, the recent implementation by Ticketmaster of technology that prevented "deep linking" to its interior pages.

For discussion of this case in the context of trespass, *see* Chapter 9, page 274.

Hyperlink Patent Dispute

A federal court has ruled that British Telecommunications (BT) does not hold a patent on hyperlinking. The U.K. phone company claimed it had held the patent for linking online documents since 1989, but only discovered it owned the patent in 1996. The patent, which details a method for accessing documents by hyperlinking "from a central location," was discovered, BT said, during a routine check. In December 2000, BT filed a patent infringement complaint in the United States District Court for the Southern District of New York against Prodigy, a U.S. Internet service provider (ISP), asserting that Prodigy infringed BT's patent by using the hyperlinking method and by providing access to its customers to use the hyperlinking method on the Internet. In March 2002, the court issued its decision defining the scope of the patents and ordered the parties to file motions for summary judgment based on its ruling on the scope of the patents. The court held that the patents described a system in which documents were retrieved from a central computer, a single device in one location. *British Telecommunications PLC v. Prodigy Communications Corp.*, 189 F. Supp. 2d 101 (S.D.N.Y. 2002).

In August 2002, the court granted Prodigy's motion for summary judgment, finding that no jury could reasonably find patent infringement because the Internet is a decentralized network, not a system centralized around a single device. Therefore, BT does not hold a patent on the process of hyperlinking via the Internet. *See* 217 F. Supp. 2d 399 (S.D.N.Y. 2002).

Better Business Bureau Controversy

The Better Business Bureau (BBB) has instituted a linking policy under which it is attempting to require any for-profit website that wishes to link to the BBB to get prior authorization. The first method of gaining authorization is to become a member of the BBB (after which no specific linking authorization is necessary). To become a member, a business must submit an application, along with background information "sufficient to enable the BBB to provide inquirers with factual reports which bear on the reliability of the business." Non-members will only be granted the right to link by demonstrating that the link will not reflect unfavorably on the BBB, that the company has a clean record with the BBB, that the public interest is served by allowing the link notwithstanding the company's non-member status, and that the link is limited to the context of general resource information. Not all companies have complied with this policy and the BBB has not taken legal action against those who have refused to comply.

Framing

The practice of framing, in which one website displays the content of another site within its own pages, is described in greater detail in the context of copyright in Chapter 3 at pages 100-101. Framing, like linking, can potentially infringe a trademark where the use of the frame creates confusion as to origin, affiliation, endorsement, or sponsorship.

 *Washington Post Co. v. Total News, Inc.*, No. 97 Civ. 1190 (PKL) (S.D.N.Y. 1997).

The Washington Post and other news organizations filed suit in February 1997 to preclude the defendant online news service from framing their websites. The plaintiffs alleged that the defendants had designed a parasitic website: instead of creating its content, Total News simply "republished" the news and editorial content of other Web publishers within a frame. Among other causes of action, the plaintiffs asserted federal trademark dilution, claiming that the defendants' actions diluted and detracted from the distinctiveness of the plaintiffs' famous trademarks. The case settled with the defendant agreeing to remove its frame and the plaintiffs allowing access to their websites through simple hypertext links, without any framing.

Metatags and Hidden Code

To achieve favorable positioning in lists of search results displayed to users of search engines, many websites place key words in data fields invisible to users but routinely surveyed by the search engines.

Courts have grappled with the question of whether the inclusion of a competitor's trademark in such "metatags" violates federal trademark law.

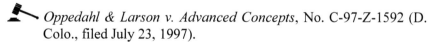 *Oppedahl & Larson v. Advanced Concepts*, No. C-97-Z-1592 (D. Colo., filed July 23, 1997).

The plaintiff, a patent law firm, filed suit claiming that the five defendants' use of the plaintiff's marks as metatags infringed and diluted the value of those marks. The case settled with an agreement that precluded further use of the plaintiff's marks in the defendants' metatags.

See also Playboy Enters., Inc. v. Calvin Designer Label, 985 F. Supp. 1220 (N.D. Cal. 1997) (ordering the defendant to cease use of the trademarks "Playmate" and "Playboy" in its metatags, as well as the registered mark "Playmate" as part of its domain name).

🔨 *The New York State Society of Certified Public Accountants v. Eric Louis Assocs.*, 79 F. Supp. 2d 331 (S.D.N.Y. 1999).

The plaintiff, a nonprofit organization for certified public accountants, has been using the common law service mark "NYSSCPA" since 1984 and registered the domain name nysscpa.org in 1994. The defendant operates a placement firm for accountants and other financial professionals;it registered the domain name nysscpa.com in 1999, along with two other domain names. Each of these three sites used the term "NYSSCPA" in its metatag field so that the defendants' sites would be listed among the search results when those using search engines searched the term "NYSSCPA." Although the defendant had stipulated to the entry of a permanent injunction, the court addressed the merits of the claims and found that the defendant's domain name and use of metatags constituted trademark infringement and dilution; the court found that the use of domain name NYSSCPA.com and use of NYSSCPA in metatags created "initial interest confusion." Although the defendant's website included a notice that it was not affiliated with NYSSCPA, the court found that the user's momentary initial confusion was sufficient to establish a likelihood of confusion and was also relevant in showing dilution.

🔨 *Brookfield Communications, Inc. v. West Coast Entertainment Corp.*, 174 F.3d 1036 (9th Cir. 1999).

As discussed above at page 38, Brookfield Communications, a movie-industry vendor and operator of moviebuffonline.com, filed suit against video rental chain West Coast Entertainment Corp. to prevent its planned launch of a website at moviebuff.com. The court found Brookfield to be the senior user of the mark, and the defendant was enjoined from using the "moviebuff" trademark in either a domain name or in metatags. The court commented that "using another's trademark in one's metatags is much like posting a sign with another's trademark in front of one's store."

🔨 *Bihari v. Gross*, 119 F. Supp. 2d 309 (S.D.N.Y. 2000).

The defendant registered several domain names, which he used to criticize the plaintiff's interior design business. The defendant voluntarily relinquished the two domain names that included the plaintiff's service marks, but continued to use the plaintiff's marks in the metatags of the remaining sites. The court held that the ACPA does not apply to metatags. The court also rejected the plaintiff's trademark infringement claim holding that defendant used plaintiff's marks in the metatags of his websites as a fair description of the content of those sites, not as marks.

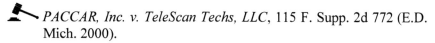

PACCAR, Inc. v. TeleScan Techs, LLC, 115 F. Supp. 2d 772 (E.D. Mich. 2000).

As discussed above at page 39, Telescan Technologies was enjoined from using PACCAR's marks in any of its domain names, Web pages, metatags, or website "wallpaper." The court embraced the notion of "initial interest confusion" and stated that "a disclaimer that purports to disavow association with the trademark owner after the consumer has reached the site comes too late."

Trans Union LLC v. Credit Research, Inc., 142 F. Supp. 2d 1029 (N.D. Ill. March 27, 2001).

The plaintiff succeeded on a number of trademark infringement claims involving the defendant's use of domain names and logos that infringed Trans Union's trademarks. The court, however, found that the use of "trans union" in a single metatag constituted fair use of the trademark. The court distinguished this case, in which there was only one such metatag, from "cyber-stuffing," the practice of repeating a term numerous times in a website's metatags in order to lure the attention of Internet search engines. Such cyber-stuffing is not fair use because it serves to misdirect the user to the stuffer's page rather than the page that the consumer was initially seeking.

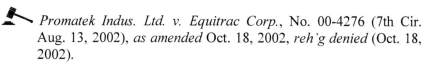

Promatek Indus. Ltd. v. Equitrac Corp., No. 00-4276 (7th Cir. Aug. 13, 2002), *as amended* Oct. 18, 2002, *reh'g denied* (Oct. 18, 2002).

The U.S. Court of Appeals for the Seventh Circuit recently ruled that a company may not include a competitor's trademark in metatags when such use will cause users initial confusion. The plaintiff, Promatek, and the defendant, Equitrac, compete in the cost-recovery equipment market. Equitrac provides services for "Copitrak" equipment, to which Promatek owns the trademark. Equitrac included the word "Copitrack" in the metatags field on its website, prompting Promatek to file suit. Equitrac subsequently removed the Copitrack metatags from its website, but Promatek persisted in its suit, seeking an injunction to prevent Equitrac from using the term Copitrack on its site. The trial court granted the injunction and ordered Equitrac to include language on its website (1) indicating that it is not affiliated Copitrack, and (2) directing users seeking Copitrak to Promatek's website via a link. Although the court found it likely that Equitrac did not intend to confuse or mislead consumers, it nevertheless found a strong likelihood that the Copitrack metatag would lead to initial confusion. This potential confusion was actionable under the Lanham Act. The court of appeals affirmed the injunction on August 13, 2002. The court later issued a modification to its opinion, clarifying that the use of another party's metatags is permissible if used in a legitimate and nondeceptive way.

Mark Nutritionals Inc. v. FindWhat Services Inc., No. SA-02-CA-0085-OG (W.D. Texas complaint filed January 31, 2002); *Mark Nutritionals Inc. v. Overture Services Inc.*, No. SA-02-CA-0086-OG (W.D. Texas complaint filed January 31, 2002); *Mark Nutritionals Inc. v. Alta Vista Co.*, No. SA-02-CA-0087-EP (W.D. Texas complaint filed January 31, 2002); *Mark Nutritionals Inc. v. Innovative Marketing Solutions Inc. d/b/a Kanoodle.com*, No. SA-02-CA-0088-OG (W.D. Texas complaint filed January 31, 2002).

Mark Nutritionals, the company that markets the Body Solutions weight-loss program, has filed suit against multiple search engines claiming that their practice of allowing advertisers to purchase the rights to have their websites listed first when users enter the search terms "body" and "solutions" violates the Lanham Act (§§ 1114 and 1125).

Spam

Several suits have been filed to prevent companies and individuals from sending out "spam," or junk e-mail, with another company's trademark as a return address. Through this practice, known as forgery, "spammers" avoid detection and prevent their own Internet service providers' systems from being clogged by returned e-mail. Some companies have successfully sued spammers on the grounds that such forgery constitutes trademark infringement.

Many states have enacted anti-spam laws, and others are considering them. In addition, there are several pending federal bills that would address spam. For a more detailed discussion of spam and spam laws, *see* Chapter 7.

CompuServe, Inc. v. Cyber Promotions, Inc., 962 F. Supp. 1015 (S.D. Ohio 1997).

A preliminary injunction was granted to prevent Cyber Promotions, Inc. from inserting any false reference to the plaintiff in any e-mail, falsely causing any e-mail to appear as if it were sent by or originated from the plaintiff or one of the plaintiff's accounts, or using the plaintiff's services in connection with the transmission of e-mail.

Hotmail Corp. v. Van$ Money Pie, Inc., 41998 U.S. Dist. LEXIS 10729 (N.D. Cal. April 16, 1998).

A "forged header" suit was filed seeking injunctive relief and damages against spammers, alleging Lanham Act claims, computer fraud and abuse claims, and trespass. The court entered a preliminary injunction on April 16, 1998. On June 16, 1998, the court issued a permanent injunction against three of the eight spammers named as defendants in the suit. The company settled with two of the defendants. *CNET News.com*, June 16, 1998.

Liability of Domain-Name Registrars and Internet Service Providers

Liability for Third-Party Trademark Infringement

Although there is no "safe harbor" immunity for Internet service providers (ISPs) with regard to third-party trademark infringement (as there is for third-party copyright infringement, *see* Chapter 3 at pages 104-105), courts appear to have been reluctant to hold ISPs liable for the infringing conduct of users.

 Gucci America, Inc. v. Hall & Associates, 135 F. Supp. 2d 409 (S.D.N.Y. 2001).

The defendant Internet service provider operated the goldhaus.com website on behalf of its client Hall. The plaintiff, Gucci, informed Mindspring, an ISP, that the material posted on Hall's website infringed Gucci's trademark rights and demanded removal of the material. When Mindspring failed to remove the material, Gucci sued both Hall and Mindspring. The court denied Mindspring's motion to dismiss, holding that an ISP may be liable for contributory trademark infringement where the ISP exercised "direct control and monitoring of the instrumentality used by a third party to infringe the plaintiff's mark." The court declined to extend the ISP immunity that exists for contributory copyright infringement, legislatively granted under the Digital Millennium Copyright Act (DMCA), to cases involving trademark infringement. The court noted that the plaintiff would have a high burden in establishing that the defendant had sufficient knowledge of the infringement for the plaintiff to prove a claim of contributory infringement.

▲ *Lockheed Martin Corp. v. Network Solutions, Inc.*, No. 4:00-CV-0405-A, 2001 U.S. Dist. LEXIS 5459 (May 1, 2001).

The defendant domain-name registrar permitted a third party to register domain names that were identical or confusingly similar to the plaintiff's trademarks. The plaintiff sued the defendant domain-name registrar, claiming that the registrations were obtained in violation of the ACPA. A federal judge in Texas dismissed the action, holding that domain-name registrars have no duty to perform gatekeeper functions when registering domain names. The court held that the language in the ACPA that prohibits improper "registration" was intended only to apply to the party *obtaining* the domain name. The court noted that the purpose of the UDRP was to handle domain-name disputes efficiently, because it is difficult to prevent improper registrations but simple to transfer domain names.

See also Bird v. Parsons, 2002 U.S. App. LEXIS 9543 (6th Cir. May 21, 2002) (finding that domain-name registrars and companies that provide an auction site for registered domain names are not liable for third-party infringement); *Ford Motor Co. v. Greatdomains.com*, No. 00-CV-71544-DT (E.D. Mich. December 20, 2001) (finding that an Internet auction site cannot be held liable for third-party violations of the ACPA).

Liability of Domain-Name Registrars for "Coming Soon Pages"

Domain-name registrars often link registered domain names to a placeholder page that announces that the registrant's site is under construction and will be "Coming Soon." These "Coming Soon Pages" may include banner advertisements for the registrar's services, as well as advertisements for the registrar's sponsors. Many domain-name registrants may not be aware that registrars engage in this practice.

Until recently, no registrant had challenged the registrars' right to post these pages. However, in July 2001, a domain-name registrant named Zurakov filed suit against Register.com alleging that the Coming Soon Page that Register.com linked to Zurakov's domain name was a breach of the parties' service contract and a violation of the implied covenant of good faith and fair dealing and General Business Laws (GBL) §§ 349 and 350 ("Deceptive Acts and Practices"). *Zurakov v. Register.com*, No. 600703/01 (N.Y. Sup. Ct. July 25, 2001). Zurakov also claimed that the page allowed Register.com to profit unjustly from the domain name. The court disagreed.

Zurakov had registered the domain name www.laborzionist.org with Register.com, and while Zurakov was constructing his site, Register.com linked the domain name to a Coming Soon Page containing banner advertisements for Register.com and its sponsors. Zurakov claimed that his domain-name registration gave him an exclusive property right in the domain name and that the Coming Soon Page interfered with that right and deprived him of the benefits of the contract. However, the court held that Zurakov only had a contract right, not a property right, in www.laborzionist.org because the domain name was merely a product of the service contract with Register.com and was not a registered patent or trademark. Because the service agreement governed the parties' contract rights, it alone governed Zurakov's rights in the domain name. The court found that Zurakov "received everything he bargained for under the service contract" because the contract explicitly provided that "register.com may suspend, cancel, transfer or modify [Zurakov's] use of the services at any time, for any reason, in register.com's sole discretion." *Zurakov*, No. 600703/01 at 4-5. Further, the court noted that Register.com fully disclosed its practice of displaying a Coming Soon Page in both the "Frequently Asked Questions" and the "Help" sections of the Register.com website, and Zurakov had the ability to delete the Coming Soon Page by following the instructions set forth in those sections. Accordingly, the court granted Register.com's motion to dismiss.

Search Engine Liability

Two search engine companies have been accused of improperly exploiting the trademarks of others by selling companies the right to have their banner advertisements served up to users who include the trademarks of other companies in their search terms:

 Estee Lauder, Inc. v. Fragrance Counter, Inc. and Excite, 189 F.R.D. 269 (S.D.N.Y. 1999).

Estee Lauder sued the Excite portal, alleging that users who searched for "Estee Lauder" on Excite's WebCrawler service were presented with banner ads for retailers The Fragrance Counter and Cosmetics Counter, and that Estee Lauder's name was used in the banner without the company's permission. Neither The Fragrance Counter nor Cosmetics Counter is licensed to sell Estee Lauder merchandise. The case was dismissed without prejudice on August 16, 2000, after the defendants agreed to stop "keying" their banner ads to searches for the plaintiff's trademarks.

➤ *Playboy Enters., Inc. v. Netscape Communications Corp.*, 55 F. Supp. 2d 1070 (C.D. Cal. 1999), *aff'd*, 1999 U.S. App. LEXIS 30215 (9th Cir. Nov. 15, 1999), and *Playboy Enters., Inc. v. Netscape Communications Corp.*, 2000 U.S. Dist. LEXIS 13418 (C.D. Cal. Sept. 12, 2000).

Playboy alleged in a federal lawsuit that Excite and Netscape were violating its trademark rights by displaying banner ads for other companies to users who run a search for "Playboy." On June 24, 1999, the U.S. District Court for the Central District of California refused Playboy's request for a preliminary injunction. The court ruled narrowly that the terms "playboy" and "playmate" are generic, that Playboy Enterprises has no monopoly on those words in all forms, and that the sale of those search keywords to third-party advertisers that operate adult-entertainment sites therefore does not constitute trademark infringement or dilution. The Ninth Circuit affirmed the denial of the preliminary injunction. Subsequently, the district court entered judgment for the defendants finding no dilution, no likelihood of confusion, and no use of the plaintiff's marks to identify the defendants' goods. An appeal is pending in the U.S. Court of Appeals for the Ninth Circuit.

Domain-Name Slamming

➤ *Register.com v. Domain Registry of Am., Inc.*, No. 02 Civ. 6915, 2002 U.S. Dist. LEXIS 24795 (S.D.N.Y. Dec. 26, 2002).

Domain-name registrar Register.com won a preliminary injunction against Domain Registry of America (DROA) for causing customers to change unwittingly their Internet domain service from Register.com to DROA. The defendant sent e-mails to the plaintiff's customers suggesting that they renew their domain-name registrations. Those who did had their registrations transferred from Register.com to DROA. The e-mails, the court said, misled customers by implying that DROA was somehow assisting Register.com. In issuing the preliminary injunction, the court dubbed the unlawful practice "domain name slamming" because of its similarities to long-distance telephone services' attempts to cause customers to switch long-distance companies, commonly called "slamming."

COPYRIGHT ISSUES

Copyright Basics

The need to protect the works of authors was considered so fundamental to the nation's well-being that the framers of the Constitution explicitly granted Congress the power to provide copyright protection in Article I, Section 8, Clause 8 of the United States Constitution. However, Congress and the courts also have attempted to balance the rights of authors against the countervailing constitutional right of the public to engage in free speech under the First Amendment. Thus, while copyright law generally grants authors the exclusive right to copy, display, reproduce, and distribute their works, it also limits the scope of these rights. For example, copyright law limits the duration of copyright protection, and permits certain unauthorized uses of copyright protected material under statutory exemptions and the "fair use" doctrine.

Protected Works

The Copyright Act of 1976 affords copyright protection to "original works of authorship fixed in any tangible medium of expression ... ." 17 U.S.C. § 102. Such works include, for example, literature, music, motion pictures, artistic works, photographs, computer programs, websites, and sound recordings. They can also include collective works and other compilations. Copyright does not protect facts, ideas, procedures, or discoveries.

The Digital Millennium Copyright Act of 1998 expressly extends copyright protection to works created in digital media. 17 U.S.C. §§ 1201 et seq., Pub. L. 105-304, 112 Stat. 2863, Oct. 18, 1998, § 512. Works created in digital media are considered "fixed" if they can be perceived, reproduced, or otherwise communicated for more than a transitory period, including fixation on a computer disc or in a computer's random access memory (RAM).

Scope of Protection

The owner of a copyright has the exclusive right to reproduce the copyrighted work, prepare derivative works from it, distribute copies, and publicly display or perform it. 17 U.S.C. § 106. Since the passage of the Copyright Term Extension Act of 1998, copyright protection generally lasts for the life of the author plus 70 years, or, in the case of works for hire and anonymous works, the shorter of 95 years from the date of first publication or 120 years from the creation of the work. 17 U.S.C. § 302.

On January 15, 2003, the U.S. Supreme Court decided the case *Eldred v. Ashcroft*, No. 01-618 (U.S. Jan. 15, 2003), upholding a 20-year extension of existing copyrights. The Court held that the Copyright Term Extension Act of 1998 (CTEA) did not exceed Congress' power under the Copyright Clause of the Constitution. The CTEA extends the duration of existing copyrights from life of the author plus 50 years to life of the author plus 70 years. The ruling keeps works such as Disney's Mickey Mouse and the poems of Robert Frost out of the public domain for an additional 20 years. It was not within the Court's power, Justice Ginsberg wrote for the seven-member majority, to question Congress' actions with respect to intellectual property matters. The opinion indicated that the Constitution afforded broad powers to Congress to legislate with respect to intellectual property matters, authority that it exercised within appropriate limits when enacting the CTEA.

Registration

Copyright registration is not a condition to obtaining copyright protection. Rather, copyright protection applies automatically when an original work of authorship is fixed in a tangible medium of expression. 17 U.S.C. § 102. However, copyright registration obtained before or within five years after a work's first publication is evidence of the validity of the copyright in the work and of the facts stated in the certificate of registration. 17 U.S.C. § 410(c). In addition, copyright registration is ordinarily required in order to sustain a copyright infringement lawsuit.

Available Remedies

The Copyright Act authorizes injunctive relief and damages. Available damages include not only the copyright owner's lost profits, but also any profits gained by the infringer as a result of the copyright violations. 17 U.S.C. §§ 502, 504(b). If the works were registered at the time of the infringement, statutory damages of up to $30,000 per work for non-willful infringement and up to $150,000 per work for willful infringement are available as an alternative to actual damages. 17 U.S.C. § 504(c). An award of attorney fees is also possible. 17 U.S.C. § 505.

Limits on Protection

The rights of the copyright holder are limited by the right of others to make "fair use" of copyrighted material—that is, to use it in public discussion or for other permitted purposes. In determining whether a use of copyrighted material is "fair," courts are directed by the Copyright Act to consider (1) the purpose for which the material was used, (2) the nature of the material, (3) the amount used, and (4) the effect of the use on the market for or value of the copyrighted material. 17 U.S.C. § 107.

The Digital Millennium Copyright Act grants Internet "service providers," as defined in the Act, a limited immunity from copyright infringement claims. This limited immunity is discussed in detail below.

Obtaining and Protecting Rights to Web Site Content

Methods of Obtaining Rights

A Web publisher can make content available to its users in three ways: (1) by developing original content, (2) by licensing content provided by others for display on its website, and (3) by linking to or framing material developed by others. Web publishers have encountered legal issues involving each of these methods.

Possession of Print Media Rights Does Not Necessarily Imply Online Rights

In *Ryan v. CARL Corp.*, 23 F. Supp. 2d 1146 (N.D. Cal. 1998), freelance journalists successfully sued an Internet service that had allowed subscribers to search an electronic database for articles, then select particular articles to be delivered by fax.

In its landmark decision in *New York Times Company v. Tasini*, 533 U.S. 483 (2001), the U.S. Supreme Court held that publishers that licensed articles by freelance writers for republication without obtaining the writers' permission or providing further compensation were violating copyright law.

Various periodicals, including *The New York Times*, *Newsday*, and *Sports Illustrated*, were sued after they made available in searchable online electronic databases freelance articles they had previously published in print. The freelancers claimed that this practice infringed upon the copyrights they held in their individual articles. The Court of Appeals for the Second Circuit, in *Tasini v. The New York Times Co.*, 206 F.3d 161 (2d Cir. 2000), reversed a trial court ruling against the freelance journalists. The Second Circuit held that, in the absence of a contractual agreement with its freelance contributors, the publisher of a collective work (such as a magazine) may not grant an electronic database (such as NEXIS) the right to republish in electronic form the individual freelance articles that make up the collective work. While a publisher's right of copyright in the collective work allows the publisher to create "revisions" of that work, the inclusion of individual freelance articles in electronic databases was more than mere revision under the Copyright Act and thus beyond the scope of the publishers' rights of copyright.

In affirming the court of appeals decision, the Supreme Court stated that in determining whether an electronic database would be deemed a permissible revision of the original collective work, a court should look to "whether the database itself perceptibly presents the author's contribution as part of a revision of the collective work." *Tasini* at 504. The Court made it clear that a microfiche reproduction of issues of a magazine is a permissible revision of the original, because articles appear in microform "writ very small, in precisely the position in which the articles appeared in the [original print publication]." *Id.* at 501. Though the user of a microfilm version of a newspaper "can adjust the machine lens to focus only on the [a]rticle, to the exclusion of surrounding material," the user "first encounters the [a]rticle in context." *Id.* By contrast, the databases in which the plaintiff authors' works were reproduced "store[d] and retrieve[d] articles separately within a vast domain of diverse texts." *Id.* at 503. The articles, as reproduced in these databases, "appear[ed] disconnected from their original context." The case was remanded to the district court to determine the appropriate remedies.

On July 2, 2001, in the wake of the Supreme Court's *Tasini* ruling, the Authors Guild and two freelance writers filed a class-action lawsuit against *The New York Times* claiming copyright infringement. The National Writers Union, which was a party in the *Tasini* case and for which Tasini serves as president, has also indicated that it plans to sue *The New York Times* again based on the newspaper's new freelance policy.

Marx v. Globe Newspaper Co., Inc., No. 00-2579-F (Mass. Super. Ct. Nov. 26, 2002).

In response to the Supreme Court's decision in *Tasini*, the Boston *Globe* newspaper required all freelancers to sign a license agreement granting the newspaper a non-exclusive license to use all of the freelancer's past and future works, including the right to reproduce the works, or derivatives of the works, in any medium, including electronic databases. Any freelancer who did not sign the new license would be ineligible for future freelance work from the *Globe*. Six of the freelancers sued the newspaper, contending that the license agreement was an unfair or deceptive act in violation of Massachusetts consumer protection and fair business dealing laws. The Massachusetts Superior Court granted the newspaper's motion for summary judgment; because the plaintiffs were independent contractors, the newspaper had no duty to continue using their services. In the court's view, the *Globe* was free to comply with the *Tasini* ruling by requiring its freelancers, as a condition of continued assignments, to grant the newspaper the right to republish their prior works "even if one were to characterize this modification as 'extortion' obtained through the Globe's strong bargaining position, the legitimate commercial reason for the Globe to have demanded this modification placed its demand within the rough and tumble, yet reasonable, commercial standards of fair dealing in the trade."

 Greenberg v. National Geographic Soc'y, 1998 U.S. Dist. LEXIS 18060 (S.D. Fla. 1998), *rev'd*, 244 F.3d 1267 (11th Cir. 2001), *cert. denied*, 122 S. Ct. 347 (Oct. 9, 2001).

On October 9, 2001, the Supreme Court declined to review an appeals court decision that found that the National Geographic had infringed the plaintiff's rights in his photographic works. The National Geographic Society had produced a 30-CD-ROM set that included every issue of *National Geographic* published from 1888 through 1996; some of plaintiff's photos were included in the work. National Geographic argued that its reproduction of Greenberg's work in the collection of CD-ROMs did not make the photos "new work." The district court agreed, holding that the CD-ROM constituted a permissible revision of National Geographic's print compilations, but the U.S. Court of Appeals for the Eleventh Circuit reversed. The Eleventh Circuit assumed, without deciding, that to the extent the CD-ROM set merely reproduced digitally previously published issues of the magazine, it constituted a permissible revision, but found that the inclusion of a brief video sequence featuring various *National Geographic* covers and certain computer code that facilitated access to the images made the CD-ROM collection more than a mere revision. The case was remanded to determine the amount of damages due and whether injunctive relief is appropriate.

Using Content from Other Web Sites and the Doctrine of "Fair Use"

As noted above, one of the ways copyright law limits the exclusive rights of authors is through the doctrine of "fair use." Fair use, codified in the Copyright Act at 17 U.S.C. § 107, permits the use of copyrighted works for limited purposes of comment, criticism, teaching, scholarship, and research without the permission of the copyright owner. Whether a use is a fair use is determined by looking at four factors: (1) the purpose and character of the use, (2) the nature of the original work, (3) the amount and substantiality of the portion of the original work used, and (4) the effect of the use on the potential market for or value of the copyrighted work. The fourth factor is generally considered the most important. These four factors apply in the context of the Internet in essentially the same way they do in the context of print use.

⚖ *Kelly v. Arriba Soft Corp.*, 77 F. Supp. 2d 1116 (C.D. Cal. 1999), *aff'd in part and rev'd in part*, 280 F.3d 934 (9th Cir. 2002), *reh'g granted*, No. 00-55521 (9th Cir. Oct. 10, 2002).

The defendant operated a website that would collect images based on search terms entered by users of the site. Each image could then be viewed without visiting the website on which the picture was located. The plaintiff was a photographer who objected to his work being copied and re-displayed via the defendant's search engine. The lower court acknowledged the copyright implications of the defendant's search engine, but found that the search engine's use of the works satisfied the requirements of the fair-use defense. The court also dismissed the plaintiff's claim that the search engine violated the Digital Millennium Copyright Act, 17 U.S.C. § 1202, which prohibits the removal of copyright management information.

On appeal, the U.S. Court of Appeals for the Ninth Circuit ruled that the creation and use by a search engine of low-quality, "thumb-nail," electronic reproductions of images fell within the fair-use doctrine. However, the court found that by displaying, within an Arriba frame, high-quality images posted on the photographer's website, and by establishing inline links to those images, Arriba had violated the photographer's exclusive right to display his work. The court has agreed to rehear the case with respect to other copyright infringement issues.

For further discussion of this case in the context of framing, *see* pages 98-99, below.

⚖ *CNN v. GoSMS.com, Inc.*, 2000 U.S. Dist. LEXIS 16156 (S.D.N.Y. Oct. 30, 2000).

Several major news organizations, including Gannett, The New York Times Co., The Washington Post Co., and CNN, filed suit against GoSMS.com, Inc., a company whose technology would allow the transmission of headlines and news stories to wireless phones and other wireless devices. The lawsuit claimed direct and contributory copyright infringement, false advertising, trademark infringement, and dilution.

This "short message service" technology allows for the transmission of data 160 characters at a time. The transmissions would reproduce the plaintiffs' news stories and strip their Web content of its original advertising. After the court denied GoSMS.com's motion to dismiss, the case settled.

 Los Angeles Times v. Free Republic, 2000 U.S. Dist. LEXIS 5669 (C.D. Cal. 2000), *stipulation for entry of final judgment*, 56 U.S.P.Q.2d (BNA) 1862, 2000 U.S. Dist. LEXIS 20484 (C.D. Cal. Nov. 14, 2000).

The U.S. District Court for the Central District of California ruled that posting articles from the *Los Angeles Times* and *The Washington Post* on an Internet bulletin board so that visitors could comment on and criticize them was not a fair use. In rejecting the fair-use defense, the court concluded that the use was not transformative, the Free Republic website profited from the exploitation of the copyrighted material by attracting more users who made donations, the articles were posted verbatim rather than excerpted, and there was an adverse effect on the market for the newspapers, whose ability to sell or license the articles was diminished. There has been no reported activity on the defendant's appeal. *Free Republic et al. v. LA Times et al.*, U.S. Court of Appeals for the Ninth Circuit, Docket No. 00-57211, filed April 16, 2001.

 Video Pipeline, Inc. v. Buena Vista Home Entertainment, Inc., 192 F. Supp. 2d 321 (D. N.J. 2002).

The plaintiff, Video Pipeline, provides previews of home videos to home-video wholesalers and retailers through its videopipeline.net network. Video Pipeline originally filed suit against Buena Vista seeking a declaratory judgment that its use of movie "trailers" to make its own video clips does not constitute copyright infringement under the doctrine of fair use. The court disagreed, holding that Video Pipeline's making of its own video-clip previews for transmission over the Internet is not protected from the copyright holder's claim of copyright infringement by the fair-use defense or by the first-sale doctrine.

For a discussion of this case in the context of video streaming, *see* page 114, below.

Linking and Framing

Linking

Hypertext links lie at the heart of the Internet. As one commentator has noted, "if the Web's creators hadn't wanted linking, they would have called it the World Wide Straight Line." *See* "Linking, A Fundamental Premise of the Web, is Challenged," Siliconvalley.com (June 9, 2002), *available at* http://www.siliconvalley.com/mld/siliconvalley/news/editorial/3435606.htm.

Without more, a simple link to a website is generally not understood to implicate the copyrights of the site being linked to. However, disputes have risen in cases of "deep linking," where one website links to particular, internal pages of another site rather than the homepage, enabling visitors to bypass certain site features, including advertising. Technology also exists for sites to prevent unauthorized deep-linking by only allowing deep-linking from specific sites. For a discussion of hyperlinks in the trademark context, *see* Chapter 2, pages 78-80.

Intellectual Reserve, Inc. v. Utah Lighthouse Ministry, Inc., 75 F. Supp. 2d 1290 (D. Utah 1999).

The plaintiff is the owner of the copyright in a Mormon church work. In response to complaints from the plaintiff, the defendant removed the copyrighted work from its website, but posted a notice that the work was available online at three other sites and provided hyperlinks to those websites. In addition, the defendant's website encouraged users to visit those sites, and one of the linked sites encouraged the copying and posting of the work. The court noted that "browsing" a website created a copy of the work on the user's computer sufficient to support a copyright claim. The court found that the defendant could be found liable for the actions of the users who displayed the copyrighted work on their computers under a theory of contributory copyright infringement, and granted a preliminary injunction against the website operator.

Ticketmaster Corp. v. Tickets.Com, Inc., 2000 U.S. Dist. LEXIS 4553, 54 U.S.P.Q.2d (BNA) 1344 (C.D. Cal. March 27, 2000), *preliminary injunction denied*, 2000 U.S. Dist. LEXIS 12987 (C.D. Cal. Aug. 10, 2000).

Ticketmaster sued Tickets.com, alleging that it had provided false and misleading information and illegally linked to the Ticketmaster website. Among other claims, Ticketmaster accused Tickets.com of "deep linking," offering an unauthorized connection from the Tickets.com site to a location several pages within the Ticketmaster site. The court dismissed several of the plaintiff's claims. Although the court did not dismiss the copyright infringement, passing-off, reverse passing-off, or false advertising claims, the court concluded that "hyperlinking does not itself involve a violation of the Copyright Act" and that "deep linking by itself (*i.e.*, without confusion of source) does not necessarily involve unfair competition."

For discussion of this case in the context of trespass, *see* Chapter 9, page 274.

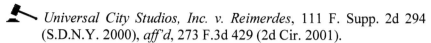 *Universal City Studios, Inc. v. Reimerdes*, 111 F. Supp. 2d 294 (S.D.N.Y. 2000), *aff'd*, 273 F.3d 429 (2d Cir. 2001).

The district court permanently enjoined a hacker website from, among other things, "knowingly linking" to any website containing any program, file, or device used to circumvent the encryption technology protecting DVDs. The court fashioned a test that would permit liability for linking to a website with knowledge that the site contains information on how to circumvent copyright protections with the purpose of disseminating information on the illegal circumvention methods.

On November 28, 2001, the U.S. Court of Appeals for the Second Circuit affirmed the decision of the district court. For discussion of this case in the context of anti-circumvention under the Digital Millennium Copyright Act of 1998, *see* page 105, below.

 "Dutch Papers Fail in Internet Copyright Case," Financial Times, (Aug. 23, 2000).

PCM and other major Dutch publishers sought an injunction against Kranten.com, a website that offers news headlines consolidated from the major newspapers. The injunction sought would have prevented Kranten.com from deep-linking into the publishers' Web pages and by-passing the advertising on their homepages. The court in Rotterdam found that the links in fact directed extra traffic to the plaintiffs' sites and that the plaintiffs could easily place advertisements next to individual stories as well as on their home pages. The court denied the injunction.

"Linking, A Fundamental Premise of the Web, is Challenged," Siliconvalley.com (June 9, 2002), *available at* http://www.siliconvalley.com/mld/siliconvalley/news/editorial/3435606.htm.

Homestore.com has sued Bargain Network in a federal court in California for unauthorized use of its real-estate listings. Homestore is seeking an injunction against Bargain Network's alleged practice of deep-linking from Bargain.com to detailed real-estate listings contained within the Realtor.com website.

For discussion of this case in the context of trespass, *see* Chapter 9, page 273.

⚖ *Danish Newspaper Publishers Association v. Newsbooster.com*
(Bailiff's Court of Copenhagen, decided July 5, 2002).

The Danish Newspaper Publishers Association recently won an injunction against a web service called Newsbooster. Newsbooster provides users who sign up for membership the ability to use keyword searches to obtain links to news stories. Newsbooster claims to "make news stories easier to find by presenting links to items with a keyword search." The Danish publishers objected to Newsbooster's practice of providing its members with deep-links to their content. The case must now be presented to the Danish Maritime and Commercial Court to confirm the injunction. This case is available at http://www.news booster.com/?pg=judge&lan=eng

Framing

Framing technology allows a website to display the content of a third-party website without actually delivering the user to the third-party site. The framed content is displayed within the framing site, which may continue to display its branding and navigation to the user. To fit within the frame, the framed page may be reduced proportionately in size, content that appears "above the fold" may be pushed down "below the fold," or some of the framed content may actually be obscured by the frame. These modifications to the manner in which the framed site is displayed might arguably constitute the creation of derivative works, a right that is exclusive to the copyright holder.

⚖ The practice of framing was challenged in *Washington Post v. Total News*, No. 97 Civ. 1190 (PKL) (S.D.N.Y. filed Feb. 20, 1997), in which Total News displayed the websites of various news organizations within a Total News frame and sold advertising in the frame. The case was settled in June 1997, with the defendant's agreement to stop framing the plaintiffs' content. For a discussion of this case in the context of trademark dilution, *see* Chapter 2, pages 81.

⚖ *Kelly v. Arriba Soft Corp.*, 77 F. Supp. 2d 1116 (C.D. Cal. 1999) *aff'd in part and rev'd in part*, 280 F.3d 934 (9th Cir. 2002), *reh'g granted*, No. 00-55521 (9th Cir. Oct. 10, 2002).

The plaintiff, a professional photographer, sued Arriba, the operator of a image search engine, over Arriba's unauthorized display of copyrighted photographs from Kelly's website.

Arriba's website displayed each search result with a link to the identified website. When a user clicked on the link, the linked page was sometimes displayed in a frame generated by the Arriba website. On other occasions, images from the linked-to pages were imported—linked-to directly—to be displayed as part of a Web page generated by Arriba. This practice is known as "inline" linking.

The Court of Appeals for the Ninth Circuit held that Arriba's framing and inline linking infringed Kelly's exclusive right to *display* his copyrighted works publicly. This is the first case to state unambiguously that framing or inline linking violates any of the exclusive rights of a copyright owner.

The court in *Kelly* rejected Arriba's fair-use defense with respect to its use of full-sized images from Kelly's website because Arriba used the entirety of Kelly's images for commercial gain and without any transformative purpose. By contrast, the court found that Arriba's use of "thumbnail" images in its search results, which linked directly to Kelly's website without any framing, was a fair use.

Kelly filed a motion for rehearing of the infringement ruling. On October 10, 2002, the Ninth Circuit ordered additional briefs from the parties, asking them to respond to inquiries related to Kelly's exclusive rights to display and create derivatives of his work.

For further discussion of this case in the context of fair use, *see* page 94 above.

Protecting Electronic Databases of Factual Material

In *Feist Publications, Inc. v. Rural Telephone Service Co.*, 499 U.S. 340 (1991), the Supreme Court defined the scope of copyright protection afforded to compilations of factual information. The Court ruled that "if the selection and arrangement" of the compilation are "original," then the elements of the work that embody this originality can be protected under copyright law. The Court ruled that the "white pages" telephone listings at issue in *Feist* did not meet this standard of originality and were not subject to copyright protection. *But see Key Publications, Inc. v. Chinatown Today Publ'g Enters., Inc.*, 945 F.2d 509 (2d Cir. 1991) (finding that a "yellow pages" telephone directory of Chinese businesses met the *Feist* test for original selection and arrangement and was eligible for copyright protection).

If material is not eligible for copyright protection, an electronic publisher may nevertheless attempt to place restrictions on its use by contract. *See* Chapter 6, pages 195-201, for a discussion of the enforceability of "shrinkwrap" or "click-through" licenses.

An electronic publisher may also attempt to restrict the use of its material through technological means. The Digital Millennium Copyright Act of 1998 (DMCA), discussed more thoroughly at pages 102-108 below, makes it unlawful to attempt to circumvent certain technological means of copy protection. 17 U.S.C. § 1201, Pub. L. 105-304.

⚖ *Mist-On Systems, Inc. v. Gilley's European Tan Spa*, No. 02-C-0038-C, 2002 U.S. Dist. LEXIS 9846 (W.D. Wis. May 2, 2002).

The defendant tanning salon posted on its website a series of frequently asked questions (FAQs) about spray-on tanning that resembled the FAQs on the same subject on the plaintiff's website. The plaintiff, Mist-On Systems, sued for copyright infringement. Citing *Feist* for the proposition that the "stereotypical" Q&A format of a FAQ page is not copyrightable "as such," the court went on to find that, even though the two pages contained some similarities, "these superficial similarities fall short of proving copying." The court found that many of the similarities between the two pages were factual (*i.e.*, descriptions of processes and ingredients of the product described), and that the differences in layout, phrasing of questions, and arrangement of the two FAQ pages precluded a finding of copyright infringement.

⚖ *Telstra Corporation Limited v Desktop Marketing Systems Pty Ltd.*, [2001] FCA 612 (May 25, 2001).

The defendant challenged a lower court ruling that it had infringed Telstra's copyright in its white- and yellow-page listings by making CD-ROMs from the data. A trial judge in Australia held that the Australian Copyright Act of 1968 gave Telstra copyright in its telephone white pages, yellow pages, and lists of headings used in the yellow pages. In May 2002, the Australian Federal Court dismissed the defendant's appeal. The defendants have sought leave to appeal to the High Court of Australia. This case is available at http://www.fedcourt.gov.au/judgments/judgmts.html *See* "Telstra May Face Court Over Copyright Issue" (June 25, 2002), at http://www.smh.com.au/articles/2002/06/25/102386457097.html.

Liability of Electronic Publishers for Infringing Content Posted by Others

Web publishers often provide forums, chat rooms or bulletin boards, where website visitors can upload and display content. This practice can sometimes expose the website operator to copyright infringement claims—for instance, when the publisher (1) directly commits infringing acts, (2) knows of infringing activity and materially contributes to it (contributory infringement), or (3) has the capacity to control or police the infringer's activities and gets direct financial benefit from them (vicarious infringement). These issues have been litigated in a number of cases, including the following:

⚖ In *Playboy Enters., Inc. v. Frena*, 839 F. Supp. 1552 (M.D. Fla. 1993), the defendant bulletin board operator insisted that (1) he had not known about the infringing photos being distributed through his bulletin board, and (2) he had taken the photos down as soon as he had learned of the infringement. The court nevertheless granted summary judgment for Playboy on its copyright claims, on the ground that because copyright infringement is a "strict liability" offense, the defendant's awareness or lack of awareness was irrelevant.

⚖ In *Sega Enters. Ltd. v. MAPHIA*, 857 F. Supp. 679 (N.D. Cal. 1994), the defendant was a bulletin board operator who had asked his fee-paying subscribers to upload certain types of files, including some subject to copyright protection, so that others could download them. The court issued a preliminary injunction, explaining that though the owner had not himself performed any of the specific infringing acts, it had enough knowledge of and involvement in such practices to establish a *prima facie* case of contributory copyright infringement.

⚖ In *Religious Technology Center v. Netcom*, 907 F. Supp. 1361 (N.D. Cal. 1995), the court set limits on Internet service provider liability. Netcom was the Internet access provider for a bulletin board operator at whose site an individual user had posted material copyrighted by the Church of Scientology. The church's Religious Technical Center (RTC) sued the user, the bulletin board operator, and Netcom. The court found no direct infringement by Netcom. Furthermore, it found no vicarious infringement, reasoning that Netcom had no policy of failing to enforce copyrights and had not benefited financially from the arrangement. However, the court refused to dismiss the case entirely, saying the access provider might be contributorily liable because RTC had given Netcom and the bulletin board operator notice of the violation, and the providers might not have acted reasonably upon receipt of this notice.

⚖ In *Playboy Enters., Inc. v. Webbworld, Inc.*, 968 F. Supp. 1171 (N.D. Tex. 1997), a website owner had devised an automated electronic process that searched his website for photos, including copyrighted *Playboy* photos, uploaded by users; the photos were then posted in a separate area of the website for paying subscribers. The court found the website owner liable for copyright infringement.

The Digital Millennium Copyright Act of 1998

Safe-Harbor Provisions

Section 512 of the Digital Millennium Copyright Act, 17 U.S.C. § 512, limits the liability of service providers for their role in providing online material. The Act contains four limited exemptions from liability, known as the "safe harbor" provisions. Each has its own requirements:

Section 512(a) protects service providers from liability for transmitting infringing material. A service provider is protected so long as it does not initiate the transmission, does not select or modify the material that is transmitted, does not select the recipients, and does not maintain a copy on its system that is ordinarily accessible to others or is retained for a period longer than is necessary to make the transmission.

Section 512(b) protects service providers from liability for system caching, the process some service providers use to copy, store and re-post web pages for their users. Among the many requirements to qualify for this immunity, service providers are not allowed to modify the content or prevent the originating website from collecting information or receiving credit for traffic it would have received if the service provider's user had accessed the page directly. The caching must also not interfere with any password or fee requirements on the originating website. The service provider must also comply with the originating website's rules concerning refreshing, reloading or updating the material so the original website's content is accurately represented. The service provider must also take down any infringing material that the originating website has been asked to remove under Section 512(c)(3).

Section 512(c) protects service providers from liability for content that users post and store on their systems. The protection is only provided if the service provider can demonstrate that: (1) it does not have actual or constructive knowledge of the allegedly infringing material, or upon obtaining knowledge or awareness of infringing activity, it acted expeditiously to remove the material; (2) it does not receive a direct financial benefit from the infringing material if it has the "right and ability to control" the material; and (3) it promptly removed the allegedly infringing material upon receiving notification in the manner provided by Section 512(c)(3). As one of the prerequisites for protection, the service provider must designate with the Copyright Office an agent to receive such notices of copyright infringement.

Section 512(d) provides protection for service providers for linking users to online locations that contain infringing material. The prerequisites to qualifying for protection under this section are similar to those required in Section 512(c). Other copyright issues involving linking are discussed above.

ISP Lawsuits Under the DMCA

In *Hendrickson v. eBay, Inc.*, 165 F. Supp. 2d 1082 (C.D. Cal. 2001), the U.S. District Court for the Central District of California ruled that the Internet auction company eBay was protected by one of the safe-harbor provisions of the DMCA. The auction company was sued by the plaintiff when it refused to remove allegedly pirated DVDs and videotapes of the plaintiff's documentary that were being offered for sale. The court held that eBay was entitled to safe-harbor protection under § 512(c) of the DMCA because all three safe-harbor prerequisites were met. The court found that the evidence demonstrated that eBay did not have actual or constructive knowledge of the particular listings, nor did it have the "right and ability to control" the allegedly infringing activity. The court stated that the "right and ability to control" language of the DMCA "cannot simply mean the ability of a service provider to remove or block access to materials posted on its website or stored in its system [because] ... [t]o hold otherwise would defeat the purpose of the DMCA and render the statute internally inconsistent." *Hendrickson* at 1093. Finally, the court held that Hendrickson had failed to comply substantially with the notice requirements of § 512(c)(3). The court therefore granted eBay's motion for summary judgment.

Ellison v. Robertson, et al., 189 F. Supp. 2d 1051 (C. D. Cal., 2002).

The plaintiff, novelist Harlan Ellison, alleged that the defendant, Steven Robertson, scanned large sections of the plaintiff's copyrighted works and posted them to a USENET newsgroup alt.binaries.e-book. The U.S. District Court for the Central District of California held that the failure of Internet service provider America Online to track down and eliminate copyright infringers on USENET services did not negate AOL's safe-harbor protection under the DMCA.

ISP Liability

Despite the DMCA's general treatment of Internet Service Providers (ISP) as "passive conduits" that are not held accountable for the online activities of customers, a few recent court cases have required ISPs to cooperate more fully with authorities.

⚖ In November 2001, a Finnish judge ordered an ISP to take down a site accused of posting serial numbers and passwords that could be used to crack popular business software programs. In June 2002, movie distribution sites Film88.com and Movie88.com, hosted in Taiwan and the Netherlands, respectively, were similarly shut down for copyright infringement through cooperation by their ISPs. For further discussion of Film88.com and Movie88.com in the context of video streaming, *see* page 112, below.

⚖ In May 2002, a German court held the Microsoft Network Internet service provider responsible for content (pictures of tennis celebrity Steffi Graf's face pasted onto photos of naked bodies) placed on its server by private users. *Graf v. Microsoft GmbH, OLGZ Cologne*, No. 15 U 221/01 (May 28, 2002), available at http://www.terhaag.de/ra/bnawash-main.html. The court said that from the point of view of an objective user, the content of the online community where the pictures were posted could be attributed to Microsoft because Microsoft provided the infrastructure, established the topic, permitted the posting on its Web pages, framed the community page with advertisements, and stipulated basic rules for participation.

⚖ *Perfect 10 Inc. v. Cybernet Ventures Inc.*, 2002 U.S. Dist. LEXIS 7333, Copy. L. Rep. (CCH) P28,423 (C.D. Cal., April 22, 2002).

In April 2002, the defendant, Cybernet Ventures, operators of the Adult Check service (AC), an age-verification service for adult websites, was preliminarily enjoined for contributory and vicarious copyright infringement. The plaintiff, Perfect 10, which holds the copyright in a number of photos of nude women and publishes them in a magazine and on the Web, argued that AC encouraged and financially benefited from unauthorized posting of its photos on websites operated by the defendants' member companies. The court found that the plaintiff was likely to be able to prove AC benefited from the infringement because an access fee was paid directly to AC by its members based on the popularity of each member's site. Unlike *Religious Technology Center v. Netcom Online*, discussed at page 101, above, where the operator of a news server was not held vicariously liable because the fee paid was not related to server content, AC was found to receive income in direct proportion to the popularity of the sites it serviced. The court found AC's monitoring program, which gave sites detailed instructions on layout, appearance, and content, provided evidence of AC's control over the content of its member sites. The court found the DMCA safe-harbor provisions would be unlikely to protect AC because of AC's failure to implement a policy terminating repeat infringers. The injunction has resulted in AC's dropping support for thousands of pornography websites. *See* "Dirty Sites Jittery After Ruling," *Wired* (May 10, 2002), *available at* http://www.wired.com/news/business/0,1367,52429,00 .html.

Liability for Circumventing Technological Copyright Protection Measures

While generally limiting the liability of certain online service providers, the DMCA also creates new liability with its anti-circumvention provision. Section 1201 of the DMCA outlaws conduct and devices aimed at circumventing technological measures put in place to control access to works and protect the rights of copyright owners. *See* 17 U.S.C. § 1201. The DMCA provides both civil and criminal penalties for such conduct. *See id.* at §§ 1203-1204.

On May 3, 2002, the Electronic Frontier Foundation published a report on the "unintended consequences" of the DMCA over the past three years, including accounts of various researchers withholding electronic security research results for fear of prosecution under the DMCA's anti-circumvention provision. The report is available at http://www.eff.org/IP/DMCA/20020503_dmca_consequences.pdf.

 Universal City Studios, Inc. v. Reimerdes, 111 F. Supp. 2d 94 (S.D.N.Y. 2000), *aff'd*, 273 F.3d 429 (2d Cir. 2001).

Members of the motion-picture industry brought suit under the DMCA's anti-circumvention provisions against 2600 Magazine/The Hacker Quarterly for posting and linking to "DeCSS" on its website. DeCSS is a utility designed to defeat the CSS encryption technology used to protect Digital Versatile Discs (DVD).

The U.S. District Court for the Southern District of New York permanently enjoined defendants from posting DeCSS on their own website and from linking to any other website containing DeCSS. The court ruled that the defendants' actions did not fall within any of the DMCA exceptions. The court also found that fair use is not a defense to the anti-circumvention provisions of the DMCA. The court ruled that the defendants violated the anti-circumvention provision not only by posting DeCSS on their website, but also, under the particular facts of this case, by linking to other websites where DeCSS was available for download. The court also rejected the defendants' claims that the anti-circumvention provisions of the DMCA are unconstitutional.

On November 28, 2001, the Court of Appeals for the Second Circuit affirmed the decision of the district court, and in May 2002, the same court declined to rehear the case.

➤ *DVD Copy Control Ass'n v. Bunner*, 93 Cal. App. 4th 648 (Cal. Ct. App. 2001).

A California Court of Appeals reversed a lower court's injunction to stop the Internet publication of the source code for DeCSS. The court stated that the DVD Copy Control Association's right to protect its trade secret does not outweigh the First Amendment right to freedom of speech. The California Supreme Court is currently reviewing the appellate court's determination that the DeCSS computer code is "pure speech" for purposes of First Amendment protection. 41 P.2d 2 (Cal. 2002) (granting petition for review).

➤ *Norwegian Economic Crime Unit (OKOKRIM) v. Johansen, Byrett* (Norway) (2002).

Jon Johansen, a teenager in Norway, is being criminally prosecuted for allegedly creating DeCSS software that can enable DVD playback using the Linux operating system. The case is set for trial in December 2002. This case is available at http://www.eff.org/IP/Video/DeCSS_prosecutions/Johansen_DeCSS_case/20030109_johansen_decision.html.

➤ *RealNetworks Inc. v. Streambox, Inc.*, No. C99-2070P, 2000 U.S. Dist. LEXIS 1889 (W.D. Wash. Jan. 18, 2000).

RealNetworks Inc. filed suit against Streambox, Inc. in December 1999, alleging that three Streambox products violated the anti-circumvention provisions of the DMCA. The U.S. District Court for the Western District of Washington granted a preliminary injunction against two of these products, the Streambox VCR and the Ferret. The Streambox mimics a RealNetworks product, RealMedia, circumvents the authentication procedure created by RealNetworks (the "Secret Handshake"), and allows users to downloan RealMedia files that are streamed over the Internet. The court found that the Secret Handshake is a technological measure that effectively controlled access to copyrighted works, and that the Streambox VCR is primarily, if not exclusively, designed to circumvent this protection. The court found that the Streambox VCR had no significant commercial purpose other than to enable users to access and to record protected content. The court also granted a preliminary injunction against the Ferret (a plug-in that alters the RealPlayer). The court found a likelihood of success on the plaintiff's copyright infringement claim because the Ferret created an unauthorized derivative work. The court denied a preliminary injunction against another product, the Ripper (a file conversion tool that allows users to convert files from one format to another), because it did not circumvent any technological measure and had independently significant commercial purposes.

This case was settled in September 2000. In addition to a cash settlement, Streambox agreed to modify its Streambox VCR and Ripper software to prevent the unauthorized modification of RealMedia files. It also agreed to stop distributing the Ferret plug-in.

 United States v. Elcom Ltd. a/k/a Elcomsoft Co., Ltd. and Dmitry Sklyarov, No. CR 01-20138 RMW, 203 F. Supp. 2d 1111 (N.D. Cal. May 8, 2002).

In the first indictment under the criminal provisions of the DMCA, Russian citizen Dmitry Sklyarov was charged with trafficking in a software product primarily designed or produced for the purpose of circumventing technological copyright protection. The DMCA provides criminal penalties for such conduct when it is perpetrated for purposes of commercial advantage or private financial gain. The indictment alleges that Sklyarov and his Russian employer, Elcomsoft, developed and marketed, for commercial advantage and financial gain, a program called the Advanced eBook Processor (AEBP) for use in circumventing the Adobe Acrobat eBook Reader. The Adobe Acrobat eBook Reader allows reading of electronic books on personal computers, and it permits publishers and distributors to restrict or limit the purchaser's ability to copy, distribute, and print the text, or to have it read audibly by the computer. Sklyarov's AEBP program removes such limitations, allowing the purchaser freely to copy, distribute, and print the text or to have it read by the computer. The maximum statutory penalty for violation of the DMCA's anti-circumvention provisions is five years in prison and a fine of $500,000. Sklyarov, a Ph.D. student who studies cryptography, was arrested and jailed on July 17, 2001, in Las Vegas. He had come to Las Vegas to deliver a lecture on e-book security. In December 2001, the case against Sklyarov was dismissed in exchange for his testimony against his employer, Elcomsoft.

On May 8, 2002, a federal trial court judge denied motions to dismiss the lawsuit against Sklyarov's employer, Elcomsoft, on grounds that the anti-circumvention provisions of the DMCA violate the First Amendment. The judge stated that, while computer programs can legally qualify as speech, the DMCA is content-neutral because it controls the function of the programs it restricts, not their content. (For a discussion of content-based versus content-neutral speech restrictions, *see* Chapter

1, pages 3-4.) The court found that the DMCA does not prohibit more speech than necessary to promote the government's legitimate interests in preventing electronic piracy. The court also found that, while the DMCA may make it more difficult for an individual to exercise fair-use rights (such as making back-up copies for personal use), the DMCA does not ban or eliminate fair use. On December 17, 2002, a jury acquitted Elcomsoft of all criminal charges. ("Not guilty" verdicts are not subject to appeal.)

Video and Music on the Web

Webcasting

The proliferation of music on the Web has prompted the music industry to consider how best to regulate webcasting of copyright-protected musical works. Musical works are subject to two separate copyrights: the copyright in the musical composition (the notes and lyrics) and the copyright in the musical performance (the musicians' and producer's recorded rendition of the musical composition). Typically, publishing companies own the copyrights to musical compositions, and record companies hold the rights to musical performances.

Radio stations pay royalties for blanket licenses for their rights to broadcast musical compositions. They have been statutorily exempt from paying royalties for the musical performances, because Congress believed that radio air-play promotes record sales. As many radio stations began making their broadcasts available on the Internet, copyright holders sought to be compensated for their work. Radio broadcasters argued that their existing blanket licenses should apply to Webcasting the musical compositions, and that the promotional value of their Webcasting should exempt them from paying performance royalties, as it exempted them from paying royalties with respect to their broadcasts. However, in December 2000, under the DMCA, the Copyright Office ruled that Webcasting requires additional licenses for musical compositions, and that Webcasters must pay royalties for the musical performances, as well.

Bonneville International Corp. v. Peters, 153 F. Supp. 2d 763 (E.D. Pa. 2001).

In 2001, radio station operators filed suit in a federal court in Pennsylvania against the U.S. Copyright Office asking the court to review the Copyright Office ruling that imposed an obligation to royalties for musical performances on FCC-licensed broadcasters that Webcast their signals over the Internet. The Recording Industry

Association of America (RIAA) joined the Copyright Office as an intervenor-defendant. The court did not directly consider whether broadcast stations' Webcasting activities should be exempt from royalties for musical performances in digital audio transmissions, but instead deferred to the Copyright Office's determination that they are not exempt. The court granted the motion for summary judgment filed by the Copyright Office and RIAA.

The court's decision has serious implications for radio broadcasters who stream their own radio broadcast signals over the Internet: they must now (1) comply with the requirements of the DMCA to be eligible for a statutory license; (2) negotiate a separate license with the sound recording copyright owner; or (3) cease Webcasting.

Royalty Fees for Internet Radio Broadcasts—History

The DMCA provides that the statutory license fees and terms for Internet Webcasts of musical performances are to be set by voluntary agreement as a result of industry negotiations, or by a Copyright Arbitration Royalty Panel (CARP) if the parties cannot agree. Since negotiations between Webcasters and the recording industry did not result in an agreement, a CARP was convened. More than 15 Webcasters and several broadcast groups proposed a royalty rate of $0.0015 per music webcast listener hour, while the Recording Industry Association of America, Inc. (RIAA) proposed that Webcasters pay $0.0004 per streamed performance, that is per song per listener. Radio stations currently pay $0.0022 per listener hour for their terrestrial broadcasts to performance rights societies such as SESAC, BMI and ASCAP. On February 20, 2002, the CARP announced its recommended rates of $0.0007 for retransmissions of terrestrial broadcasts, and $0.0014 for all other Internet broadcasts.

On April 22, 2002, a bipartisan group of 20 lawmakers asked the Copyright Office to review the proposal in light of arguments that the fee structure would force small Internet broadcasters out of business.

On June 20, 2002, at the recommendation of the Registrar of Copyrights, the Librarian of Congress rejected the CARP's determination, stating that significant portions of it were arbitrary or contrary to law. The Librarian accepted the CARP's conclusion that an agreement negotiated between RIAA and Yahoo! represented the best evidence of what rates would have been negotiated in the marketplace between a willing buyer and a willing seller, but rejected the CARP finding that Internet broadcasts have less promotional impact for the record companies than traditional broadcasts. The Librarian set a

$0.0007 rate (a low $0.0002 rate was for non-commercial stations) for each song performance, regardless of whether the performance is a retransmission of a terrestrial broadcast or an Internet-only transmission. The rate will be applied retroactively to 1998, with initial payments due in October 2002. Either side can appeal the decision to the U.S. Court of Appeals for the District of Columbia Circuit.

On December 4, 2002, President Bush signed into law the Small Webcaster Settlement Act of 2002 (SWSA) (Pub. L. No. 107-321). The SWSA applies to "Noncommercial Webcasters" and to "Small Commercial Webcasters." The SWSA is intended to address Congressional concerns that Noncommercial and Small Commercial Webcasters were not adequately represented in the process that resulted in the Copyright Office's July 8, 2002, decision establishing royalty rates for Webcasting digital sound recordings. The SWSA delays until June 2003, the date by which noncommercial and small commercial Webcasters must make their initial royalty payments. The extra time is to allow noncommercial and small commercial Webcasters to negotiate new royalty rate agreements with SoundExchange, the royalty receiving agent designated by the recording industry, with royalty fees to be based on a percentage of revenue rather than on a per performance basis.

Since the enacting of the SWSA, SoundExchange has entered into an agreement with a group of small Webcasters, establishing new Webcasting performance royalty rates, based on a percentage of revenue for Webcasters operating within certain revenue caps. Any small Webcaster that satisfies the eligibility requirements set forth in the agreement may join the agreement and operate under its terms, or it may opt to continue to pay the per-performance royalty rates established by the Copyright Office.

The European Commission approved plans to allow radio broadcasters to secure one blanket license for their Webcasting activities. The license will cover the entire copyrighted musical work and will be valid across 18 countries (the 15 EC members plus European Economic Area members Iceland, Norway, and Liechtenstein).

Non-Broadcasting Webcasters

In 2002, Congress considered legislation that would apply to music Webcasters that do not also broadcast over-the-air signals under an FCC license. The bill, the Small Webcaster Amendments Act of 2002 (H.R. 5469), would allow "small webcasters," defined by revenue caps, to enjoy some exemptions from the statutory royalty fees imposed by the recent Copyright Office mandate, as well as reduced rates. The measure stalled in the Senate before Congress recessed for the November 2002 elections.

Retransmission of Television Broadcast Signals

With the increased use of broadband Internet connections in homes and businesses, entrepreneurs have sought to develop services that will allow users to view broadcast television signals on the Web. In 1999, the Canadian Radio-television and Telecommunications Commission (CRTC) exempted Internet-based operations from the regulations of the country's Broadcasting Act. According to Canada's Copyright Act, a company whose operations are "comparable" to those of cable television providers may retransmit a live signal "in its entirety" if its operations are "lawful under the Broadcasting Act." Two companies, JumpTV and iCraveTV, argued that the exemption makes their operations automatically lawful under Canada's Broadcasting Act.

 Twentieth Century Fox Film Corp., et al. v. iCraveTV, No. 2000 U.S. Dist. LEXIS 11670, 53 U.S.P.Q.2d (BNA) 1831 (W.D. Pa 2000).

A Canadian Internet publisher, iCraveTV.com, was capturing U.S. television programming by picking up the signals of television stations, converting the signals to digital form, and then streaming the broadcasts over its website. Several major U.S. motion-picture studios, the National Football League, the National Basketball Association, and three major broadcasters filed suit to stop the Webcasts, alleging copyright infringement and Lanham Act violations. After a court-ordered preliminary injunction, iCraveTV.com announced in February 2000 that the parties had settled the lawsuit. iCraveTV.com halted its retransmission practices, and, in June 2000, announced its intention to relaunch using a software called "iWall" that would identify users by country and block users in the United States from receiving transmissions. Additionally, iCrave stated that it plans to pay copyright holders by charging a subscription fee, functioning much like a cable-television system. As this edition went to press, in November 2002, www.iCraveTV.com did not resolve to a functioning website.

 JumpTV

Arguing that current royalty rates under retransmission tariffs, which can be as high as 75 cents per subscriber per month, are inequitable for Internet Webcasters dealing with advertising-based revenue of pennies per subscriber, JumpTV and representatives of the rights-holder collectives have worked out a two-part schedule for Internet tariffs. At the same time, proposed amendments to the Canadian Copyright Act have been passed by the House of Commons and now move on to the Canadian Senate. The amendments would force Internet broadcasters to obtain a license from the CRTC, making it more complicated to launch such services. *See* Ian Jack, "Web-TV Broadcasting Needs License," *National Post* (June 19, 2002). JumpTV currently provides feeds of several content providers, including NASA TV and Thai TV Global Network, that do not oppose the rebroadcasts.

Video Streaming

Video streaming refers to the process of providing users the ability to view (but not download) individual video files, such as feature-length films, over the Internet. Video streams are made available by the sender and are accessed by the recipient.

 *Video Pipeline, Inc. v. Buena Vista Home Entertainment, Inc.*, 192 F. Supp. 2d 321 (D. N.J. 2002).

The plaintiff, Video Pipeline, provides previews of home videos to home-video wholesalers and retailers. It entered into a master clip license agreement with defendant Buena Vista, allowing it to exhibit certain video clips and promotional videos provided by Buena Vista through its videopipeline.net network. These previews could be viewed, but not downloaded by Video Pipelines' retail clients. Video Pipeline originally filed suit against Buena Vista seeking a declaratory judgment that its use of the trailers to make its own video clips does not constitute copyright infringement. The court held that Video Pipeline's making of its own video-clip previews for transmission over the Internet is not protected from a copyright infringement claim by the fair-use defense or the first-sale doctrine. Thus, Buena Vista had a likelihood of success on the merits and an injunction against operation of the service was appropriate.

For a discussion of this case in the context of fair use, *see* page 97, above.

Movie 88.com/Film88.com

Taiwan-based Movie88.com sold unauthorized access to thousands of feature-length movies for $1 each. Taiwanese authorities shut down the site in February 2002 through cooperation with Movie88.com's Internet service provider under international provisions of the U.S. Digital Millennium Copyright Act. A replacement, Film88.com, appeared in June 2002. Although Film88 was headquartered in Iran, its servers were based in the Netherlands. The Motion Picture Association of America worked with Film88's Netherlands-based Internet service provider to shut down the site. The sites remain inactive.

Internet Music Technology

Music-file swapping has become widely popular in recent years. Using programs such as KaZaA, Morpheus, Napster, and Gnutella, users transfer and download many thousands of files a day over peer-to-peer networks. While the recording industry and file-swapping supporters argue over whether Internet file sharing increases or decreases music sales (one recent study by Forrester Research shows that Internet piracy is not to blame for the 15 percent decline in record sales since 2000, but that the economy and competition from other media outlets are the source), the record industry has sued several file-swapping services for copyright infringement. Both the record industry and software companies are struggling to develop a business model for online file delivery that meets the demands of consumers and allows them to download files over the Internet without violating the copyright rights of content owners.

Distribution of Digital Audio "MP3" Files

 A&M Records, Inc. v. Napster, Inc., No. C99-5183 (N.D. Cal. 2000), and *Leiber, et al. v. Napster, Inc.*, No. C00-0074 (N.D. Cal. filed January 7, 2000), *modified injunction aff'd*, 284 F.3d 1091 (9th Cir. 2002).

The Recording Industry Association of America, Inc. (RIAA) sued Napster, Inc., for contributory and vicarious copyright infringement. Napster operated a website and offered software enabling users to easily find and download MP3 music files stored on the hard drives of other users.

In May 2000, the U.S. District Court for the Northern District of California held that the Napster online music system is not a "service provider" entitled to the exemption from contributory and vicarious copyright infringement liability provided to service providers under § 512(a) of the Digital Millennium Copyright Act. The court found that Napster "enables or facilitates" connections between its users, but does not "transmit, route, or provide connections through its system," as required to qualify for the exemption. In July 2000, the court entered a preliminary injunction against Napster, rejecting its defenses that the Napster system was lawful because it was capable of being used for substantial non-infringing uses and that the file sharing Napster users engaged in constituted a protected fair use under copyright law.

In February 2001, the U.S. Court of Appeals for the Ninth Circuit ruled that Napster users infringed at least two of the copyright holders' exclusive rights: the rights of reproduction and distribution. The court remanded the case to the district court to modify the injunction in accordance with its ruling, allowing Napster to continue operating in the meantime. The district court issued the modified injunction in March 2001, requiring the recording industry to provide Napster with a list of copyrighted songs that it was required to remove from its servers. In July 2001, the district court ruled that Napster had to remain off-line until it could demonstrate that it could operate a music sharing service that effectively screened out musical works identified by the plaintiff record companies with 100 percent effectiveness. The U.S. Court of Appeals for the Ninth Circuit affirmed the district court's injunction on March 25, 2002.

The U.S. Court of Appeals for the Ninth Circuit ruled that the trial court did not abuse its discretion in ordering the continued shutdown of Napster until it could demonstrate that none of the files identified as containing copyrighted work was being shared via the Napster service. The court also affirmed the lower court's injunction requiring Napster to put in place a screening mechanism that could not easily be defeated by users.

In a related matter, on September 26, 2001, Napster announced that it would pay $26 million to settle its ongoing legal disputes with music publishers and songwriters about the copyrighted musical compositions. *See In Re Napster Inc. Copyright Litigation*, No. MDL 00-1369 MHP (N.D. Cal., settlement announced Sept. 26, 2001). The agreement is subject to approval by the plaintiffs and the trial judge.

In February 2002, the U.S. District Court for the Northern District of California ruled that Napster's allegations of copyright misuse by the major recording labels was sufficient to warrant further discovery of the recording companies' joint online music-distribution ventures. *See* 2002 U.S. Dist. LEXIS 2963 (N.D. Cal, February 21, 2002). Napster based its argument on (1) the licensing agreement between Napster and the MusicNet digital music licensing venture, formed by EMI, BMG, Warner, and RealNetworks; and (2) the actions of the major labels in setting up MusicNet and Pressplay, formed by Sony and Universal.

Napster filed for bankruptcy in June 2002, putting the unconcluded copyright infringement suit on hold. Media conglomerate Bertelsmann initially agreed to purchase Napster, but the bankruptcy court blocked the purchase and the deal subsequently dissolved. On November 27, 2002, Roxio, creators of CD-burning technology, purchased Napster's assets without taking on Napster's legal liabilities, including liabilities stemming from the record labels' pending suit.

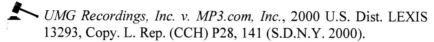 *UMG Recordings, Inc. v. MP3.com, Inc.*, 2000 U.S. Dist. LEXIS 13293, Copy. L. Rep. (CCH) P28, 141 (S.D.N.Y. 2000).

The plaintiffs brought a copyright infringement action against MP3.com, Inc., which operated a commercial service (My.MP3.com) that allowed users to copy their own music CDs onto servers under MP3.com's control and then to access the music at any time from any place over the Internet. The defendant viewed its service as a "virtual CD player" and asserted a fair-use defense, stating that MP3.com provided a "transformative 'space shift' by which subscribers can enjoy the sound recordings ... without lugging around the physical discs themselves." In April 2000, the court granted the plaintiffs' motion for partial summary judgment, rejecting the defendant's fair-use defense. The court concluded that the use was not transformative but rather repackaged the recordings to facilitate their transmission through another medium.

By mid-August 2000, MP3.com had settled with all of the plaintiff recording companies except UMG. MP3.com agreed to pay large sums of money, between $75 and $100 million in one of the deals, in exchange for the right to use music distributed by various record companies as part of its My.MP3.com service. Some of the deals also involved a per-song or per-CD fee.

In September 2000, the court determined that MP3.com had willfully violated UMG's copyrights and awarded statutory damages of $25,000 per CD. While UMG's suit originally claimed 10,000 CDs were copied, in a November 2000 settlement, MP3.com admitted responsibility for 4,700 CDs and paid UMG $50 million in damages plus $3.4 million in legal fees.

Based on this decision, MP3.com subsequently was prohibited from arguing in a similar case brought against it that its My.MP3.com service did not willfully infringe copyrights. *See Teevee Toons v. MP3.com, Inc.*, 134 F. Supp. 2d 546 (S.D.N.Y. 2001).

MP3.com was eventually purchased by Vivendi Universal, one of its former major label legal opponents.

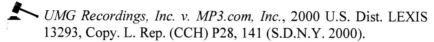 Copyright.net Music Publishing Inc. v. MP3.com Inc., No. 01-CIV-7321 (S.D.N.Y. filed Aug. 8, 2001).

More than 50 music publishers and songwriters, including Copyright.net Music Publishing, filed suit against MP3.com alleging copyright infringement based on MP3.com's distribution of digital audio files. The plaintiffs' complaint maintained that MP3.com willfully, contributorily, and vicariously infringed their copyrights by converting their works from compact discs to MP3 format, storing the allegedly infringing digital audio files on its servers, creating "on demand" access to the digital audio files by subscribers, and facilitating the "viral distribution" or rapid spread of the allegedly infringed works by allowing subscribers to download the files when it should have known that subscribers would distribute them to others in a "viral manner." The suit sought actual damages and profits of MP3.com, statutory damages in the amount of $25,000 for each musical composition infringed, attorney fees and costs, and a permanent injunction against MP3.com.

MP3.com filed a legal malpractice suit against its former outside counsel, Cooley Godward LLP. *MP3.com, Inc. v. Cooley Godward LLP*, No. BC 266625 (Cal. App. Dep't Super. Ct., filed Jan. 18, 2002). MP3.com is suing Cooley Godward for allegedly failing to warn it of its potential liability and assuring it that it was protected by the fair-use defense. MP3.com is seeking more than $175 million in damages. Cooley Godward has stated that it plans to defend the action vigorously. *See* Brenda Sandburg, *The Recorder*, "MP3.com Sues Cooley Over Advice," Jan. 22, 2002, available at http://www.law.com/regionals/ca/stories/edt0122d.shtml.

In early October 2002, it was reported that Sony recording artists Bob Dylan, Billy Joel, and James Taylor had filed a lawsuit against Vivendi Universal's MP3.com website. The plaintiffs assert that the site is distributing their songs without authorization. The suit, filed in U.S. District Court for the Southern District of New York, claims that MP3.com copied tracks from their commercial compact discs and made them available to website users.

➤ *Metro-Goldwyn-Mayer Studios Inc. v. Grokster, Ltd.*, Case No.: 01-08541 SVW (C.D. Cal., filed Oct. 2, 2001).

The recording industry and several recording studios filed a copyright infringement lawsuit against Music City, KaZaA, and Grokster, popular peer-to-peer MP3 file-trading networks that gained popularity after Napster ran into legal troubles. Unlike Napster, these services do not require users to connect to a central server that houses an index of downloadable files. Instead, these services provide downloadable software that allows users to search through individual computers in the network without ever using a centralized server. Therefore, it is possible that even in the absence of companies like Music City, KaZaA, and Grokster, the file-swapping network could survive because users now have the software necessary to communicate directly with others' computers. The plaintiffs claim that the defendants are facilitating infringement by providing users with the technology and infrastructure to make unauthorized copies of motion pictures, music, and other content. The plaintiffs are seeking actual damages and the defendants' profits, statutory damages in the amount of $150,000 for all individual infringements involved, attorney fees and costs, and an injunction against the defendants.

As of June 2002, StreamCast (formerly Music City) was seeking new counsel because one of its lead attorneys, Andrew Bridges, who successfully defended Diamond Multimedia against RIAA claims that the Rio MP3 player violated copyright law, is withdrawing from the case. KaZaA has announced that it will accept a default judgment in the case because it no longer has the money needed to continue a defense. The case was originally set for trial in October 2002. On January 8, 2003, the court denied KaZaA's motion to dismiss for lack of personal jurisdiction. For further discussion of this decision in the context of personal jurisdiction, *see* pages 226-227. On January 27, 2003, Sharman filed suit against the copyright holders, alleging antitrust violations and seeking to enjoin them from enforcing their copyrights.

 In re Aimster Copyright Litigation, No. 1:01cv 8933 (N.D. Ill., Sept. 4, 2002).

A federal trial court entered a preliminary injunction barring Aimster from continuing to operate its file-sharing service. The court ruled that Aimster was not entitled to a fair-use defense for the vicarious and contributory infringement claims against it. Aimster, now called "Madster," used instant-messaging technology to allow users to trade audio files. By facilitating infringement by end-users, Aimster vicariously and contributorily infringed the rights of the copyright holders. It could not defend its actions as "fair use." Aimster's reliance on the Supreme Court's discussion in the "Betamax" case (*Sony Corp. v. Universal City Studios*, 464 U.S. 417 (1984)) was misplaced, the court said, because Aimster was in complete control of its ongoing service, and was not merely a manufacturer or seller of a potentially infringing device. Madster remained in operation, ignoring the preliminary injunction. In December 2002, the court ordered Madster to disconnect its website and any computers it used for the file-sharing service. As of January 31, 2003, the website was still in operation, allowing users to download its file-sharing software.

➤ *Buma/Stemra v. Kazaa*, Amsterdam Court of Appeals (March 28, 2002).

On March 28, 2002, a Dutch appeals court ruled that Internet software company KaZaA was not liable for any individual's abuse of its software, which is used around the world to locate copyright protected games, music, pictures, and films. KaZaA had been sued by Dutch music rights organization Buma/Stemra. The ruling came too late to save KaZaA as an independent company; its principal assets were sold to an Australian company, Sharman Network, after the initial ruling in favor of the music industry in 2001. The Dutch court found that the technology behind KaZaA did not require a Napster-like central service under control of the software developers. The court also found that it was important that the software was being used for non-infringing purposes. Sharman continues to offer the KaZaA software and to litigate and lobby vigorously in favor of the right to distribute the software. This case is available at http://www.eff.org/IP/P2P/BUMA_v_Kazaa/20020328_kazaa _appeal_judgment.html.

➤ *Zomba Recording Corp., et al. v. Audiogalaxy, Inc.*, No. 02 Civ. 3999 (LTS) (S.D.N.Y., filed May 24, 2002).

In May 2002, RIAA members filed suit against the online music service Audiogalaxy, claiming the company willfully and intentionally encouraged millions of users to copy and distribute the copyrighted works of its artists and facilitated that distribution and copying. The music search service allows users to download cover artwork and software in addition to songs. Audiogalaxy settled the suit in June 2002, agreeing to obtain appropriate permission or consent from songwriters, music publishers, and recording companies before using or sharing copyrighted works. Additionally, the company will pay the recording industry an undetermined amount of money to settle the lawsuit. *See* Gwendolyn Mariano, "Audiogalaxy to Ask First, Trade Later," CNET News.com (June 18, 2002), *available at* http://news.com.com/2100-1023-936932.html.

➤ *Arista Records, et al. v. AT&T Broadband Corp.*, et al., No. _____ (S.D.N.Y., filed Aug. 16, 2002).

Record labels filed suit against several large Internet Service Providers, alleging that the defendants provide "backbone routers" that allow Internet users in the U.S. to access an offshore website, listen4ever.com, from which they unlawfully download music from a centralized server containing thousands of copyrighted music files. The plaintiff record companies are unable to identify who owns listen4ever.com, but evidence indicates its operations are based in China. Regardless of the site's connections to China, the plaintiffs contend that because it uses an American .com domain name, is in English, and targets American users, its owners are trying to circumvent U.S. copyright law.

> *RIAA v. Verizon*, No. 02-MS-0323 (JDB) (D.D.C. Jan. 21, 2003) (Mem.).

The recording industry filed suit against Verizon, an Internet service provider, seeking an order compelling Verizon to identify a subscriber accused of illegally trading copyrighted musical recordings in digital format using KaZaA software. Verizon argued that because the subscriber's infringing conduct takes place entirely on the individual's hard drive and not at any Verizon facility, Verizon should not be required to reveal its customer's identity. Verizon also contended that the definition of "service providers" subject to subpoena does not include general access providers, such as Verizon. On January 21, 2003, the federal trial court ordered Verizon to identify the alleged copyright infringer.

On January 30, 2003, Verizon asked the trial court to stay its order until the U.S. Court of Appeals for the District of Columbia can review the case.

> *Arista Records et al. v. MP3Board Inc.*, No. 00 Civ. 4660 (S.D.N.Y. Aug. 29, 2002).

The plaintiffs were several record companies that held copyrights in sound recordings. They alleged that the website mp3board.com enabled listeners to locate and download digital musical files from the Internet without authorization, and sued the defendant for contributory and vicarious copyright infringement. The court rejected some of the plaintiffs' claims because they had not provided sufficient notice to the defendant under the DMCA. Of the three cease-and-desist letters that the plaintiffs sent to the defendant, the court found that only one provided sufficient notice under the DMCA. The two that did not provide sufficient notice included only the names of the artists whose songs they claimed were made available on the site, and did not provide adequate notice for the defendant to locate and remove any infringing links. The letter that provided sufficient notice, on the other hand, included artist names and song titles, and was accompanied by printouts of pages from the MP3Board website, on which the plaintiffs indicated which links it believed were infringing its copyrights. The court indicated that for notice to be sufficient under the DMCA, the copyright holders had to provide, at a minimum, the names of the specific sound recordings they were seeking to protect.

Industry Initiatives to Secure Digital Audio Files

Screening technologies, including encryption and watermarking systems, offer technical solutions to protecting copyright in digitally distributed works. The Secure Digital Music Initiative (SDMI), organized by the RIAA, and composed of major computer companies, consumer electronic companies, and record labels is working to develop and implement a multi-industry base to provide secure electronic music. Technology, such as RealNetworks' extensible media commerce language (XMCL) and Microsoft's extensible rights markup language (XRML), that enables copyright-protection systems to work with one another, is also in development. This technology will present entertainment companies with the option of switching among various rights-management systems without having to reformat all of their content.

Other CD copy-protection methods are being implemented that prevent discs from being read by computer CD-ROM drives, some portable CD players, and even some car stereo systems. While these methods can sometimes be defeated using a felt-tip pen, Apple Macintosh users have reported that playing the copy-protected discs in their computer hard drives has caused the computers to crash. *See* "CD Crack: Magic Marker Needed," *Wired* (May 20, 2002), *available at* http://www.wired.com/news/technology/0,1282,52665,00.html.

➤ An out-of-court settlement has been reached in *Karen Delise, et al. v. Fahrenheit Entertainment, Inc., et al.*, Case No. CV 014297 (Cal. App. Dep't Super. Ct. 2001), a case charging that Music City Records, Fahrenheit Entertainment, and Suncomm, a digital rights management firm, violated California's consumer-protection laws by failing to include an adequate disclaimer on the packaging for copy-protected CDs. Buyers complained that the copy protection prevented them from fully enjoying the CDs they purchased. As part of the settlement, distributors will include a warning on CD labels that the affected discs are not designed to work in DVD players or CD-ROM players, and that electronic copies of the songs made available for downloading by purchasers of the CDs are not compatible with MP3 players. They will also stop requiring consumers to enter their names and e-mail addresses as a condition of downloading electronic copies of the songs. A copy of the settlement agreement is available at http://www.techfirm.com/sunnk.pdf.

Dickey v. Universal Music Group, et al. (L.A. Superior Court, filed June 11, 2002), *available at* http://www.milberg.com/pdf/audiocds/complaint.pdf.

A class-action lawsuit has been filed against the five major record companies for producing and distributing copy-protected music CDs that have problems being played on some players and computers. The complaint alleges the record companies made false and misleading statements and distributed CDs that carry the "Compact Disc" logo but do not meet the industry's "Red Book" standards for CDs established by Sony and Philips. The suit seeks a court order to either force the defendants to cease the manufacture, distribution, and sale of the copy-protected discs or to make them carry warning labels differentiating them from standard CDs.

Government Involvement in the Digital Audio Debate

In an effort to understand the paradigm of music on the Web, the U.S. Senate held a fact-finding session in July 2000 on the issue of digital downloading and copyright law. The hearing, entitled "Music on the Internet: Is There an Upside to Downloading?" was chaired by Sen. Orrin Hatch (R-Utah), who is, incidentally, a country songwriter. Many vocal players from both the Internet and recording industries testified before the committee, including Metallica's Lars Ulrich, Napster CEO Hank Barry, and Gene Kan, developer of Gnutella. Hatch has clearly stated that the Senate is not interested in interfering with the ongoing litigation surrounding digital downloading, but rather in pursuing a mutually beneficial relationship between music creators and the companies that make music available to distributors.

Congress considered several bills that would address the use of copy-protection technology. In March 2002, the Security Systems Standards and Certification Act, S. 2048, also known as the Consumer Broadband and Digital Television Promotion Act or the Hollings Amendment, proposed government-mandated copy-protection technology in consumer electronic devices. The Anticounterfeiting Amendments of 2002, S. 2395, would expand existing counterfeit laws to cover digital media. It would make it a criminal violation to copy authentication devices such as holograms or watermarks, as well as create a civil cause of action for copyright owners to recover damages.

Internet Music Licensing

In October 2000, Napster and Bertelsmann came together in an effort to launch an online music-sharing service with membership fees that would go toward compensating artists and record labels for use of their copyright protected materials. Although Napster has filed for bankruptcy, the program is inactive, and Bertelsmann controls its assets, the goal endures. MusicNet, a venture involving AOL Time Warner, Bertelsmann, and EMI Group, has joined in the effort. Pressplay, formed between Sony Corporation and Vivendi Universal, has similar plans.

Pressplay and MusicNet are subscription services backed by record labels. In the fall of 2002, Pressplay and MusicNet announced they are close to reaching licensing agreements to offer songs from all five major recording labels. However, the services offer limited downloads that are not in the popular MP3 file format and usually cannot be transferred to portable MP3 playing devices or burned to CDs. Universal and Sony have announced plans to make large portions of their music catalogs available for download at a discount via independent distributors Liquid Audio Inc. and RioPort Inc. Prices are expected to be $0.99 per song, or $9.99 per album, in a format that allows the downloads to be burned onto CDs a limited number of times. Additionally, Listen.com has reached agreements with all five major recording labels to sell online music.

Sony is now using Scour.net, a company it once sued over copyright infringement, to promote some of its artists. The new owner of Scour, CenterSpan Communications, allows users to download free songs and listen to them for 30 days, after which the songs are no longer accessible. Song files can be sent to friends, but the recipient of a song must register with Scour.com and would be subject to the same restrictions. Song files cannot be burned onto a CD or listened to on other devices such as MP3 players. *See* Lisa M. Bowman, "Sony to Send Songs Via Scour," CNET News.com (May 14, 2002), *available at* http://news.com.com/2100-1023-913534.html.

In November 2002, the EMI record label announced it would distribute its music to nine online music providers, including Liquid Audio, Listen.com, MusicNet, PressPlay, Roxio, and others. This agreement significantly expands legal access to its catalog. The new agreement allows users not only to download songs, but also to transfer songs to other devices, such as MP3 players, and to burn songs onto CD up to three times. This mass licensing is uncharacteristic of the major labels' licensing agreements to date.

Both Pressplay and MusicNet have also faced difficulty with the U.S. government. In August 2001, the Justice Department revealed that it is conducting an antitrust investigation of the online music business, focusing on the alleged use of copyright rules and licensing practices to control music distribution. The investigation targets the online music ventures Pressplay and MusicNet, which were formed in Napster's wake with the backing of the music industry's largest record labels. The Justice Department investigation seeks to determine whether the record labels worked together, using their exclusive copyright power over musical recordings, to control the development of the online music marketplace. *See* Kelly Donohue, "MusicNet & Pressplay: To Trust or Antitrust?," 2001 Duke L. & Tech. Rev. 0039 (Nov. 12, 2001), *available at* http://www.law.duke.edu/journals/dltr/articles/2001DLTR0039.html.

Audio Mills tried to bypass these issues altogether through its BitBop Tuner, which is an online service that searches streaming radio broadcasts for any song a user wishes to hear. If the song is not currently being streamed, the Tuner will search past playlists to predict which station is most likely to play the requested song soonest. Streamed audio is typically of lesser quality than downloaded audio and the Tuner is not always successful in finding the requested song right away. Distribution of the Tuner had been discontinued as of March 29, 2002.

File swapping service KaZaA and telephone company Verizon have teamed up to lobby Washington to create a compulsory license for Webcasting. The companies claim that a compulsory Webcasting license would allow file sharing to flourish while ensuring artist compensation. *See* Jefferson Graham, "KaZaA, Verizon Propose to Pay Artists Directly," *USA Today* (May 13, 2002), available at http://www .usatoday.com/life/cyber/tech/2002/05/14/music-kazaa.htm. The RIAA has expressed doubts about the plan, calling it "ridiculous." *See id.* Another proposed idea, the creation of an Intellectual Property User Fee, would potentially add a charge onto the purchase of CD burners, computers, or ISP subscriptions that would be put into a fund for artists to pay for lost revenue. *See* John Borland, "KaZaA Finds Friends in File-Swapping Fight," CNET News.com (May 16, 2002), *available at* http://news.com.com/2102-1023-914983.html. Such a model is already in place, with blank audiotape sales to compensate record companies to compensate them for album taping.

For a discussion of music licensing requirements for FCC-licensed radio broadcasters transmitting their signals via the Internet, *see* pages 108-110, above.

The E-Books Debate

The issues surrounding digital music distribution—compensating authors and copyright owners and preventing piracy—are also at the center of the electronic book-publishing debate. Including explicit digital media rights provisions in contracts between freelance writers, artists, and their employers has become increasingly important.

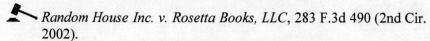 *Random House Inc. v. Rosetta Books, LLC*, 283 F.3d 490 (2nd Cir. 2002).

Random House brought a copyright infringement action against electronic publishing start-up Rosetta Books, claiming that Rosetta Books had offered for online sale eight works to which Random House owned the exclusive publishing rights. Random House asserted that, in signing over the rights to publish their works in "book format," authors also relinquished the rights to publish their works in electronic form, *i.e.*, e-book rights. A number of large traditional publishers jointly filed an *amicus* brief in support of Random House's position. Rosetta Books maintained that the authors in question still owned the e-book rights to their works and that they contracted with these authors for those rights. The authors simply chose to enter agreements with Rosetta rather than Random House. Rosetta argued that Random House's contracts with these authors preceded the advent of the Internet and thus could not have contemplated electronic publication.

On March 8, 2002, the U.S. Court of Appeals for the Second Circuit held that the district court had not abused its discretion by denying Random House's motion for a preliminary injunction against the sale of Rosetta's e-books. Citing *Tele-Pac Inc. v. Grainger*, 570 N.Y.S.2d 521 (1st Dep't. 1991), the court said that Random House did not have a likelihood of success on the merits, a requirement for obtaining an injunction, because New York law, which controlled the dispute, narrowly construes the grant of rights when the contracting parties do not specify that the grant of rights extends to future media. Therefore, Random House's licensing agreements with the authors did not make Random House the beneficial owner of the right to publish the books in electronic format.

Licensing/Royalty Systems

In January 2001, BarnesandNoble.com created a new division that will pay authors royalties of 35 percent of the retail price of works sold in digital format.

In March 2001, National Writers Union and Brill's Contentville jointly launched a Web-based licensing system, under which writers register their copyrights through a Publications Rights Clearinghouse and receive as royalties 30 percent of the fees paid by Contentville's customers. The clearinghouse operates in much the same was as ASCAP does for collecting fees and distributing royalties for musical compositions.

AOL Time Warner has recently announced an e-book publishing division, iPublish. The Author's Guild has criticized iPublish because it perceives the terms it is offering to authors to be unfair. According to the Guild, iPublish would own the rights to any future digital format of the work, as well as audio book rights, but would insufficiently compensate authors by awarding them only 25 percent of its net sales as royalties. The Guild asserts that this amount is too low, considering the low cost involved in distributing e-books. AOL perceives the digital conversion of these works to be a major investment and feels authors should share some of the risk.

A new Internet clearinghouse called the Creative Commons has been launched at http://www.creativecommons.org. The site encourages copyright holders to donate their material for royalty-free, noncommercial use.

Digital Video Recording

Digital Video Recorders (DVR) are the digital version of VCRs. Using computer hard drives instead of video tape, DVRs allow users seemingly to pause and rewind live television while the DVR continues to record. Some DVRs have the ability to skip forward at preprogrammed intervals, effectively skipping commercials, or to send recorded programs to other DVR machines.

In an interview appearing in the April 29, 2002 issue of *CableWorld*, Turner Broadcasting CEO Jamie Kellner said that skipping commercials amounts to theft of the programming, but that there is "a certain amount of tolerance for going to the bathroom."

 Paramount Pictures Corp. v. ReplayTV Inc., Case No. 01CV-9358 (C.D. Cal., filed Oct. 31, 2001); *Time Warner Enter. Co. v. ReplayTV Inc.*, No. 01CV-9693 (C.D. Cal., filed Nov. 9, 2001); *Metro-Goldwyn-Mayer v. ReplayTV Inc.*, No. 01CV-9801 (C.D. Cal., filed Nov. 15, 2001); *Columbia Pictures v. ReplayTV Inc.*, No. 01CV-10221 (C.D. Cal., filed Nov. 28, 2001).

These suits were consolidated pursuant to an August 15, 2002, Court Order Denying Motion To Dismiss; Order Denying Motion to Stay; Order Granting Motion To Consolidate, *Newmark, et al. v. Turner Broadcasting Network, et al.*, No. CV 02-0445 FMC (C.D. Cal. Aug. 15, 2002).

Paramount and a number of other media companies have brought suit against ReplayTV for contributory and vicarious copyright liability. The lawsuit challenges features of ReplayTV's 4000 series DVR. The plaintiffs specifically oppose the "send show" feature, which allows users to distribute recorded programs to other ReplayTV users, and the "autoskip" feature, which automatically deletes commercials during the playback of a recorded program.

In early May 2002, a federal magistrate ordered ReplayTV's owner, SonicBlue, to develop software that would allow it to monitor the viewing habits of its ReplayTV set-top box owners and turn the information over to the plaintiffs. Without addressing the possible privacy implications, on May 31, 2002, the District Court for the Central District of California overturned the ruling, saying it impermissibly required SonicBlue to create new data that is not currently in existence.

Newmark v. Turner Broadcasting System Inc. (C.D. Cal., filed June 6, 2002).

. A group of ReplayTV 4000 DVR owners filed suit against entertainment-industry companies, seeking a declaratory judgment that use of a DVR to record and time-shift programs, skip commercials, and distribute copies of programs to other ReplayTV owners does not violate copyright law. The complaint also names ReplayTV, Inc. and Sonicblue Inc., manufacturers and distributors of the ReplayTV DVR as defendants. DVR owners are worried that the outcome of Replay's lawsuit with Paramount may force Replay to disable some DVR features.

Limiting the Scope of the DMCA

The DMCA's strict copyright protection of digital materials has been under intense criticism since the statute was enacted. Because the DMCA lacks a fair-use defense or other means to rationalize some legitimate uses of copyrighted digital materials, a movement is afoot to limit the scope and reach of the DMCA.

Proposed Legislation and Regulations

Congress is considering several bills that would amend the DMCA.

On October 2, 2002, Rep. Lofgren (D-Cal.) introduced the Digital Choice and Freedom Act (H.R. 5522). The bill would provide protections for consumers who make backup copies or give away digital material they have purchased. Additionally, it would permit consumers to bypass technological protections on copyrighted materials in order to use the copyrighted work for a legal purpose.

Rep. Boucher (D-Va.) introduced a bill on October 3, 2002, called the Digital Media Consumers' Rights Act of 2002 (H.R. 5544). The bill would amend the Federal Trade Commission Act to provide that the advertising or sale of a copy-protected music disc that is not clearly identified as copy-protected is an unfair method of competition and an unfair and deceptive act or practice. It would also amend the DMCA to include a fair-use defense for circumventing technological protections (*e.g.*, by passcode or other security measure) of copyrighted digital works for noninfringing or otherwise defensible uses. When the 108th Congress convened in January 2003, Rep. Boucher (D-Va.) reintroduced the Digital Media Consumers' Rights Act of 2002 (H.R. 107), which is identical to the bill he introduced in November 2002 (H.R. 5544).

Two days after H.R. 5522 was introduced in Congress, the Copyright Office issued a Notice of Inquiry, seeking comments related to the DMCA's prohibition on circumventing technical-protection measures controlling access to copyrighted materials. *See* Library of Congress, Copyright Office, Docket No. RM 2002-4 (Oct. 4, 2002). The Copyright Office requested that comments be filed by December 18, 2002, addressing whether consumers would be adversely affected if they were unable lawfully to make non-infringing uses of particular classes of technologically protected copyrighted materials. This notice of inquiry marks only the second time since the DMCA's enactment that the Copyright Office has elicited public comment on the statute.

Copyright Law Versus Contract Law

Courts have addressed whether copyright law trumps contract provisions that limit or otherwise alter legitimate uses, and defenses to unauthorized uses, of copyright-protected works.

Softman Products Co. v. Adobe Systems, Inc., 171 F. Supp. 2d 1075 (C.D. Cal. 2001).

To encourage customers to buy multiple Adobe programs at the same time, Adobe bundled its software into various boxed collections, which it sold for less than the included programs would have cost if purchased separately. Each copy of each program contained a license agreement that popped up on installation, purporting to prohibit a buyer from breaking up the collections and selling the individual programs separately. When Softman Products Co., a Los Angeles-based software distributor, did just that, Adobe sought an injunction prohibiting sale of the "unbundled" software. By re-selling the individual programs, Adobe argued, Softman was breaching the license agreement under which Adobe had distributed the boxed collection.

Softman countered that the license agreement could not prohibit the company from selling the unbundled programs because it had bought copies of the software collections, not licensed them. And as the owner of the copies, Softman argued that it had a right under copyright law to sell those copies regardless of any restriction Adobe sought to impose under the license agreement. The court agreed.

Though Adobe characterized each transaction in the chain of commerce—from Adobe to its distributors to Softman, and eventually to the consumer—as a license, the court looked to the "economic realities" of these exchanges to conclude that Adobe had actually sold, not licensed, the copies of its software Softman obtained: "Adobe transfers ... merchandise to distributors. Distributors pay full value for the merchandise and assume the risk that the software may be damaged or lost. The distributors also assume the risk that they will be unable to sell the product. The distributors then resell the product to other distributors in the secondary market. The secondary market and the ultimate consumer also pay full value for the product and accept the risk that the product may be damaged or lost." And the rights are transferred in perpetuity; the buyer does not have to return the software to the seller upon expiration of some specified period of time. All in all, the court concluded, the transactions looked more like sales of copies of the software than like licenses to use the software.

One of the exclusive rights that copyright law grants to the owner of copyright in a work is the right to distribute copies of that work. But copyright law has long provided that the owner of a copy of a work has a right to sell that copy without any permission from the copyright owner. In other words, the owner of the copyright in a work has the exclusive right to sell each copy of the work the first time it is sold, but once a copy is sold, the buyer has the right to dispose of that copy as he sees fit. Adobe could not use its license agreement to compel Softman to relinquish rights granted to Softman by copyright law under this "first sale doctrine."

Adobe Sys., Inc. v. Stargate Software, Inc., 216 F. Supp. 2d 1051 (N.D. Cal. 2002).

Adobe sued Stargate alleging that the defendant was selling its software without authorization. The U.S. District Court for the Northern District of California held that the agreement between Adobe and Stargate, which characterized each software transaction as a license rather than a sale, was valid. The court rejected the conclusion of the *Softman* court that such a license was a sale.

Bowers v. Baystate Technologies, Nos. 01-1108, 01-1109 (Fed. Cir. Aug, 20, 2002), *modified by Bowers v. Baystate Technologies*, Nos. 01-1108, 01-1109 (Fed. Cir. Jan. 29, 2003) (dissenting opinion added).

Bowers, a software designer, and Baystate entered into a license agreement, which included a provision that prohibited Baystate from reverse engineering[‡] of the software. Baystate reverse-engineered the software, and Bowers sued, claiming damages for both breach of contract and violation of the Copyright Act. The federal trial court awarded only the contract claim damages, refusing to award copyright claim damages because, the trial court said, such damages would be duplicative of the contract damages.

The U.S. Court of Appeals affirmed the trial court's ruling that Baystate had breached its contract with Bowers, and held that the trial court did not abuse its discretion in omitting copyright damages as duplicative. This holding indicates that state contract law authorizing shrinkwrap licenses that prohibit reverse-engineering is not preempted by federal copyright law.

[‡] "Reverse engineering" is taking apart an object to see how it works in order to duplicate or enhance the object. Software reverse engineering involves reversing a program's machine code back into source code in order to: (1) retrieve the source code of a program because it was lost; (2) study how the program performs certain operations; (3) improve the performance of a program; (4) fix a bug; (5) identify malicious content in a program, such as a virus; or (6) adapt a program written for use with one type of microprocessor for use with a different type of microprocessor. Reverse engineering for the sole purpose of copying or duplicating programs constitutes a copyright violation and is illegal. In some cases, the licensed use of software specifically prohibits reverse engineering. From whatis.com on the TechTarget Network at http://whatis.techtarget.com/definition/0,,sid9_gci507015,00.html.

DEFAMATION

Libel Basics

A defamatory statement is one that injures the reputation of another. The common-law torts of libel and slander punish the publication of statements that are both defamatory and false. A libelous statement was traditionally a false and defamatory statement published in writing. A slanderous statement is a false and defamatory statement uttered orally. (False and defamatory oral statements broadcast over radio or television are now widely considered libel, rather than slander.) Money damages may be awarded to compensate the victim of libel or slander for the reputational injury caused by publication of the false and defamatory statement.

There is an unavoidable tension between the common-law protections of reputation and the mandate of the First Amendment to the Constitution that "Congress shall make no law ... abridging the freedom of speech, or of the press. . . ." To ensure that debate on public issues remains "uninhibited, robust and wide-open," *New York Times v. Sullivan*, 376 U.S. 254, 270 (1964), the Supreme Court has found that the First Amendment limits the circumstances under which a speaker or publisher may be punished for making false and defamatory statements: "Neither lies nor false communications serve the ends of the First Amendment ... [b]ut to insure the ascertainment and publication of the truth about public affairs, it is essential that the First Amendment protect some erroneous publications as well as true ones." *St. Amant v. Thompson*, 390 U.S. 727, 732 (1968).

Public Officials

In *New York Times Co. v. Sullivan*, 376 U.S. 254 (1964), the Supreme Court ruled that the First Amendment limits common-law defamation claims brought by public officials. The Court held that to recover for publication of a defamatory falsehood, a public official must prove that the challenged statement was "of and concerning" the public official plaintiff, that the statement was false, and that the defendant acted with "actual malice." The Court defined "actual malice" as publication with knowledge that the statement was false or with reckless disregard of whether the statement was false or not.

Public Figures

Later, the Supreme Court extended the standard announced in *New York Times Co. v. Sullivan* to defamation cases brought by "public figures." Public figures include individuals who voluntarily inject themselves into public controversy, as well as those who are involuntarily thrust into the limelight, even if only with respect to a particular activity or incident.

Private Individuals

A private-figure defamation plaintiff can recover damages based on the defendant's negligence (or a more speech-protective standard, under the law of some states). In no instance, however, can a private-figure plaintiff recover damages for defamation without a showing of fault amounting, at least, to negligence. Any lesser standard, the Court concluded, would unduly burden free speech. *Gertz v. Robert Welch, Inc.*, 418 U.S. 323, 347 (1974). And, at least when the speech relates to an issue of public concern, a private-figure plaintiff must bear the burden of proving falsity; the defendant speaker is not obligated to prove the truth of the challenged statements. *Philadelphia Newspapers, Inc. v. Hepps*, 475 U.S. 767, 768 (1986).

Online Service Provider Liability

General Background

At common law, one who repeats the statements of another is as responsible for the defamatory content of those statements as the original speaker. *See, e.g., Cianci v. New Times Publ'g Co.*, 639 F.2d 54, 60-61 (2d Cir. 1980). This common-law rule, however, is subject to the federal constitutional limitation against imposing liability without fault. *See Gertz v. Robert Welch, Inc.*, 418 U.S. 323, 347 (1974). One cannot be held liable in a defamation action unless he or she has "'tak[en] a [r]esponsible part in the publication.'" *Lewis v. Time, Inc.*, 83 F.R.D. 455, 463 (E.D. Cal. 1979), *aff'd*, 710 F.2d 549 (9th Cir. 1983) (citation omitted).

Publishers, Distributors, and Common Carriers

Courts have long recognized a distinction among one who publishes or republishes a defamatory statement, one who "delivers or transmits" material published by a third party, and one who merely provides facilities used by a third party to publish defamatory material. *See, e.g., Lerman v. Chuckleberry Publ'g, Inc.*, 521 F. Supp. 228, 235 (S.D.N.Y. 1981), *rev'd on other grounds*, 745 F.2d 123 (2d Cir. 1984), *cert. denied*,

471 U.S. 1054 (1985); *Anderson v. New York Telephone Co.*, 361 N.Y.S.2d 913 (N.Y. 1974). "Publishers," such as newspapers, magazines, and broadcasters, control the content of their publications and are, accordingly, held legally responsible for any defamatory material they publish. *Restatement (Second) of Torts* § 578 (1977). "Distributors," such as bookstores, libraries, and newsstands, cannot be held liable for a statement contained in the materials they distribute unless "[they knew] or had reason to know of the defamatory [statement at issue]." *See, e.g., Auvil v. CBS "60 Minutes,"* 800 F. Supp. 928, 931-32 (E.D. Wa. 1992). Distributors are under no duty to examine the publications that they offer for sale to ascertain whether they contain defamatory statements. *See Lewis*, 83 F.R.D. at 463. Common carriers, such as telephone companies, which do no more than provide facilities by which third parties may communicate, cannot be held liable for defamatory statements communicated through those facilities unless they have participated in preparing the defamatory material. *See Anderson*, 361 N.Y.S.2d at 913 (adopting dissenting opinion in *Anderson v. New York Telephone Co.*, 345 N.Y.S.2d 740, 750-752 (N.Y. App. Div. 1973)).

Development of the Law

Whether an online service provider is properly classified as a publisher or distributor was one of the first major issues to arise in Internet libel jurisprudence. Initially, two courts in New York addressed this issue, with contrary results. Then, in the Communications Decency Act of 1996, Congress immunized providers and users of "interactive computer services" from liability for statements made by other information content providers. 47 U.S.C. § 230(c)(1).

Liability of Interactive Service Providers Prior to the Enactment of the Communications Decency Act of 1996

 Cubby, Inc. v. CompuServe Inc., 776 F. Supp. 135 (S.D.N.Y. 1991).

CompuServe operated a bulletin board that contained a daily newsletter called "Rumorville." When the plaintiff, Cubby, began a competing electronic publication called "Skuttlebutt," Rumorville published various unflattering statements about Skuttlebutt, including an allegation that Skuttlebutt was a "start-up scam." 776 F. Supp. at 141. Cubby sued the creators of Rumorville for libel and sued CompuServe on the grounds that it had republished the statements.

The court found that CompuServe was properly deemed a distributor, rather than a publisher. *Id.* at 141. In reaching this conclusion, the court focused on the fact that CompuServe did not exercise control over the bulletin board, but instead had contracted with an independent entity to "manage, review, create, delete, edit and otherwise control the contents" of the bulletin board. *Id.* at 143. The court further noted that CompuServe had "no opportunity to review" content before it was uploaded and made available to subscribers, and thus had "no more editorial control ... than does a public library, bookstore, or newsstand." *Id.* at 140. Based on these findings, the court granted CompuServe's motion for summary judgment. *Id.* at 144.

Stratton Oakmont, Inc. v. Prodigy Servs. Co., 23 Media L. Rep. (BNA) 1794 (N.Y. Sup. Ct. 1995).

An anonymous user of Prodigy's "Money Talk" bulletin board posted statements claiming that Stratton Oakmont, a securities firm, had committed criminal and fraudulent acts and was a "cult of brokers who either lie for a living or get fired." 23 Media L. Rep. at 1795. Stratton Oakmont sued Prodigy and, anticipating the "distributor" defense that had been successful for CompuServe, moved for summary judgment on the limited issue of whether Prodigy had exercised sufficient editorial control over its online services to be deemed a publisher.

The court, in ruling for Stratton Oakmont, found that Prodigy exercised substantial control over the bulletin board and thus should be classified as a publisher rather than a distributor. *Id.* at 1795. Specifically, the court stated that Prodigy "held itself out to the public and its members as controlling the content of its computer bulletin boards" and controlled the content of its bulletin boards through the use of screening software and by engaging bulletin-board leaders charged with monitoring content for compliance with specific guidelines. *Id.* at 1797. The court added that Prodigy had made a "conscious choice" to regulate the content of its bulletin boards and thereby exposed itself to greater potential liability than other computer networks that undertook a less active role. *Id.* at 1798.

Lunney v. Prodigy Servs. Co., 683 N.Y.S.2d 557, *aff'd*, 94 N.Y.2d 242 (1999), *cert. denied*, 120 S. Ct. 1832 (2000).

A Boy Scout sued Prodigy after an allegedly defamatory e-mail message was sent in his name (but not by him) to his Scout master. The trial court ruled that the ISP could not be held liable simply because it provided the facilities used by a third party to communicate a defamatory message. Thus, the court treated the ISP not as a publisher or distributor, but rather as a common carrier, such as a telephone company, for purposes of defamation suits. The court declined to decide whether an

ISP is immune under the Communications Decency Act of 1996, presumably because the suit had been filed prior to the enactment of that statute.

The New York Court of Appeals affirmed the ruling, noting that "an ISP, like a telephone company, is merely a conduit." 99 N.Y.2d at 242. Accordingly, "Prodigy was not a publisher of the electronic ... messages." *Id.*

The United Kingdom has not adopted this approach. *See Godfrey v. Demon Internet Ltd.*, 3 W.L.R. 1020 (Q.B. 1999) (holding that ISPs sued over defamatory messages posted by a third party are protected by the innocent-dissemination defense up to a point; however, once the provider is notified about the defamatory message, it becomes responsible for it, and thus can be sued for defamation as the publisher of the statement), available at http://www.haledorr.com/pdf/Godfrey _v_Demon.pdf.

Communications Decency Act of 1996

Statutory Provision. Following the *Stratton Oakmont* decision, discussed above, Congress recognized the increased potential for liability for speech published online. In an attempt to encourage continued private investment and free discussion on the Internet, Congress enacted sweeping and far-reaching protections from liability for Internet service providers (ISP) and those operating websites through § 230 of the Communications Decency Act of 1996, Pub. L. No. 104-104, 110 Stat. 133, 138 (1996) (codified at 47 U.S.C. § 230), which provides, in relevant part, as follows:

"No provider or user of an interactive computer service shall be treated as the publisher or speaker of any information provided by another information content provider." 47 U.S.C. § 230(c)(1).

Legislative History. The Conference Committee Report states that the legislation was intended to overrule the *Stratton Oakmont* holding that online service providers can be held liable as publishers of third-party comments. *See* Joint Explanatory Statement of the Congressional Conference Committee, H.R. Conf. Rep. No. 104-458 (1996), published in 142 Cong. Rec. H1078, 1130 (Jan. 31, 1996).

Liability of Interactive Service Providers and Users After the Enactment of the Communications Decency Act of 1996

Courts have applied the protection of § 230 broadly, ruling that ISPs and those operating websites generally enjoy immunity from liability. As long as the material complained of was written by a third party, rather than an agent or employee of the ISP or website, the ISP or website is immune from liability. At the same time, the operator of a website may choose to exercise control over the content of its site by removing or editing content provided by third parties without becoming liable as the "publisher" of the third-party statements. Local governments, however, do not enjoy the same level of immunity under the statute as private providers.

Aquino v. Electriciti, Inc., 26 Media L. Rep. (BNA) 1032 (Cal. Super. Ct. 1997).

The plaintiffs sued Electriciti, Inc., an ISP, and one of its employees for negligence and intentional infliction of emotional distress for disseminating statements posted by an anonymous individual that the plaintiffs were "ring leaders" of an "international conspiracy" to further "Satanic Ritual Abuse" of children and that the plaintiffs engaged in kidnapping, cannibalism, and murder of anyone who stood in the way of the "international conspiracy." Plaintiffs' First Amended Complaint ¶ 10 (filed June 23, 1997). After the court dismissed the plaintiffs' claims on grounds that the plaintiffs' action was barred by § 230 of the Communications Decency Act, the plaintiffs filed an amended complaint, which, in addition to reasserting their original claims, set forth causes of action for breach of contract and violation of civil rights. Specifically, the plaintiffs asserted that the defendants breached a purported contract with them by failing to disclose to the plaintiffs the name of the third-party who posted the defamatory statements and violated the plaintiffs' civil rights by aiding and abetting the third-party in an effort to discriminate against the plaintiffs based on their religious beliefs.

The defendants again moved to dismiss, asserting that all of the plaintiffs' causes of action, including their claims for breach of contract and violation of civil rights, were inconsistent with § 230, which was designed to immunize online service providers from liability arising from third-party content. In a brief order, the court again dismissed the plaintiffs' claims, apparently adopting the defendants' broad interpretation of § 230. 26 Media L. Rep. at 1032.

Zeran v. America Online, Inc., 129 F.3d 327 (4th Cir. 1997), *cert. denied*, 118 S. Ct. 2341 (1998).

An unidentified person posted messages on an America Online bulletin board offering t-shirts featuring tasteless slogans relating to the bombing of the federal building in Oklahoma City. Those interested in purchasing the shirts were instructed to call the plaintiff's home phone number in Seattle, Washington. The plaintiff requested that AOL remove the postings, and AOL agreed to do so. AOL declined, however, to print a retraction as a matter of policy. The parties disputed the date that AOL actually removed the posting from its bulletin board. The plaintiff filed suit against AOL for negligence, alleging that it had unreasonably delayed removing the defamatory messages, refused to post retractions, and failed subsequently to screen for similar postings.

The district court granted judgment for AOL on grounds that § 230 of the Communications Decency Act barred the plaintiff's claims. On appeal, the plaintiff argued that § 230 left intact distributor liability for interactive computer service providers who possess notice of defamatory material posted through their services and fail to remove such material.

The Court of Appeals for the Fourth Circuit affirmed the judgment for AOL: "[b]y its plain language, § 230 creates a federal immunity to any cause of action that would make service providers liable for information originating with a third-party user of the service. ... Thus, lawsuits seeking to hold a service provider liable for its exercise of a publisher's traditional editorial functions—such as deciding whether to publish, withdraw, postpone or alter content—are barred." *Id.* at 330. The court noted, among other things, that holding AOL liable in these circumstances would directly contradict one of the important purposes of § 230—namely, "to encourage service providers to self-regulate the dissemination of offensive material over their services." *Id.* at 331. *See also Doe v. America Online, Inc.*, 25 Media L. Rep. (BNA) 2112 (Fla. Dist. Ct. App. 1997) (holding that § 230 immunizes AOL from liability for statements made by subscribers in chat rooms), *aff'd*, 718 So. 2d 385 (Fla. Dist. Ct. App. 1998).

Blumenthal v. Drudge, 992 F. Supp. 44 (D.D.C. 1998).

The plaintiffs, Sidney Blumenthal, a former White House aide, and his wife, sued Matt Drudge, publisher of an electronic publication known as the "Drudge Report," and AOL for libel, invasion of privacy, and intentional infliction of emotional distress. The plaintiffs alleged that Drudge libeled them by reporting that "top GOP operatives" believed that "Blumenthal ha[d] a spousal abuse past." *Blumenthal*, 992 F. Supp.

at 46. The plaintiffs asserted that AOL, which had entered into a license agreement with Drudge by which it paid him a monthly royalty in exchange for the right to make the "Drudge Report" available to AOL users, jointly published the allegedly defamatory statements with Drudge and thus was not immune from liability pursuant to § 230. The plaintiffs also alleged that AOL could be held liable on grounds that Drudge was an employee or agent of AOL.

AOL filed a motion for summary judgment, and Drudge filed a separate motion to dismiss or transfer for lack of personal jurisdiction (jurisdictional issues are discussed in Chapter 8). AOL, which based its motion entirely on § 230, asserted that, as an interactive computer service, it was immune from liability for any cause of action arising from material prepared by a third party. In granting AOL's motion, the court held that the fact that AOL had the right to make changes in the "Drudge Report" was not sufficient to make it a joint publisher of the report. Rather, the plaintiffs were required to present evidence that AOL had some role in creating or developing the information in the "Drudge Report." They failed to do so. "Indeed, plaintiffs affirmatively state that 'no person, other than Drudge himself, edited, checked, verified, or supervised the information that Drudge published in the Drudge Report.'" *Id.* at 50. The court also found that "there is no evidence to support the view originally taken by plaintiffs that Drudge is or was an employee or agent of AOL ... ." *Id.*

Mainstream Loudoun v. Board of Trustees of the Loudoun County Library, 2 F. Supp. 2d 783 (E.D. Va. 1998).

Citizens of Mainstream Loudoun sued their public library because the library installed filtering software on its computers as part of the Library Board's "Policy on Internet Sexual Harassment." *Mainstream Loudoun*, 2 F. Supp. 2d at 787. The plaintiffs claimed the policy impermissibly blocked their access to protected speech, and sought declaratory and injunctive relief. The library moved for summary judgment, claiming it was immune from suit under § 230.

In denying the motion, the court held that the public library was not immune from suit because § 230(c)(2), providing immunity from suit for providers who restrict access to certain content, should apply only to private Internet content providers. *Id.* at 790. The purpose of the CDA was to protect ISPs from government regulation, not to insulate government regulation from judicial review. *Id.* Therefore, § 230 does not protect government entities.

The court also noted that even if § 230 were construed to apply to public libraries, the "tort-based" immunity from "civil liability" would not bar an action for declaratory and injunctive relief. *Id.* at 790. The court emphasized this line of reasoning in denying the library's motion for reconsideration. *See Mainstream Loudoun v. Board of Trustees of the Loudoun County Library*, 24 F. Supp. 2d 552, 561 (E.D. Va. 1998) (holding that § 230 provides immunity for actions for damages, but does not immunize a defendant from an action for declaratory and injunctive relief).

For discussion of this case in the context of First Amendment issues, *see* Chapter 1, page 11.

 Ben Ezra, Weinstein, and Co. v. America Online, Inc., 27 Media L. Rep. (BNA) 1794 (D.N.M. 1999), *aff'd*, 206 F.3d 980 (10th Cir. 2000), *cert. denied*, 531 U.S. 824 (2000).

The plaintiff, a publicly traded company, sued AOL for defamation, among other things, on the grounds that AOL repeatedly published inaccurate information regarding the value of the plaintiff's stock. AOL moved for summary judgment pursuant to § 230. The court found that the allegedly defamatory information was created by third-party content providers, not by AOL. Accordingly, the court found that § 230 provided AOL with immunity from the plaintiff's claims and entered summary judgment for AOL.

The Court of Appeals for the Tenth Circuit subsequently affirmed the ruling, stating that "Plaintiff presents no evidence to contradict Defendant's evidence that [the third-party content providers] alone created the stock information at issue." *Ben Ezra, Weinstein, and Co. v. America Online, Inc.*, 206 F.3d 980, 986 (10th Cir. 2000), *cert. denied*, 121 S. Ct. 69 (2000). The court added that there also was no evidence that AOL was "'responsible, in whole or in part, for ... the creation and development of information' published on its Quotes & Portfolios area." *Id.* (quoting 47 U.S.C. § 230(f)(3)).

For discussion of this case in the context of requests to stay discovery, *see* page, below 142.

 Doe v. America Online, Inc., 718 So. 2d 385 (Fla. Dist. Ct. App. 1998), *aff'd*, 783 So. 2d 1010 (Fla. 2001), *cert. denied*, 122 S. Ct. 208 (2001).

A mother sued AOL and Richard Lee Russell, an AOL user, for emotional injuries caused by Russell's publication and marketing in an AOL chat room of videotapes depicting the mother's 11-year-old son in sexual activities. The plaintiff claimed that AOL had notice of Russell's Internet activities, and yet did not warn or advise Russell to stop, nor did it suspend or terminate his service. The trial court found that "making AOL liable for Russell's chat room communications would treat AOL as the publisher or speaker of those communications," and therefore AOL was immune from suit under § 230. *Id.* at 387. The Florida Supreme Court agreed with both the appeals court and the trial court, and Doe's complaint against AOL was dismissed.

As in *Zeran*, the court held that the plaintiff's attempt to hold AOL liable as a distributor, rather than as a publisher or speaker, in order to avoid preemption by § 230 was ill founded. Because of the sheer number of postings, subjecting ISPs to distributor liability would create an impossible burden to investigate each time a potentially defamatory statement is brought to AOL's attention. *Id.* at 389. Thus, receiving notice of an unlawful posting does not mean that ISPs lose the protection of § 230. The court also held that the Act applies retroactively, meaning that complaints instituted after the Act's effective date are subject to its provisions, regardless of when the relevant conduct giving rise to the claim occurred. *Id.* at 383.

Schneider v. Amazon.com Inc., 31 P.3d 37; 2001 Wash. App. LEXIS 2086 (Wash. Ct. App. Sept. 17, 2001).

The plaintiff, Jerome Schneider, author of several books, filed suit against the defendant, Amazon.com, an online bookseller, alleging defamation and tortious interference with business expectancy based on negative comments about the author contained on the Amazon.com website. The Amazon.com website allows visitors to post comments about the books made available on the site, and at least ten anonymous comments were posted that were critical of the plaintiff and his books.

The court held that Amazon.com was immune from suit under § 230 of the Communications Decency Act because it qualified as an "interactive service provider" within the meaning of § 230's "good samaritan" immunity section (47 U.S.C.S. § 230(c)). The court relied heavily on *Zeran v. America Online Inc.*, 129 F.3d 327 (4th Cir. 1997), discussed at page 136, above, which held that AOL was immune from liability for material posted on its online bulletin boards. Comparing the two cases, the court noted that reader postings on Amazon.com "appear indistinguishable from AOL's message board for § 230 purposes." 31 P.3d 37, 40. The fact that Amazon.com was not providing access to the Internet was irrelevant to the court because "[u]nder the statutory definition [in § 230(f)], access providers are only a subclass of the broader definition of interactive service providers entitled to immunity."

Id. The court also rejected the plaintiff's arguments that § 230 immunity only applies to tort claims and that Amazon.com, by reserving the right to edit visitors' postings and claiming license rights in the content, became the content provider. Instead, the court concluded that the requirements of § 230 were met, and it barred the plaintiff's claim accordingly.

Barrett v. Clark, No. 833021-5 (Cal. Super. Ct. July 25, 2001).

A California Superior Court ruled that an individual's continued re-postings to newsgroups of an allegedly defamatory statement originally authored and posted by another person is protected under § 230's "good samaritan" immunity (47 U.S.C.S. § 230(c)). The plaintiffs, Stephen Barrett and Terry Polevoy, operate consumer advocacy websites, one of which is called "Quackwatch," that are designed to inform consumers about health fraud. They sued the defendant, Ilena Rosenthal, who runs support groups for women who were harmed by breast implants, for libel based on her postings about them on Internet newsgroups. The court found that only one statement by Rosenthal was arguably defamatory, and that was a statement, authored by someone else, that she had re-posted to a newsgroup. Since she did not "create" or "develop" the allegedly defamatory statement, the defendant was not the "publisher speaker" of that statement. Accordingly, she was protected from liability by § 230's "good samaritan" provision. *See Barrett*, No. 833021-5.

Carafano v. Metrosplash.com, 207 F. Supp. 2d 1055 (C.D. Cal. 2002).

The plaintiff, Christianne Carafano a/k/a Chase Masterson, a professional actor who appeared in the television show "Star Trek: Deep Space Nine," sued the operator of a matchmaking website for publishing a false dating profile that included her real telephone number and address. The site, "Matchmaker.com," asked users to complete an extensive questionnaire, including an essay and as many as 62 multiple-choice questions, that was used to gather information from which the matchmaking profile was created. The site also screened all photographs submitted by users for posting, but did not screen the text of the profiles. Carafano alleged that the website's publication of the false profile constituted invasion of privacy, libel, misappropriation, and negligence on the part of the matchmaking service.

A federal district court in California ruled that the operator of the matchmaker website was not eligible for immunity under § 230. The court found that the service was responsible for the content of its online dating profiles because its extensive work in constructing the questionnaire used to create the profiles amounted to taking an active role in developing the information that was ultimately published.

Requests to Stay Discovery Under § 230 Pending Ruling on Dispositive Motion

Ben Ezra, Weinstein, and Co. v. America Online, Inc., 27 Media L. Rep. (BNA) 1794 (D.N.M. 1999), *aff'd*, 206 F.3d 980 (10th Cir. 2000), *cert. denied*, 531 U.S. 824 (2000).

In this case, described in more detail above at page 139, AOL moved to delay discovery until after the court decided AOL's motion for summary judgment under § 230. The court granted AOL's motion, holding that the immunity afforded to ISPs under § 230 should also relieve ISPs from the burdens of litigation, which include discovery. *Id.* at 2213. However, the court noted that the discovery bar is not necessarily absolute. Plaintiffs may file a Fed.R.Civ.P. 56(f) affidavit, showing what discovery they wish to take and how that discovery will assist in defeating the defendant's invocation of § 230. *Id.*

On appeal, the plaintiff alleged that the district court abused its discretion by overruling the plaintiff's objection to the magistrate judge's order denying the plaintiff additional discovery beyond the 25 interrogatories and four depositions initially permitted. The court of appeals rejected this argument, stating that the plaintiff failed to "demonstrate precisely how additional discovery [would] lead to a genuine issue of material fact." 206 F.3d at 987.

Other Defamation Issues Peculiar to the Internet

Two attributes that attract users to online chat rooms are anonymity and the feeling of freedom that comes from that anonymity, giving users a sense that they are free to speak their minds. Anonymity raises unique issues when a plaintiff alleges injury arising out of the statements of an anonymous user.

Discovery of the Identities of Anonymous Defendants

As discussed in Chapter 1, pages 20-25, it is increasingly common for libel lawsuits to be brought against unknown "John Doe" defendants who post allegedly defamatory statements on Internet message boards. In these lawsuits, subpoenas are issued to the message-board hosts in an effort to obtain identifying information about the authors of the allegedly defamatory remarks. The courts must balance the plaintiff's interest in having a forum for grievances with the defendant's right to anonymous speech. This balancing test has produced varied results.

Libel Suits by Anonymous Plaintiffs

In *America Online, Inc. v. Anonymous Publicly Traded Company*, 542 S.E.2d 377, 385 (Va. 2001), a Virginia appeals court held that a company suing AOL in an attempt to discover the identity of John Does allegedly posting defamatory material on AOL message boards must reveal its own identity. Mere possibility of economic harm, without more, does not permit plaintiff to proceed anonymously. (Overruling *In re Subpoena Duces Tecum to America Online, Inc.*, 52 Va. Cir. 26 (Va. Cir. Ct. 2000)).

For discussion of this case and of First Amendment issues relating to anonymous speech generally, *see* Chapter 1, pages 22.

Sovereign Immunity as Applied to a Government Web Site

In *John Doe v. United States*, 83 F. Supp. 2d 833 (S.D. Tex. 2000), the plaintiffs, individuals associated with various temporary labor companies, initiated a suit seeking money damages from the United States pursuant to the Federal Tort Claims Act, alleging invasion of privacy and intentional infliction of emotional distress. The claims alleged that the U.S. Attorney's Office for the Southern District of Texas had posted a "News Release" on its website indicating that the plaintiffs had been charged with mail fraud and/or money laundering, when, in fact, no such charges had been filed.

The court held that the plaintiffs' allegations "arose out of" libel or slander claims regardless of how the plaintiffs had labeled their allegations. As a result, 28 U.S.C. § 2680(h), which precludes suits against the United States for libel and slander, applied, and the United States' motion to dismiss for lack of subject matter jurisdiction was granted.

Motion to Dismiss on the Pleadings and ISP Immunity

Sabbato v. Hardy, 29 Media L. Rep. 1860, No. 2000CA00136, 2000 Ohio App. LEXIS 6154 (Ohio Ct. App. December 18, 2000).

In *Sabbato*, a website manager who designed and operated a site where opinions could be read and posted by users was sued for both distribution of and participation in libelous remarks. *Id.* at *1. Citing the immunity provisions of the Communications Decency Act, the trial court dismissed the entire action. *Id.* at *2.

The Ohio Court of Appeals reversed in part, holding that the applicability of the good-faith immunity protection afforded by the

Communications Decency Act could not be determined without converting the motion into one for summary judgment, in which a decision can be reached only if there are no material facts in dispute. *Id.* at *7. The court reasoned that, because there was a question of fact concerning the website manager's participation in the creation of the libelous remarks, some evidence had to be presented concerning good faith in order to secure immunity from suit. *Id.* at *6-7. The decision of the trial court to dismiss a claim regarding the *distribution* of defamatory material by the manager was upheld. *Id.* at *6.

Global Telemedia Int'l, Inc. v. Doe, 132 F. Supp. 2d 1261 (C.D. Cal. 2001).

Two users posted allegedly libelous statements about Global Telemedia in a chat room. *Id.* at 1264. Global Telemedia and its manager, Stevens, sued the two participants over these messages. The defendants moved to dismiss the suit pursuant to California Civil Procedure § 425.16, which was designed to discourage Strategic Litigation Against Public Participation (SLAPP) lawsuits. *Id.* at 1264-65.

The anti-SLAPP procedure allows the defendant to obtain dismissal of the suit if the alleged bad acts arose from the exercise of free speech in connection with a public issue and if the plaintiff cannot show a probability of success on the claims. *Id.* at 1265. Though the court noted that competitors may not be protected by the anti-SLAPP provisions, the defendants, as small individual investors not in the same business as the plaintiffs, could properly invoke the protection of the statute. *Id.* at 1266. The court also held that, given the offhand nature of the comments and the context of the bulletin board itself, a reasonable reader would recognize the statements to be expressions of opinion, not actionable as business libel. *Id.* at 1267.

ComputerXPress v. Lee Jackson, 93 Cal. App. 4th 993, 113 (Cal. Ct. App. 2001).

On November 15, 2001, the California Court of Appeals, Fourth District, ruled that criticism of public companies on an Internet message board is protected from frivolous litigation by California's anti-SLAPP statute, which encourages early dismissal of, and can impose sanctions for, frivolous libel suits. In this case, while the defendant may have made disparaging comments, they were of public interest and couched more in the tone of opinion than fact.

⚖ *ZixIt Corp. v. Visa International*, No. 05-01-01998-CV (Tex. App., July 31, 2002).

A Dallas, Texas court dismissed a $700 million libel suit against Visa, the employer of a poster of more than 400 anonymous messages, most of them negative, about the plaintiff, ZixIt Corporation, on the Yahoo! Finance ZixIt message board. ZixIt alleged that the posting caused its stock prices to plummet. Visa asserted its employee's free-speech rights, and claimed the posting had had no ill effect on ZixIt's stock. The jury agreed with the defendant that ZixIt was not harmed by the postings, as other factors, including a troubled economy, contributed to the decline in the value of ZixIt stock.

⚖ In *Donato v. Moldow*, Docket No. BER-L-6214-01 (Sup. Ct. N.J., Bergen Cty. Div., Dec. 21, 2001), a New Jersey Superior Court dismissed a libel suit against Stephen Moldow, operator of "Eye on Emerson," a website that lets visitors anonymously criticize their town's public officials. The court also quashed a subpoena issued by four politicians who had sought the identity of 60 anonymous posters on the site. The unknown people who posted the statements, which include allegations that public officials were involved in extramarital affairs and questionable business practices, remain "John and Jane Doe" defendants.

⚖ *Melvin v. Doe*, 789 A.2d 696 (Pa. Super. Ct. 2001), *reh'g denied*, Nos. 2115, 2116 (Pa. Super. Ct., Jan. 31, 2002), *appeal filed*, Nos. 50 WAP 2002 & 51 WAP 2002 (Pa., filed Oct. 1, 2002).

The ACLU challenged a trial court order requiring AOL to disclose the identities of 13 "John Doe" defendants who had posted anonymous messages criticizing the plaintiff on a message board. The creators of the website, "Grant Street '99," posted messages on the site claiming that the plaintiff, Superior Court Judge Jane Orie Melvin, had lobbied then-governor Tom Ridge to appoint a friend to a vacant county-judge seat. Pennsylvania law prohibits judges from engaging in such political activities. Melvin denied the allegations and sued her critics for libel in 1999. The case has not progressed beyond addressing whether Melvin has a right to know the identities of the authors of the critical postings. In its appeal, the ACLU asked the court to establish a rule that would require a plaintiff to demonstrate actual economic harm before being permitted to learn the identities of anonymous critics.

Judge Melvin previously filed a defamation suit against these anonymous critics in Virginia, but the Virginia court dismissed her suit. *See Melvin*, 789 A.2d at 697, n. 3.

![gavel icon] *America Online, Inc. v. Nam Tai Electronics, Inc.*, 571 S.E.2d 128 (Va. 2002).

More than 50 anonymous bulletin board posters criticized Nam Tai Electronics and its directors on a Yahoo! message board. One of the anonymous posters accessed the Internet through AOL. Nam Tai subpoenaed Virginia-based AOL to identify the anonymous poster. AOL moved to quash the subpoena, citing the poster's First Amendment right to anonymous free speech; the California court denied AOL's motion to quash. AOL then asked a Virginia court to quash the subpoena. AOL again argued that Nam Tai's rights to pursue its suit did not overcome the poster's free-speech rights. The Virginia court declined to revisit issues already decided by the California court and denied the motion to quash.

International Forum Shopping

The Global Nature of Cyberspace

While many U.S. media companies may distribute their print publications only in the United States and in a few select foreign countries, those same publications, if available online, may be accessed around the world. Thus, the likelihood that a statement will be deemed published in a distant country, subjecting the publisher to foreign defamation laws, is substantially heightened. U.S. media companies are likely to face a growing number of defamation lawsuits abroad.

The Appeal of International Forum Shopping

In the United States, publishers enjoy unparalleled protection against libel suits. The First Amendment requires, among other things, that a public figure or public-official plaintiff prove by clear and convincing evidence that a defendant published the challenged statements with "actual malice," that is, with knowledge of falsity or serious subjective doubt as to truth. *See St. Amant v. Thompson*, 390 U.S. 727, 729 (1968); *New York Times Co. v. Sullivan*, 376 U.S. 254, 279-80 (1964). Defendants in libel actions also enjoy numerous protections afforded by state constitutions, state statutory and common law, and, following enactment of the Communications Decency Act of 1996 (47 U.S.C. § 230), federal statutory law.

Outside the United States, libel laws are not so forgiving. Both British and Canadian law, for example, apply a strict liability standard, meaning that libel plaintiffs need not prove negligence or some other degree of fault on the part of the publisher to prevail on a libel claim, just publication of a false and defamatory statement. British and Canadian courts also do not distinguish between public and private figures; even libel plaintiffs who are in the public eye are not required to prove negligence. In addition, British and Canadian law presume that a statement capable of conveying defamatory meaning is false unless the defendant proves the statement is true. And, Internet service providers do not have the protection of the Communications Decency Act. *Compare Godfrey v. Demon Internet Ltd.*, 3 W.L.R. 1020 (Q.B. 1999), available at http://www.haledorr.com/pdf/Godfrey_v_Demon.pdf. (holding that in the United Kingdom, the common-law defense of innocent dissemination offers ISPs protection for messages posted by third parties, but if the provider receives notice of the posting, then it acquires the responsibility of a publisher and can be held liable if the posting is not promptly removed) with *Doe v. America Online, Inc.*, 718 So. 2d 385 (Fla. Dist. Ct. App. 1998) (holding that under the Communications Decency Act, an ISP is immune from liability for a third-party posting, regardless of notice), *juris. accepted*, 729 So. 2d 390 (Fla. Apr. 12, 1999), *approved*, 783 So. 2d 1010 (Fla. 2001).

In the United Kingdom, the impact of the *Godfrey* decision may have spurred a movement to limit ISP liability. The *Godfrey* rule, coupled with the European Union's E-Commerce Directive requiring member states (including the U.K.) to adopt laws prohibiting ISP liability for transmitting tortious or illegal information, led the U.K.'s Internet Service Providers Association (ISPA) to sponsor a forum to address ISP liability. Conference participants proposed alternatives to the *Godfrey* rule. For example, they proposed that an ISP would only be liable for failure to remove materials after a court has ruled the materials to be illegal or defamatory. This would create a doctrine by which only a court's decision would provide "notice" to the ISP triggering a removal obligation. The EU directive provides an important opportunity for Parliament to reconsider the potentially unreasonable exposure ISPs face under the current strict-liability regime. Patrick J. Carome & C. Colin Rushing, "Online Defamation Law Abroad: Developments in the United Kingdom," *Libel Defense Resource Center Libel Letter*, April 2001, at 23.

 Dow Jones & Co. v. Harrods, Ltd., No. 02-CIV-3979, 2002 U.S. Dist. LEXIS 19516 (S.D.N.Y., Oct. 15, 2002).

Harrods department store of the United Kingdom issued a fake press release as an April Fool's joke stating it was offering shares in a new venture to create a mobile Harrods store on a ship. When Dow Jones' *Wall Street Journal* discovered that the story was a joke, it countered with a story warning readers to question Harrods' future disclosures. Dow Jones sued Harrods in the U.S. District Court for the Southern District of New York, seeking declaratory judgment to preclude the store from pursuing a defamation claim against the publisher that Harrods had already filed against Dow Jones in the U.K. The court granted Harrods motion to dismiss. Dow Jones is vulnerable to a suit outside the U.S. for its publication by virtue of the story's availability on the Internet, at wsj.com.

A Zimbabwe court is scheduled to hear a criminal case in which a journalist for *The Guardian*, a London-based newspaper, is accused of "publishing falsehoods." Under Zimbabwe law, this could lead to conviction for the crime of "abusing journalistic privilege," which is punishable by up to two years in prison and loss of the mandatory license required of reporters and editors in Zimbabwe. The prosecution contends the law allows for strict liability over reporters, meaning if an article is proved to have been false, the reporter is criminally liable no matter what lengths the reporter went to ensure the accuracy of his report. The court must first determine whether the article was "published" in London or Zimbabwe to determine whether it has personal jurisdiction over the defendant. Hearings have been held on this issue, but the court has yet to rule. *See* Geoffrey Robertson, "Mugabe Versus the Internet," *The Guardian* (June 17, 2002), *available at* http://www.guardian.co.uk/internetnews/story/0,7369,739026,00.html.

For further discussion of the international jurisdiction issues in this case, *see* Chapter 8, page 263.

In Thailand, a man has been found guilty of posting defamatory messges on the Internet. Thanet Songkran was given a two-year suspended sentence and was ordered to pay fines and perform community service for violating Thailand's cyber-defamation criminal statute. The defendant was convicted of posting a note on a Web bulletin board listing contact information for a young woman and claiming she was a prostitute. This case marks the first time a Thai court has ruled on online defamation. *See* ABC News (Australia) Online, "Man found guilty in Thailand's first case of cyber-defamation," Aug. 7, 2002, *available at* http://abc.net.au/news/newsitems/s642477.htm.

Potential Limitations on International Forum Shopping

The United Kingdom and Canada, as English speaking countries lacking the speech protections afforded under the U.S. Constitution, are attractive forums for defamation suits brought against U.S. publishers.

For a discussion of the limits of international jurisdiction in such cases, *see* Chapter 8, pages 264-269.

Choice of Law

The Importance of Choice of Law in Libel Cases

Even if a libel plaintiff can obtain jurisdiction over a non-resident defendant, that does not necessarily mean that the law of the forum state will be applicable. Although the First Amendment provides certain rights to libel defendants in all jurisdictions, many aspects of libel law vary by state. Accordingly, a court's decision as to which state's law to apply in an online libel action will often be significant.

Basic Choice of Law Principles Applied in Traditional Libel Cases

States employ a variety of choice-of-law principles. Most states, however, have adopted the approach set forth in the *Restatement (Second) of the Conflict of Laws*, which provides that the law of the jurisdiction with the most significant relationship to the occurrence and the parties applies. *Restatement (Second) of the Conflict of Laws* § 145 (1971).

The *Restatement* sets forth several factors designed to inform a court's analysis of the "most significant relationship" test, including, among other things, the place where the injury occurred, the place where the conduct causing the injury occurred, and the place where the relationship between the parties is centered. *Restatement (Second) of the Conflict of Laws* § 145.

The *Restatement* approach in multistate libel cases often results in applying the law of the state where the defamed is domiciled if the defamatory statement was published in that state. *Restatement (Second) of the Conflict of Laws* § 150.

Application of Choice of Law Principles in International Libel Cases

In addition to the principles outlined above, U.S. courts may consider U.S. public policy as a factor when choosing between a foreign country's law and U.S. law. For example, in *Ellis v. Time, Inc.*, 26 Media L. Rep. (BNA) 1225 (S.D.N.Y. 1997), the court refused to apply English libel law, although the plaintiff claimed that the defendant defamed him in England through a message transmitter on the Internet, because applying English libel standards would violate the First Amendment's protection of free speech. *Id.* at 1234. The court reasoned that U.S. courts must apply rules of law consistent with the Constitution, regardless of where the alleged wrong occurs. Although principles of international comity give the United States the choice of whether to acknowledge the laws of another nation, they do not impose a duty to do so. *Id.* at 1235. For further discussion of international choice of law principles, *see* Chapter 8 at page 267.

Application of Traditional Choice of Law Principles in the Context of Internet Libel

So far, courts have applied traditional choice-of-law principles to the cyberspace context without analyzing the complexities created by cyberspace defamation. *See Dahl v. Muller*, No. 99L6585 (Ill. Ct. Cl., Jan. 19, 2001) (existence of a licensing agreement with an Illinois business provided sufficient notice to the defendants that Illinois could exercise proper jurisdiction over non-resident radio stations Webcasting a syndicated program in which allegedly defamatory statements were made about the plaintiff's minor son); *Wells v. Liddy*, 186 F.3d 505 (4th Cir. 1999) (publication on website is another example of a multistate defamation and thus under traditional choice-of-law doctrine, the law of the plaintiff's domicile should apply because that is where the harm occurred), *cert. denied*, 528 U.S. 1118, 120 S. Ct. 939 (Jan. 18, 2000). *See also Isuzu Motors Ltd. v. Consumers Union*, 12 F. Supp. 2d 1035 (C.D. Cal. 1998), and *Hitchcock v. Woodside Literary Agency*, 15 F. Supp. 2d 246 (E.D.N.Y. 1998) (finding that under traditional choice-of-law doctrine, the law of the plaintiff's residence should apply because that is where the injury occurred; neither *Hitchcock* nor *Isuzu Motors* discussed the fact that the defamation occurred on the Internet).

However, the *Restatement*'s emphasis on geographical borders may be inappropriate in the cyberspace context. For instance, given the wide dissemination of speech on the Internet, injury that results from the distribution of a libelous statement may be deemed to have occurred in every jurisdiction. Moreover, it is not obvious whether the site of the conduct causing injury is the jurisdiction where the libel was written or, instead, is the jurisdiction where the server housing the libelous content is located.

These, and other similar questions, have yet to be answered definitively by the courts. Where a publisher once was able to control its area of distribution, online publication potentially subjects a publisher to the laws of every jurisdiction in which the Internet is available. An inadequate choice-of-law regime may lead to diminished predictability for online publishers, forum shopping by libel plaintiffs, and, ultimately, a chilling effect on speech.

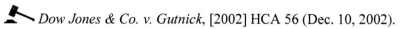 *Dow Jones & Co. v. Gutnick*, [2002] HCA 56 (Dec. 10, 2002).

On December 10, 2002, Australia's highest court rejected the efforts of Dow Jones & Company to have a libel suit against it transferred from Australia to a U.S. court. The case involved an allegedly libelous article about Australian mining magnate Joseph Gutnick, who lives and works in Victoria, Australia. Gutnick claimed to have been libeled by a February 2000 *Barron's* article that appeared on WSJ.com, the online edition of the *Wall Street Journal*. The court found that Australian courts have jurisdiction to hear a libel claim based on the article, even though few print copies of the article circulated in Australia and the online version of the article was likely accessed by a few hundred readers, at most, in Australia. Dow Jones sought to have the case transferred to a U.S. court, arguing that the online version of the article was "published" in New Jersey where Dow Jones' Web servers are located, and, therefore, a U.S. court, not an Australian court, should hear any challenge to the article. Dow Jones contended that subjecting a Web publisher to suit in every nation in the world from which its website could be accessed would severely curtail freedom of speech on the Web. The High Court of Australia, however, disagreed, finding that "the spectre which Dow Jones sought to conjure up in the present appeal, of a publisher forced to consider every article it publishes on the World Wide Web against the defamation laws of every country from Afghanistan to Zimbabwe is seen to be unreal when it is recalled that in all except the most unusual of cases, identifying the person about whom material is published will readily identify the defamation law to which that person may resort." This case is available at http://www.austlii.edu.au/cgi-bin/disp.pl/au/cases/cth/high%5fct/2002/56.html?query=%22dow%22+and+%22jone%22+and+%22gutnick%22.

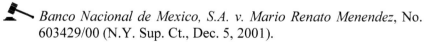 *Banco Nacional de Mexico, S.A. v. Mario Renato Menendez*, No. 603429/00 (N.Y. Sup. Ct., Dec. 5, 2001).

Banco Nacional brought libel claims in New York against defendant Mario Menendez-Rodriguez, a Mexican resident, and journalist, Marco News, a website whose purpose is to educate users about the drug trade, and Al Giordana, publisher of the Marco News website, over articles accusing Roberto Hernandez-Ramirez, the bank's largest shareholder, general director, and chairman of the board of directors, of involvement in illegal drug trafficking and money laundering, and contending that the bank was funded with the proceeds of drug trafficking. The bank claimed these assertions were false. In the court's view, the First Amendment demanded that the court apply New York libel law and not Mexican criminal or tort law. Claims against Menendez-Rodriguez were dismissed because the court lacked personal jurisdiction. Although the defendant, Giordana, lived in Mexico, the court found he had sufficient business interest in New York for the court to have jurisdiction. The court determined that the bank was not a public figure, but that the defendants were media defendants requiring the plaintiffs to prove "actual malice," or knowledge of falsity or reckless disregard for the truth to prevail in a libel case. The allegations published by the defendant had all been previously published in a Mexican newspaper. The court found that the defendants were entitled to rely on those published reports and therefore dismissed the libel claims for failure to state a claim.

Public Figure Doctrine

General Background

Federal constitutional law requires courts to determine whether a libel plaintiff is a public figure or official, on the one hand, or a private figure, on the other; the degree of fault that the plaintiff must establish to prevail depends on this determination. A public figure or official must establish constitutional "actual malice" (publication with knowledge of falsity or subjective awareness of probable falsity), while a private figure need only demonstrate that the defendant was "at fault" in publishing the false statement at issue (a showing of negligence is sufficient in most states).

Public Officials

Public officials are, at the very least, "those among the hierarchy of government employees who have, or appear to the public to have, substantial responsibility for or control over the conduct of government affairs." *Rosenblatt v. Baer*, 383 U.S. 75, 85 (1966). In general, public figures include elected officials, candidates for elected office, most law enforcement officers, and other public servants with discretionary authority, as opposed to purely ministerial functions.

Public Figures

The United States Supreme Court has identified three types of public figures:

Pervasive Public Figure. A pervasive or all-purpose public figure is an individual who has achieved such pervasive fame or notoriety that he becomes a public figure for all purposes and in all contexts. *Gertz v. Robert Welch, Inc.*, 418 U.S. 323, 351 (1974).

Limited Purpose Public Figure. A limited purpose public figure is an individual who voluntarily injects himself into a particular public controversy and thereby becomes a public figure for a limited range of issues related to that controversy. *Id.*

Involuntary Public Figure. An involuntary public figure is someone who becomes a public figure through no purposeful action of his or own but is, instead, involuntarily drawn into public events. *Id.* at 345.

. The Supreme Court has identified two factors for courts to evaluate in determining whether an individual is a public figure. First, public figures are those individuals who "invite attention and comment" through their actions and thus have "voluntarily exposed themselves to increased risk of injury from defamatory falsehood concerning them." Second, public figures "usually enjoy significantly greater access to the channels of effective communication and hence have a more realistic opportunity to counteract false statements than private individuals normally enjoy." *Gertz*, 418 U.S. at 344-45.

Applying the Public Figure Doctrine in Cyberspace

In light of the *Gertz* analysis, a plaintiff who claims to have been libeled in an online chat room or on an electronic bulletin board may more readily be deemed a limited-purpose public figure than a plaintiff claiming to have been libeled through a more traditional means of communication.

Inviting Attention and Comment

The Internet is widely known as a free-wheeling environment in which the unrestrained comments of one speaker may well be met with vigorous rebuttal. Arguably, anyone who regularly posts electronic messages, whether on a bulletin board or in a chat room, may be deemed to have "invite[d] attention and comment" about himself or herself and thus to have voluntarily assumed an increased risk of defamation.

For example, in *Ellis v. Time, Inc.*, 26 Media L. Rep. 1225, Richard Ellis, a photographer for Reuters, posted a series of messages on CompuServe in the National Press Photographers Association discussion group accusing a photographer at *Time* magazine of staging several pictures depicting child prostitution. Ellis also met with the head of the prostitution ring and allegedly tried to bribe him into admitting the photos were faked. *Time* later published a letter to its readers admitting that some of the photos were, in fact, staged. Ellis claimed, among other things, that he was defamed by certain internal and external publications by *Time* questioning the manner in which Ellis attempted to prove that the photos were staged.

The court granted *Time's* motion for summary judgment on the libel claim. The court found that Ellis was a limited purpose public figure because he thrust himself into the forefront of a particular public controversy (*i.e.*, whether *Time* had staged photographs) in order to influence the resolution of the issues involved. *Id.* at 1228. The court found that Ellis voluntarily injected himself into this debate by posting messages for discussion among his press colleagues and by meeting with the head of the prostitution ring. *Id.* at 1228-29. The court, however, was careful to note that a person who posts messages on an electronic bulletin board is not by definition a limited-purpose public figure. *Id.* at 1229. *See also Norris v. Bangor Publishing Co.*, 53 F. Supp. 2d 495, 499, 505 (D. Me. 1999) (finding that one of the reasons that the plaintiff, a political consultant, was a limited-purpose public figure was his access to traditional and electronic media.).

Greater Access to Channels of Effective Communication

The Internet also provides a readily accessible forum for an individual who has allegedly been defamed to respond to the defamation widely and effectively. Indeed, where the allegedly defamatory statements were made on a particular bulletin board or in a particular chat room, the defamed individual may be able to respond almost instantly to the very audience that received the defamatory statement.

The community with respect to which a plaintiff's private or public status is determined is the audience to whom the alleged defamation was actually published or broadcast. *See, e.g., Harris v. Tomczak*, 94 F.R.D. 687, 701 (E.D. Cal. 1982) ("The relevant population in considering the breadth of name recognition is to be measured by the audience reached by the alleged defamation."); *Reliance Ins. Co. v. Barron's*, 442 F. Supp. 1341, 1349 (S.D.N.Y. 1977) (finding the plaintiff a public figure with regard to an article published in *Barron's* magazine based on court's conclusion that "[p]robably [he] is well known among *Barron's* readership"). Thus, a plaintiff who frequents the particular chat room or posts messages to the electronic bulletin board where the allegedly defamatory statements appear may be deemed a public figure with respect to that particular cyberspace community even if he or she is not well known outside that community.

Retraction Statutes

General Background

Most states have retraction statutes of some kind. These statutes generally protect writers and publishers by requiring that notice be given to potential defendants before a libel action may be filed so that a timely correction, apology, or retraction can be published. Depending on the nature of the alleged defamation, the jurisdiction in which the suit is brought, and the plaintiff's compliance or noncompliance with the requirements of the relevant statute, application of a retraction statute may, at the least, enable a defendant to reduce the range of recoverable damages. For example, retraction statutes in many states provide that the plaintiff may recover only for actual injury (and may not recover punitive damages intended to punish the defendant) unless a retraction is demanded and not published.

Application of Retraction Statutes in the Context of Electronic Defamation

A threshold question may arise as to whether online services are covered by the provisions of a particular retraction statute. A number of retraction statutes designate only newspapers or other traditional printed matter as falling within their protections. Other statutes refer only to newspapers, radio stations, and television stations. Still others apply to defamatory statements published in any medium.

Arguably, online newspapers sharing mastheads and content with traditional print counterparts should be covered by statutes specifically applicable to "newspapers." While in theory retraction statutes should equally protect publications that exist only online, it is less clear that such publications are covered. However, determination of whether a particular online offering is covered by a retraction statute logically should be governed by the underlying purpose intended to be served by the statute.

For instance, the Florida retraction statute is based on a legislative desire to accommodate the "public interest in the 'free dissemination of news,' and the reasonable likelihood of occasional error as a result of the tremendous pressure to deliver the information quickly." *Davies v. Bossert*, 449 So. 2d 418, 420 (Fla. Dist. Ct. App. 1984) (citation omitted). Although online newspapers and magazines might fit comfortably within this underlying purpose, defamatory statements made in other online contexts might arguably not be subject to the protection of the retraction statute.

Montana's retraction statute, by contrast, is intended to apply to those members of the media capable of publishing a quick and effective retraction. Its purposes are almost surely served by offering protection to a broad array of online content. *See Fifield v. American Auto Ass'n*, 262 F. Supp. 253, 257-58 (D. Mont. 1967) (a book publisher not covered by Montana statute intended to cover situations where "a retraction would have an almost instant countering effect").

Case Law Dealing with Retraction Statutes

It's In The Cards, Inc. v. Fuschetto, 535 N.W.2d 11 (Wis. Ct. App. 1995).

The Wisconsin Court of Appeals found the state retraction statute did not apply to an online bulletin board that contained allegedly defamatory statements. At issue were statements posted by the defendant on an online sports-memorabilia-trading website. The trial court had held that the online bulletin board qualified as a "periodical" under the statute, which applies to "any libelous publication in any newspaper, magazine or periodical." Because the plaintiff failed to follow the retraction statute, the trial court granted summary judgment for the defendant.

The appellate court reversed, holding the retraction statute did not apply to bulletin-board postings because: (1) the plain meaning of the word "periodical" encompasses only "'publication[s] of which the issues appear at stated or regular intervals'"; (2) a prior judicial interpretation of the statute held it applicable only to the "print" media, a designation the Court of Appeals held inapplicable to computer bulletin-board postings; and (3) the Wisconsin retraction statute was enacted before the Internet existed and "it is for the legislature to address the increasingly common phenomenon of libel and defamation on the information superhighway." *Fuschetto*, 535 N.W.2d at 14 (citation omitted).

The decision in *Fuschetto* does not address the arguments that might be raised where an online publication serves many of the same functions and carries much of the same content as a traditional newspaper or magazine. Indeed, the typical online newspaper or magazine would qualify under the definition of a "periodical" applied by the Wisconsin Court of Appeals.

Zelinka v. Americare Healthscan, Inc., 763 So. 2d 1173 (Fla. Dist. Ct. App. 2000).

The plaintiffs brought suit in Florida alleging libel based on the publication of allegedly defamatory statements made by the defendant on an Internet message board. Section 770.01 of the Florida Statutes requires that, in certain circumstances, notice must be given to a potential defendant before a libel action can be filed. The statute is meant to allow potential defendants to avoid punitive damages by the timely publication of a correction, apology, or retraction. The defendant filed a motion to dismiss, claiming that the plaintiffs had failed to provide the proper written notice before bringing their libel suit.

Florida courts have interpreted § 770.01 as applying only to "media defendants," and not private individuals. The court held that notice was not required because the defendant was simply "a private individual who merely made statements on a website owned and maintained by someone else." 763 So. 2d at 1174. The court stated that "[i]t may well be that someone who maintains a website and regularly publishes internet 'magazines' on that site may be considered a 'media defendant' who would be entitled to notice," but this defendant was not such a person. *Id.*

Mathis v. Cannon, 556 S.E.2d 172, 252 Ga. App. 282 (Ga. Ct. App. 2001).

The plaintiff, Thomas Cannon, brought suit in Georgia against the defendant, Bruce Mathis, for statements made in an Internet chat room. The trial court awarded Cannon punitive damages. The Georgia Court of Appeals found that Georgia's retraction statutes, which state that plaintiffs cannot collect punitive damages if the publisher of the libelous item prints (or broadcasts) a retraction in as conspicuous and public a manner as the original libelous statement, do not apply to statements made in an Internet chat room. Cannon's failure to request a retraction therefore did not preclude Cannon's claim for punitive damages. In April 2002, the Georgia Supreme Court agreed to hear the defendant's appeal.

Responding to Retraction Demands

Demands for Retraction of Third-Party Content

Under the Communications Decency Act, no provider of an interactive computer service may be treated as the publisher of information provided by another information content provider. 47 U.S.C. § 230(c)(1). Treating a website operator as the publisher of allegedly defamatory statements by a third party therefore violates the Act. *Zeran v. America Online, Inc.*, 129 F.3d 327 (4th Cir. 1997), *cert. denied*, 524 U.S. 937, 118 S. Ct. 2341 (1998). *See* pages 136-137, above. Accordingly, the *Zeran* holding suggests that where an online service receives a retraction demand relating to statements it did not compose, the demanding party should be redirected to the third-party originator.

Publishing Retractions Online

Even in jurisdictions where the applicable statute does not explicitly cover all media, publishing retractions or corrections still serves the traditional functions of mitigating damages and evidencing good faith.

Traditional Publication Requirements

Retraction statutes commonly call for a correction or retraction to be published in as conspicuous a manner as the statement claimed to be libelous. *See, e.g.*, Cal. Civ. Code § 48a(2). With regard to traditional print publications, statutes often call for publication of a retraction/correction in the same editions and/or in the same position and/or in the same type size as the alleged libel originally appeared. *See, e.g.*, Fla. Stat. Ann. § 770.02(1).

Online Publication of Corrections and Retractions

What is necessary to fulfill the conspicuousness requirement depends on the specific provisions of the applicable statute. However, the underlying question is whether the correction is likely to reach substantially the same audience as did the article for which the correction was demanded. Section 6(b)(1) of the Uniform Correction or Clarification of Defamation Act (1993), for instance, requires publication "with a prominence and in a manner and medium reasonably likely to reach substantially the same audience as the publication complained of."

Correction Demands on Print Publications with Online Counterparts

Even where a correction demand served on a newspaper references only the print publication, a plaintiff may argue that failure to publish a correction in the online counterpart renders the correction ineffective. Generally, a demand for a correction or retraction is deemed sufficient if it informs the publisher of the statements claimed to be defamatory. *See, e.g., Mahnke v. Northwest Publications, Inc.*, 124 N.W.2d 411 (Minn. 1963) (demand is sufficient if it gives notice of the exact words complained of); Ky. Rev. Stat. Ann. § 411.051(2) (1996) (sufficient demand "specifies the statement or statements claimed to be false and defamatory, states wherein they are false, and sets forth the facts"). Newspapers and magazines that have online counterparts might consider whether a correction published in a print edition should also appear in their online publications.

Archived Materials

Problems Raised by Continued Archival Publication After Learning of Falsity

Maintaining an online archive raises the possibility that information that was believed to be accurate when originally published will remain available to users even though the publisher has received a correction demand and perhaps even published a correction. Once the publisher has received a retraction demand coupled with documentation demonstrating falsity, or has discovered an error through other means, the availability of the original in online archives may attract defamation claims. Plaintiffs may argue that defenses applicable at the time of initial publication do not apply to archival "republication."

Demands to "Correct" Defamatory Matter in Archival Versions

Though libel plaintiffs ordinarily recognize that a print product cannot be changed once it hits the newsstand, they may demand that an article available in an online archives be edited to remove allegedly defamatory matter or that the entire offending publication be removed permanently from the archive. Plaintiffs' attorneys may argue that an online publication's refusal to "correct" an archived online article as soon as an error is brought to the publisher's attention should be punished as an additional affront to the plaintiff. *Cf. Southern Bell Tel. & Tel. Co. v. Coastal Transmission Serv., Inc.*, 307 S.E.2d 83, 88 (Ga. Ct. App. 1983) (continued distribution of yellow pages after learning of defamatory matter contained therein held sufficient to support imposition of punitive damages).

Archived Copies as Part of the Initial "Single Publication"

Perhaps the best argument against liability for alleged defamations contained in archived material is that archiving online does not constitute republication. The "single publication" rule allows only one action for damages as to any single publication. *See Restatement (Second) of Torts* § 577A(4) (1977). Republication usually will not be found in the traditional newspaper- or book-publishing context unless a new edition of the same work containing the defamatory statements is released. *See Cox Enters., Inc. v. Gilreath*, 235 S.E.2d 633, 634 (Ga. Ct. App. 1977) (publication of different editions of a daily newspaper not deemed single publication); *Rinaldi v. Viking Penguin, Inc.*, 5 Media L. Rep. (BNA) 1295, 1297 (N.Y. Sup. Ct. 1979) (paperback edition of book deemed separate publication from hardcover edition), *modified*, 425 N.Y.S.2d 101 (N.Y. App. Div. 1980), *aff'd*, 438 N.Y.S.2d 496 (N.Y. 1981).

An archived hard copy of a newspaper is considered part of the initial publication. Similarly, producing microfilm or microfiche copies of the original editions of a newspaper on a regular basis following publication should fall within the initial publication. *Cf. Restatement (Second) of Torts* § 577A, cmt. d (1977) ("The printing and distribution of extra copies ... of a book may properly be treated as mere continued circulation of the first edition and hence as still part of the single publication, if it is done not long after the original publication as soon as the supply is exhausted. If it occurs ten years later, it is indistinguishable from a second edition and there is a new cause of action").

Print Original

Firth v. State of New York, 706 N.Y.S.2d 835 (N.Y. Ct. Cl. 2000), *aff'd*, 731 N.Y.S. 2d 244 (N.Y. App. Div. 2001).

The plaintiff, who was forced to step down from his position as the director of the division of law enforcement in New York's Department of Environmental Conservation after being accused in an Inspector General's report of orchestrating the improper sale of surplus handguns, sued the State of New York for defamation. Within 90 days of the release of the Inspector General's report, the plaintiff filed a notice of intention to file a claim for defamation. However, the plaintiff failed to file his defamation complaint within one year of the initial publication of the report. The report was placed on the Internet December 16, 1996. The suit was filed March 18, 1998.

The defendant moved to dismiss the lawsuit as being time barred pursuant to CPLR § 215(3), which requires that a cause of action for libel or slander be commenced within one year of accrual. The plaintiff asserted that his lawsuit should not be dismissed because the Inspector General made the report available on the Internet (where it remained available), thereby purportedly constituting a republication of the report each and every day and triggering a new accrual date. The Court of Claims rejected this argument, instead holding that the "single publication rule applies to defamatory publications upon the Internet." 706 N.Y.S.2d at 841.

The Court stated: "This Court sees no rational basis upon which to distinguish publication of a book or report through traditional printed media and publication through electronic means by making a copy of the text of the Report available via the Internet. While the act of making the document available constitutes a publication, in the absence of some alteration or change in form its continued availability on the Internet does not constitute a republication acting to begin the Statute of Limitations anew each day." *Id.* at 843. Accordingly, the Court of Claims dismissed plaintiff's claim.

The claimant filed an appeal contending that the statute of limitations started running anew each time that the report was accessed by an Internet user. The appellate court was not persuaded, ruling that the Court of Claims properly dismissed the complaint. Future accesses of the report by Internet users would not constitute new and actionable publications.

See also Miles Simon v. Arizona Bd. of Regents, 28 Media L. Rep. 1240 (Ariz. Super. Ct. 1999) (treating online publication of allegedly defamatory article and subsequent print edition of article as a single publication for purposes of determining commencement of statute of limitations).

Another court that has addressed this issue (in the context of a breach of contract action) found that Internet archiving of past editions does not constitute republication of articles, because an online archive, though readily available to anyone with capacity to search the Internet, is no different from other forms of archiving, such as microfiche. *Bartel v. Capital Newspapers*, 664 N.Y.S.2d 398, 25 Media L. Rep. 1959 (Small Claims Court, July 3, 1997), *aff'd*, 26 Media L. Rep. 2500 (New York County Court, July 22, 1998).

Electronic Original. The act of making an article originally published online accessible through an archive index, rather than through the index with which it was associated on the first day of publication, should not be deemed republication. Rather, it is solely a matter of making the original publication available at a different location. Just as physically moving the hard copy of a newspaper into a library does not constitute republication, changing the manner in which an online article may be accessed should not be considered a separate act of publication.

Labeling

Publishers might reduce any risk that reasonable users could misconstrue archival material as current by ensuring that their online archives are clearly labeled. Similarly, if a current story includes a link to an earlier story, dating the earlier story should reduce the risk that the earlier story will be perceived as current. A more elaborate disclaimer might specifically inform users that material in the online archive is presented in its original form, has not been updated since the original date of publication, and does not reflect information subsequently obtained by the publisher.

Mechanisms might also be employed to ensure that when errors are identified, any published correction will be electronically linked to the archived report.

DATA COLLECTION AND PRIVACY

General

Although businesses have long collected data about consumers, the rapid growth of the Internet has sparked a new debate about the collection of personal information and the consumer's right to privacy. In the online world, information can be gathered and processed quickly, often in ways that may not be immediately transparent to consumers.

On the one hand, businesses online want to gather information about their customers—as their offline counterparts do—that will allow them to serve their customers better. On the other hand, some consumers are concerned about restricting the information businesses gather and controlling how it is used.

Types of Data Collected

An online publisher may find itself collecting a variety of personal data from visitors to its website. This data most likely will take one of four forms: (1) registration information; (2) data provided by users who choose to interact with websites, for example by participating in an online promotional contest; (3) data collected through the use of cookies; (4) clickstream data; and (5) data collected through the use of "clear gifs," sometimes called "web bugs."

Registration Information

Many websites require users to register if they wish to obtain full website access. The information requested upon registration may be useful for product design, marketing, advertising sales, and other purposes. For example, *The New York Times'* website requires users to register and asks for information such as gender, household income, and zip code. Many websites also ask for e-mail addresses, home addresses, and personal interests.

Customer Information

Visitors often provide information to the websites they visit as they enter online promotional contests, participate in online surveys, make purchases, request information, or sign up for services.

Cookies

A cookie is a brief string of computer code placed by a website in the cookie file on the hard drive of a user's computer. Cookies allow websites to personalize the pages displayed to particular users by keeping track of their user names and passwords, their preferences, and even the items they have placed in their "shopping carts." websites can use cookies to keep track of the pages being accessed by each of their users and can aggregate this data to gauge the popularity and effectiveness of various website features.

The default settings on Netscape Navigator and Microsoft Explorer allow cookies to be placed on the user's computer. However, both browsers permit the user to change the default settings to alert the user when a cookie is sent or to reject all cookies entirely. Cookies come in two flavors: "session cookies" expire when the user terminates his or her browser session (*e.g.*, by closing the Web browser); "persistent cookies" persist until a specified expiration date, which may be days, weeks, or even months after they are placed.

Clickstream Data

While a user visits various sites on the Internet, each website visited and each page viewed within a site can be tracked by the user's Internet service provider. The ISP may maintain a record of a user's online activities, including websites visited, ads viewed, purchases made, and more. Website operators can also record more limited usage data through the deployment of cookies and can identify the visitor's ISP, the website through which the user linked to the site, and the site for which it left, as well as which pages on the operator's website were visited and the amount of time spent on each page.

Clear Gifs or Web Bugs

Clear gifs, sometimes called "web bugs," "single pixel gifs," or "pixel tags," are visually unnoticeable graphic files that allow websites and advertisers to identify when a visitor has accessed a Web page containing that clear gif. A clear gif is loaded as part of the Wweb page and therefore, unlike a cookie, cannot be blocked by changing the default browser settings. As the Web page that contains the clear gif is loaded, the entity that placed the clear gif can track visitors and read cookies it has previously set. Clear gifs can also be inserted into html e-mail messages, allowing an advertiser to correlate a user's e-mail address with cookies it has previously set.

▲ *In re Pharmatrak, Inc. Privacy Litigation*, No. 00-11672-JLT (D. Mass. Aug. 13, 2002).

Seven individual plaintiffs, seeking to represent a larger class of similarly situated individuals, sued Pfizer, Inc, Pharmacia Corp., SmithKline Beecham Corp., Glaxo Welcome, Inc., and American Home Products Corp., as well as a Pharmatrak, Inc., which the drug companies had hired to monitor their corporate websites and analyze their website traffic. The plaintiffs claimed that the defendants intercepted their electronic communications and accessed their hard drives in order to collect private information without their consent, all in violation of the federal Electronic Communications Privacy Act (ECPA) and the Computer Fraud and Abuse Act (CFAA). The plaintiffs complained about the defendants' use of "web bugs" and "cookies." The court dismissed the ECPA claims on technical legal grounds. But it decided the CFAA claims on a more common-sense basis.

The CFAA permits recovery for "any impairment to the integrity or availability of data, a program, a system, or information" causing damages of at least $5,000. Without addressing the merits of the plaintiffs' CFAA claims, the court found that the plaintiffs had failed to offer any evidence sufficient to establish damages that would meet the $5,000 threshold. In other words, even if the defendants had intentionally accessed the plaintiffs' computers without authorization and had obtained the private information alleged to have been collected, the plaintiffs could not produce evidence that such actions caused them each at least $5,000 in damages. Accordingly, the court granted the defendants' motion for summary judgment and dismissed the plaintiffs' claims under the CFAA.

Federal Regulations

General

With the exception of the Children's Online Privacy Protection Act (COPPA), discussed below, there are no federal laws specifically and exclusively addressing the collection and use of information from websites. However, two federal laws, the Health and Human Services Privacy Rule and the Gramm-Leach-Bliley Act, apply to certain online activities. In addition, other federal laws, including the Federal Trade Commission Act, the Electronic Communications Privacy Act, and the Computer Fraud and Abuse Act, have also been construed to apply online. With more than 100 privacy bills proposed in the 107th Congress, it is possible that more comprehensive privacy legislation will be passed in the near future.

Enforcement authority over most existing federal privacy laws has been granted to the Federal Trade Commission. As discussed in more detail below, the FTC's position on privacy laws has evolved over the past few years, especially as the value and efficacy of enforcing current laws has been called into question.

Several states have also passed privacy legislation, resulting in a concern that, absent federal legislation, a system of 50 different legal regimes for Internet privacy could take shape.

The FTC's Five Core Principles of Privacy Protection

The Federal Trade Commission's involvement with online privacy issues stems largely from its broad mandate to enforce the Federal Trade Commission Act, which prohibits "deceptive acts or practices in or affecting commerce." 15 U.S.C. § 45(a). This allows the FTC to punish, as an unfair and deceptive practice, data collection, use, or distribution practices that violate a website's own articulated privacy policy. In June 1998, the Federal Trade Commission articulated the five core principles of privacy protection that it believes any attempt at either government regulation or industry self-regulation must involve:

1. *Notice* to consumers about when, how, and for what purposes personal information will be collected.

2. *Choice* for consumers as to how any personal information collected from them may be used.

3. *Access* for consumers to data collected about them and an opportunity to contest the accuracy and completeness of the data.

4. *Security* of personal information.

5. *Enforcement* mechanisms to enforce these core principles.

In December 1999, the FTC established the Advisory Committee on Online Access and Security to provide recommendations on practices to meet the access and security principles. This committee also coordinated the Commission's 2000 Online Privacy Survey to review the nature and substance of U.S. commercial websites' privacy disclosures.

The Survey

In February and March 2000, the FTC conducted a survey of commercial sites' information practices. Two groups of sites were studied: (1) a random sample of 335 websites and (2) 91 of the 100 busiest sites. Almost all sites (97 percent in the random sample, and 99 percent in the most popular group) collected an e-mail address or some other type of personal identifying information from users. The survey analyzed the nature and substance of privacy disclosures in light of the fair-information practice principles previously articulated by the FTC. While the survey results show that there had been a steady increase in the percentage of websites that posted some form of privacy disclosure, the survey also found that only 20 percent of websites in the random sample that collected personal identifying information implemented, at least in part, all of the FTC's "fair information practice principles," and that only 41 percent of sites in the random sample and 60 percent of sites in the most popular group met the basic "notice" and "choice" standards. The survey also revealed that 8 percent of sites in the random sample and 45 percent of sites in the most popular group displayed the "privacy seal" of one of the self-regulatory bodies (such as TRUSTe and BBBOnline).

More recently, a survey conducted by Ernst & Young on behalf of the Progress & Freedom Foundation reported that online companies had become more attentive to online privacy. *See* Privacy Online: A Report on the Information Practices and Policies of Commercial Websites (March 2002), available at http://www.pff.org/publications/privacyonlinefinalael.pdf. The study found broader use of privacy policies by online companies, and found that the privacy policies surveyed were more prominent and provided greater detail on how companies use consumer information. The study is the first major examination of online privacy practices since the FTC survey of early 2002.

Relationship Between Online Privacy Statement and Offline Data Collection Practices

Speaking at a Q&A session at the Promotion Marketing Association's annual meeting in December 2001, Howard Beales, the FTC's consumer protection chief, stated that, without clear disclosure to the contrary, *a company's online privacy policy would also be assumed to govern its offline data collection and use.* This is a significant development for companies that operate websites, many of which do not currently have similar information practices for their online and offline activities. It is not certain, however, whether the FTC will commence enforcement actions against companies that have failed to treat information collected offline in a manner inconsistent with their online privacy policies.

FTC Enforcement

Some examples of past FTC enforcement actions relating to online privacy policies include:

GeoCities

In August 1998, in the FTC's first Internet privacy-related enforcement proceeding, GeoCities agreed to settle FTC charges of deceptively collecting personal information. The FTC charged that GeoCities had misrepresented how personal registration information collected on its site would be used. Rather than only using the information to provide members with the particular advertising or product information they had requested, GeoCities disclosed this information to third parties who used it to target promotional messages to GeoCities members. Also, the FTC charged that GeoCities misrepresented that GeoCities maintained information collected from children participating in the "GeoKidz Club." In fact, third parties ran the Club and maintained the collected information.

Under the terms of the settlement, GeoCities must post a clear and prominent "privacy notice" consistent with the FTC's core principles of privacy protection. The notice will tell consumers what information is being collected and for what purpose, to whom it would be disclosed, and how consumers can access and remove the information. GeoCities also agreed to institute procedures to obtain parental consent before collecting personal data from children under age 13. GeoCities must also provide its members with an opportunity to have their personal data deleted from GeoCities' and any third parties' databases. GeoCities also must provide, for five years, a hyperlink within its privacy notice to the FTC's website on consumer privacy.

DoubleClick

On February 10, 2000, the FTC commenced an inquiry into whether DoubleClick, Inc., had engaged in unfair and deceptive trade practices by tracking the online activities of Internet users and combining the tracking data with detailed personal profiles in a national marketing database. The Electronic Privacy Information Center had alleged that this was done without the knowledge of users and in violation of DoubleClick's assurances (included in versions of its privacy policy) that information would remain anonymous. The FTC announced in January 2001 that it would close its investigation (without citing any specific reasons for the closure, but maintaining its right to reopen the matter if necessary) after obtaining DoubleClick's voluntary, but not binding, assurance that it would not link users' browsing activities to their buying habits. As part of the settlement, DoubleClick modified its privacy policy to disclose its use of clear gifs, to create an opt-out for cookies, and to clarify its Internet address finder e-mail practices.

DoubleClick also came under fire from other sources. Various private lawsuits were filed, and various states considered possible suits against DoubleClick for privacy violations.

On August 26, 2002, DoubleClick announced that it had agreed to pay $450,000 and amend its policies as part of a settlement of a multi-state investigation into its use of personal data.

Toysmart

On July 10, 2000, the Federal Trade Commission filed suit against Toysmart, Inc., a Massachusetts-based Internet firm that had ceased operations in May, for allegedly trying to sell confidential, personal information collected from its customers in violation of its articulated privacy policy. *FTC v. Toysmart.com, LLC*, No. 00-11341-RGS (D. Mass. July 12, 2000). Toysmart.com's privacy policy stated that "personal information ... such as name, address, billing information and shopping practices, is never shared with a third party." But in June 2000, the company placed an ad in *The Wall Street Journal* offering its customer lists and databases for sale as part of bankruptcy proceedings.

At the end of July 2000, Toysmart settled the suit. The settlement allowed Toysmart to sell its customer information as part of a package sale of the whole website to a "qualified buyer." The qualified buyer must agree to adhere to the terms of the Toysmart privacy policy. Any changes to the policy would require notice to customers and give them an opportunity to opt-in to the change. Toysmart.com finally sold the customer list to Disney's Buena Vista Internet Group for $50,000, and the list was immediately destroyed.

Microsoft

In August 2002, Microsoft entered into a consent agreement with the FTC, under which it agreed to make substantial changes to its Passport system. The Passport system stores a computer user's log-in names and passwords so the user can visit various password-protected websites without having to log-in each time. Microsoft uses Passport to control access to its own sites, and markets it to other websites. The FTC alleged that Microsoft collected too much information, used unfair or deceptive practices, and failed to protect adequately its users' privacy and the security of the personal information it collected. Microsoft agreed (1) not to misrepresent its information practices in any way; (2) to establish and maintain a comprehensive information security program; (3) to obtain, from an objective third party, biannual reports assessing its security program; and (4) to allow the FTC to inspect its representations, plans, reports, and reviews related to the order for the next five years. *See Microsoft Corp.*, FTC No. 012-3240, Agreement Containing Consent Order (Aug. 8, 2002), available at http://www.ftc.gov/os/2002/08/microsoftagree.pdf.

The FTC's Position Regarding the Enactment of New Privacy Laws

The FTC's position regarding the enactment of new privacy laws has changed over the past few years. In June 2000, the FTC called for the passage of new, comprehensive privacy laws after it concluded that self-regulation was not working. However, since the appointment of Chairman Timothy J. Muris in 2001, the FTC has instead advocated the enforcement and strengthening of existing privacy rules, rather than the passage of new laws.

The FTC's change in position appears to have been based on several factors. Experience with COPPA and the Gramm-Leach-Blilely Act, discussed below, showed that certain types of privacy laws cannot only be costly to businesses, but may do very little to benefit consumers. The FTC also expressed concern that new online privacy laws would be of little value if the offline world is not regulated as well. On June 11, 2002, Chairman Muris reiterated these concerns in a speech at the Networked Economy Summit and emphasized that the online industry has made significant improvements in providing privacy protection to consumers without any legislative mandates.

The FTC's position does not preclude Congress or the states from adopting privacy rules, but it does affect congressional debate on the issue. *See* Daniel Sieberg, *FTC Sidelines the Call for New Privacy Laws* (Oct. 4, 2001), *available at* http://www.cnn.com/2001/US/10/04/inv.online.privacy/; Timothy Muris, *Protecting Consumers' Privacy: Goals and Accomplishments* (Remarks on June 11, 2002 at the Networked Economy Summit), *available at* http://www.ftc.gov/speeches/muris/gmason.htm.

Proposed Federal Legislation

Notwithstanding the FTC's current position on new online privacy laws, more than 100 privacy bills have been proposed in the 107th Congress. Most reiterate common themes, requiring that consumers are notified of companies' data-collection policies and requiring that companies give consumers the ability to opt-in or opt-out of such collection. A summary of some recent bills is provided below. More information can also be found at http://thomas.loc.gov.

Consumer Privacy Protection Act of 2002

The Consumer Privacy Protection Act (H.R. 4678), introduced in May 2002, would allow businesses in both the online and offline world to share information about customers who have not opted out of such data sharing. The bill would override state laws that place more restrictions on commercial use of personal information. It would grant the FTC enforcement powers but would not give individuals the right to sue for privacy violations. In September 2002, the House subcommittee on Commerce, Trade, and Consumer Protection held hearings on the bill.

Online Personal Privacy Act

Introduced by Senator Hollings (D-S.C.) in April 2002, the Online Personal Privacy Act (S. 2201) would require companies to obtain affirmative "opt-in" consent before collecting and sharing "sensitive" information from website visitors. ("Sensitive Personally Identifiable Information" is defined under the Act to include personal health information; information about the visitor's race, sexual orientation, or political beliefs; and certain financial information.) For information deemed "non-sensitive" under the Act, companies would be required to provide clear and conspicuous notice and give visitors the opportunity to decline consent ("opt-out"). The proposed Online Personal Privacy Act would attempt to create uniformity by pre-empting all state laws and regulations regarding online privacy. On May 17, 2002, the bill was approved by the Senate Commerce Committee and ordered reported favorably to the Senate. In August 2002, the bill was placed on the Senate Legislative Calendar, No. 551, and written report No. 107-240 was issued.

Who Is E-mailing Our Kids Act

The Who Is E-mailing Our Kids Act (H.R. 1846) was introduced in May 2001, and would amend the 1934 Communications Act to require schools and libraries receiving universal service assistance to block access to Internet services that enable users to access the World Wide Web and transfer electronic mail in an anonymous manner. The bill was referred to committee in May 2001.

Consumer Online Privacy and Disclosure Act

The Consumer Online Privacy and Disclosure Act, (H.R. 347) which was introduced in January 2001, would require the FTC to prescribe regulations to protect the privacy of personal information collected from and about individuals on the Internet, to provide greater individual control over the collection and use of that information, and for other purposes. The bill was referred to committee in February 2001, and to the subcommittee on Telecommunications and the Internet in May 2001.

Online Privacy Protection Act of 2001

The Online Privacy Protection Act (H.R. 89), introduced in January 2001, would require the FTC to prescribe regulations to protect the privacy of personal information collected from and about individuals that use the Internet and who are not covered by the Children's Online Privacy Protection Act of 1998. The bill would provide greater individual control over the collection and use of personally identifying information. The bill was referred to committee in February 2001, with no further activity reported.

Consumer Internet Privacy Enhancement Act

The Consumer Internet Privacy Enhancement Act (H.R. 237), also introduced in January 2001 and referred to committee in February 2001, would protect the privacy of consumers who use the Internet. The bill declares it unlawful for a commercial website operator to collect personally identifying information online from a website user unless the operator provides both notice and opportunity for such user to limit the use and disclosure of such information.

Federal Agency Protection of Privacy Act

The Federal Agency Protection of Privacy Act (H.R. 4561) was introduced on April 24, 2002, and passed by the House in October 2002. The Senate received the bill on October 8, 2002. The bill would require federal agencies to consider individual privacy issues when promulgating rules and regulations.

Constitutionality of Privacy Laws

Case law suggests that any newly enacted privacy laws may face substantial constitutional challenges. In *U.S. West v. Federal Communications Commission*, 182 F.3d 1224 (10th Cir. 1999), the U.S. Court of Appeals for the Tenth Circuit vacated an FCC order prohibiting phone companies from using customer proprietary network information (CPNI) for marketing purposes without the affirmative approval of their customers. CPNI includes such sensitive information as when, where, and to whom a customer places calls. The court found that the regulations were not narrowly tailored since the FCC required that telephone customers affirmatively opt-in (grant the carrier express approval through written, oral, or electronic means before the carrier may use the customer's CPNI data) without considering whether an "opt-out" approach (in which approval would be inferred from the customer-carrier relationship unless the customer specifically requested that his CPNI be restricted) would have been sufficient. While the ruling was relatively narrow, the court's reasoning suggests that broad privacy legislation may be unconstitutional:

> "Although we agree that privacy may rise to the level of a substantial state interest, the government cannot satisfy the second prong of the [applicable] test by merely asserting a broad interest in privacy ... In sum, privacy may only constitute a substantial state interest if the government specifically articulates and properly justifies it ... [With regard to a speech restriction imposed to protect privacy by keeping certain information confidential, the] government must show that the dissemination of the information desired to be kept private would inflict specific and significant harm on individuals, such as undue embarrassment or ridicule, intimidation or harassment, or misappropriation of sensitive personal information for the purposes of assuming another's identity ... Although we may feel uncomfortable knowing that our personal information is circulating in the world, we live in an open society where information may usually pass freely. A general level of discomfort from knowing that people can readily access information about us does not necessarily rise to the level of a substantial state interest ... for it is not based on an identified harm."

Id. at 15.

See also *Smith v. Chase Manhattan Bank*, discussed at page 180, below, in which the court held that the bother of junk mail and telephone solicitations is not an actionable harm.

Protection of Children's Personal Information

To protect against the collection of information from children who may not be sufficiently sophisticated to appreciate the significance of their information disclosures, Congress passed the Children's Online Privacy Protection Act of 1998 (COPPA).

Children's Online Privacy Protection Act of 1998

COPPA required the FTC to establish notice, parental consent, and access requirements. 15 U.S.C. §§ 6501, *et seq.* The new rules took effect on April 21, 2000 and are available at http://www.ftc.gov/privacy/index.html. They apply to commercial websites that are directed to, or that knowingly collect information from, children under 13. Operators of those websites :

1. Must provide a clear and prominent link to a statement detailing their information practices, including names and contact information for all operators who collect or maintain personal information, the types of personal information collected from children, how such personal information is used, whether personal information is disclosed to third parties, and, if information is disclosed to third parties, must describe the businesses in which these third parties are engaged. The link must be on the home page of the site or on the home page of a separate children's area, if one exists, and the link must be displayed in each area where personal information is collected. The statement must be updated if the operator's practices materially change.

2. Must obtain prior, verifiable parental consent for the collection, use, and/or disclosure of personal information from children. Discussion of the method of verifying consent occupied much of the FTC's debate leading up to the new rules. Ultimately, the FTC decided to phase in the requirements according to a "sliding scale approach." This approach allowed the use of e-mailed consent from the parent for the first two years after the effective date of the rules (April 21, 2000), unless the website uses personal information in ways that pose greater risks to children (*e.g.,* disclosing such information to a third party, or revealing it in a message board or chat room). The FTC has extended this sliding scale rule through 2005. The e-mailed consent must be confirmed by a follow-up e-mail, letter, or telephone call to the parent confirming the consent. For those activities that pose what the FTC views as greater risk to children, and for all information collected after the extension period expires, methods deemed more reliable by the FTC must be used to verify consent. These methods might include requiring parents to print and mail or fax a consent form, use of a credit card, setting up a toll-free number where trained staff can receive calls, e-mail with password or PIN, or some other technological measure that is "reasonably calculated ... to ensure that the person providing consent is the child's parent."

3. Must give parents the option to consent to the collection and use

of the child's personal information without consenting to disclosure of his or her personal information to third parties.

4. Must allow parents a chance to review the personal information about a child that is collected and to have the information deleted if they choose. The website operator may not condition a child's participation in an activity or promotional contest on disclosure of more personal information than is reasonably necessary for participation in the activity or contest.

5. Must establish and maintain reasonable procedures to protect the confidentiality, security, and integrity of the personal information collected.

Nonprofits and COPPA

Organizations that qualify as nonprofits under § 5 of the FTC Act are not subject to COPPA. The FTC has cautioned, however, that some nonprofits operating for the profit of their for-profit members would be subject to COPPA. *See California Dental Assn. v. FTC*, 526 U.S. 756 (1999).

COPPA Safe Harbor

The FTC's rules include a safe-harbor provision allowing for industry self-regulation in lieu of FTC regulation. Website operators that participate in industry "seal" programs (such as TRUSTe) that are approved by the FTC would be subject to the review and disciplinary procedures of the industry programs instead of the FTC's procedures. The FTC announced on May 23, 2001 that TRUSTe has been approved as a safe-harbor program under the terms of COPPA. Programs submitted by the Children's Advertising Review Unit of the Council of Better Business Bureaus, an arm of the advertising industry's self-regulation program, and the Entertainment Software Rating Board have also been approved as COPPA safe harbors.

Five-Year Review

Within five years of the effective date of the rules, the FTC will conduct a review to evaluate the effect of the rules, children's ability to obtain access to information of their choice online, and the availability of websites directed to children. The FTC will report its conclusions to Congress.

The Cost of Compliance

There is already significant concern over the costs of complying with COPPA. Many websites have simply stopped providing content aimed at children under age 13, citing the hassle and expense of complying with the new rules. *See* Lynn Burke, "Kids' Sites Cite COPPA Woes," Wired News, September 14, 2000, *available at* http://www.wired.com/news/politics/0,1283,38666,00.html.

Prosecution Under COPPA

On April 19, 2001, the FTC announced settlements with three website operators for violations of COPPA. The FTC charged Monarch Services, Inc. and Girls Life, Inc., operators of www.girlslife.com; Bigmailbox.com, Inc. and Nolan Quan, operators of www.bigmailbox.com; and Looksmart Ltd., operator of www.insidetheweb.com, with illegally collecting personal information from children under age 13 without parental consent. The companies agreed to pay an aggregate total of $100,000 in civil penalties and to comply with COPPA in the future. The settlements also require the operators to delete all personal information collected from children online at any time since COPPA's effective date. These three cases mark the first civil penalties levied by the FTC under COPPA. More information can be found on the FTC's website, http://www.ftc.gov/opa/2001/04/girlslife.htm.

On October 2, 2001, the FTC announced that Lisa Frank Inc., a maker of toys for girls, will pay $30,000 in fines to settle charges that it violated COPPA by soliciting information from children without first obtaining verifiable parental consent. The company allegedly asked girls to provide their first and last names, mailing addresses, phone numbers, e-mail addresses, and birth dates before they were allowed to access many areas of the website.

In April 2002, Ohio Art, noted for its product Etch-A-Sketch, was fined $35,000 by the FTC over a COPPA infraction on the Etch-A-Sketch site. According to the consent decree, the site was collecting information from children before obtaining parental consent. The consent decree and settlement can be found at http://www.ftc.gov/os/2002/04/ohioartconsent.htm.

In February 2002, the FTC reached a $10,000 settlement with American Pop Corn Company involving COPPA violations on the website www.jollytime.com. The site maintained a "Kids Club" section aimed at children under age 13. The FTC complained that American Pop Corn had collected personally identifiable information from children younger than age 13 without parental consent and in violation of COPPA and its published privacy policy.

At least 50 other operators of children's websites have received letters from the FTC warning of COPPA noncompliance.

Prosecution Beyond COPPA

Of course, in addition to the new rules announced to implement COPPA, the FTC maintains its general authority to prohibit unfair and deceptive practices with respect to the collection of information from children.

In May 1999, Liberty Financial Companies, Inc., operator of the Young Investor site (http://www.younginvestor.com), settled with the FTC over charges that the site falsely collected personal information from children. The FTC alleged that the site falsely represented that personal information collected from children in a survey would be maintained anonymously, whereas information about the child and the family's finances was maintained in an identifiable manner. The consent agreement requires the site to post a privacy notice and obtain verifiable parental consent before collecting a child's personal information. *In re Liberty Financial Companies, Inc.*, FTC File No. 982 3522 (1999), available at http://www.ftc.gov/os/caselist/9823522.htm.

Privacy of Medical Information

In November 1999, the U.S. Department of Health and Human Services published its Proposed Rule implementing the privacy requirements of the Health Insurance Portability Accountability Act of 1996 (HIPAA). In December 2000, HHS issued the Final Rule, which included significant changes received during the comment period. The Rule took effect on April 14, 2001, and requires covered entities to comply with the Final Rule's provisions within two years.

Defining protected health information as individually identifiable health information transmitted in electronic form, the Rule provides that covered entities can use or disclose protected information for purposes of treatment, payment, and health-care operations, or for other specified purposes (*i.e.*, public health, research, law enforcement). Covered entities may continue to use or disclose protected information for any purpose if individual authorization is obtained. Additionally, the Rule establishes three rights: (1) to obtain access to, inspect, and obtain a copy of information about oneself; (2) to be afforded a good-faith effort by health-care providers that they will provide written notice of their information-sharing practices; and (3) to request amendment or correction of incomplete or inaccurate information about oneself. While the Rule does not grant individuals the right to sue over violations of these rights, it does provide civil monetary penalties and criminal penalties, including imprisonment for up to ten years, for obtaining protected information under false pretenses, disclosure of protected information with intent to sell, or disclosure of protected information for malicious harm.

In 2002, the Bush Administration rolled back some of the major protections for the privacy of medical records.

The new rules abandon the requirement that doctors, hospitals, and other health-care providers obtain written acknowledgment from patients that they have received notice of the potential uses of the information they provide, and written consent from patients before disclosing personal medical information for purposes of treatment or paying claims. Instead, health-care providers are required to make a "good faith effort" to obtain written acknowledgment from their patients of the notice. The new rules limit the types of information that can be disclosed, and guarantee patients access to their medical records. HHS officials and other supporters of the new HIPAA rules explain that the new rules are intended to strike a balance between protecting patients' privacy on one hand, and maintaining quality health care on the other.

Privacy in the Financial Services Industry

The Gramm-Leach-Bliley Act (codified in relevant part at 15 U.S.C. §§ 6801-6809) Title V, subtitle A, Pub. L. No. 106-102, §§ 501-510, 113 Stat. 1338, 1436-45 (Nov. 12, 1999) was signed into law on November 12, 1999. The Act is intended to enhance competition in the financial services industry. The Act includes privacy provisions that require financial institutions to provide notice to consumers of their privacy policies regarding personal information, and to allow consumers the opportunity to opt-out of disclosures of personal information. Although the law does not directly address online privacy, it could affect certain online services because the definition of "financial institution" is quite broad.

On May 12, 2000, the FTC issued its Final Rule implementing the Gramm-Leach-Bliley Act (full text available at http://www.ftc.gov/os/2000/05/glb000512.pdf). The Final Rule mandates that "financial institutions" notify customers about the collection of personal information and offer some choice as to how that data is shared. This Rule applies to a wide range of entities (since the definition of "financial institutions" is broad), including companies that perform activities "closely related" to banking, such as financial-data processing, sales of financial software, and property-appraising services. The Rule applies to data collected as part of the sale or provision of a financial product or service. Companies covered by the Rule are required to give notice to consumers as to what personal, nonpublic information is collected, and the companies must reveal with whom they share data; this notice may not simply be posted on a website, but rather the company must verify that consumers have seen it. Additionally, the Rule states that consumers must be given the right to prohibit sharing of their personal information with unaffiliated third parties. The Rule became effective November 13, 2000, and full compliance was required by July 1, 2001.

The Final Rule was challenged in the U.S. District Court for the District of Columbia as being unlawful and unconstitutional. *Individual Reference Services Group, Inc. v. FTC*, 145 F. Supp. 2d 6 (D.D.C. 2001). In upholding the Rule, the court stated that the Rule does not contravene the plain meaning of the Gramm-Leach-Bliley Act and that it is a permissible construction of the statute. In addition, the FTC's actions in promulgating the Rule were not arbitrary and capricious. Moreover, the Rule was held not to violate the plaintiff's right to free speech under the First Amendment or to violate the plaintiff consumer-reporting agency's right either to due process or equal protection under the Fifth Amendment.

The Gramm-Leach-Bliley Act has come under fire from both industry representatives and privacy advocates. Industry representatives claim that compliance with the law, which entails mailing thousands of privacy notices, is too expensive. Privacy advocates, on the other hand, claim that the Act fails to provide enough protections for consumer privacy. *See* http://www.epic.org/privacy/financial/glb_comments.pdf. The FTC held a public workshop in December 2001 in response to concerns about the clarity and effectiveness of privacy policies. *See* http://www.ftc.gov/bcp/workshops/glb/index.html.

Two bills have been introduced in the 107th Congress that would change the way the Gramm-Leach-Bliley Act protects customer data. The Markey-Barton Consumer's Right to Financial Privacy Act provides fines and jail time for people who fraudulently obtain private consumer information from financial institutions. *See* H.R. 2720. The National Consumer Privacy Act calls for all 50 states to operate under the same general standards and would prevent states from amending the protections of the Gramm-Leach-Bliley Act, even by making them stronger. *See* H.R. 2730.

Only a few cases have been brought alleging violations of consumer privacy with respect to financial information. These include:

➤ *Federal Trade Commission v. Information Search Inc.*, No. AMD-01-1121 (D. Md.); *Federal Trade Commission v. Guzzetta*, No. 01-2335 (E.D.N.Y. February 25, 2002); *Federal Trade Commission v. Garrett*, No. 01-1225 (S.D. Tex.).

According to settlements announced on March 8, 2002, by the FTC, several information brokers who allegedly used deception to obtain consumers' confidential financial information will be required to refrain from these practices and forego their earnings.

➤ *Timothy P. Smith, et al. v. Chase Manhattan Bank, USA, N.A., et al.*, 741 N.Y.S.2d 100 (N.Y. App. Div. 2002).

The New York Appellate Division upheld the dismissal of a suit under New York consumer-protection laws complaining of the sale of personal financial information by a bank to third-party telemarketers. The plaintiffs, a group of Chase Manhattan credit card and mortgage holders, alleged that the bank violated its Customer Information Principles by selling their information to non-affiliated vendors, who, in turn, used the information to make unwanted telephone solicitations and send junk mail. Even though consumers were not given an opportunity to opt-out, the court found that receipt of junk mail and unwanted telephone solicitations did not rise to the level of actual harm, as required for recovery under the state statute. For discussion of this case in the context of spam, *see* Chapter 7, page 208.

In the fall of 2002, it was reported that some Internet merchants have been testing a new feature designed to enhance privacy options for Internet customers wary of providing credit-card numbers or other sensitive financial information over the Internet. I4 Commerce has developed a "bill me later" option, which works much like a credit card online in that a user enters information when making a purchase, but instead of the charge number, the user provides a date of birth, or some part of a Social Security number. *See* Troy Wolverton, "Web shoppers' new option: Bill me later," c/net news.com, Oct. 1, 2002, *available at* http://news.com.com/2100-1017-960380.html?tag=lh.

The Electronic Communications Privacy Act and Computer Fraud and Abuse Act

Two federal statutes, the Electronic Communications Privacy Act (ECPA) (18 U.S.C. § 2511 (2000)) and the Computer Fraud and Abuse Act (CFAA) (18 U.S.C. § 1030 (2000)), have been invoked as bases for asserting privacy claims. While neither of these laws was enacted with the goal of providing comprehensive privacy rights, they have been broadly construed to permit recovery for certain narrowly defined invasions of privacy.

The ECPA, a federal criminal statute, forbids the use of wiretaps without a court order and prohibits the unauthorized use or interception of the contents of any wire, oral, or electronic communication. 18 U.S.C. § 2511(1) (2000). The ECPA also prohibits unauthorized access to stored electronic communications. *Id.* at § 2701.

The CFAA, also a federal criminal statute, generally prohibits unauthorized access to a "protected computer" with the intent to obtain information, defraud, obtain anything of value, or cause damage to the computer. 18 U.S.C. § 1030(a). A "protected computer" is defined broadly as a computer that is used by or for a financial institution or the United States Government or is used in interstate or foreign commerce or communication.

Suits under the ECPA and CFAA

Timothy R. McVeigh v. William S. Cohen, 983 F. Supp. 215 (1998).

The plaintiff, an allegedly homosexual member of the armed forces, contended that the Navy violated his rights under the ECPA in an effort to discharge him in contravention of the statutory policy colloquially known as "Don't Ask, Don't Tell, Don't Pursue." The Navy contacted America Online under false pretenses for information that could connect the screen name "boysrch" and the accompanying user profile with McVeigh. The court found that there was a likelihood of success on the merits with regard to the issue of whether the Navy had violated or solicited a violation of the ECPA. The court said the government can obtain information concerning the identity of an online subscriber from an online service provider, but only if it (1) obtains a warrant or (2) gives prior notice to the online subscriber and then issues a subpoena or receives a court order authorizing disclosure of the requested information. The Department of Defense and the Navy were therefore enjoined from discharging or taking any adverse action against McVeigh.

Chance, et al. v. Avenue A Inc., 165 F. Supp. 2d 1153 (W.D. Wash. 2001).

The plaintiffs brought a class-action suit against Avenue A, a provider of Web advertising services, claiming that Avenue A had used cookies and pixel tags (also know as "web bugs" or "clear GIFs") to monitor their electronic communications without their consent in violation of the ECPA, the CFAA, and state law. The court granted

Avenue A summary judgment on the CFAA claims on the ground that no single act of placing or accessing a cookie on a user's computer caused that user damages in excess of the CFAA's $5,000 threshold, and that damages caused by multiple acts cannot be aggregated under the CFAA to reach the threshold. "[T]he transmission of internet cookies," the court found, "is virtually without economic harm." The court also found that Avenue A hadn't violated the wiretap provision of the ECPA, which prohibits interception of a wire, oral, or electronic communication without the consent of at least one party to the communication. Even if the users did not consent to transmit cookie data to Avenue A, the websites they were visiting had consented to the interception of such cookie data.

Crowley, et al. v. Cybersource Corp., 166 F. Supp. 2d 1263 (N.D. Cal. 2001).

The plaintiffs brought a class-action suit against Amazon.com and Cybersource, a company that verifies the identities of those making online purchases. The plaintiffs claimed that when they gave Amazon.com their names, e-mail addresses, mailing addresses, telephone numbers, and credit-card information, Amazon transmitted this information to Cybersource. Cybersource then unlawfully stored this information and used it to create a personal profile of each plaintiff. The court found that Amazon is not a provider of electronic communications services and, therefore, could not have violated provisions of the ECPA prohibiting disclosure of information by electronic information service providers. Nor did Amazon violate the provisions of the ECPA prohibiting unauthorized access to the facilities through which an electronic communication service is provided, because Amazon received voluntary e-mail transmissions from its customers: it did not access the information on their computer systems and could not have unlawfully accessed its own computer systems.

In re DoubleClick Inc. Privacy Litigation, 154 F. Supp. 2d 497 (S.D.N.Y. 2001).

In March 2001, a New York District Court dismissed a class-action suit against DoubleClick, an online advertising company. The plaintiffs challenged DoubleClick's practice of placing cookies on their users' computers, claiming violations of the ECPA, the Wiretap Act, and the CFAA. The court dismissed all of these claims.

In re Intuit Privacy Litigation, 138 F. Supp. 2d 1272 (C.D. Cal. 2001).

A California District Court issued a split decision in a class-action privacy suit in which the plaintiffs alleged that the placement of cookies on the computers of visitors to the quicken.com website violated the ECPA and the CFAA. The court held that the plaintiffs could proceed with their suit based on their claim of unauthorized access to electronic communications, but dismissed claims based on the interception of electronic communications and fraudulent computer activity.

 *Specht v. Netscape Communications Corp.*, 150 F. Supp. 2d 585 (S.D.N.Y. 2001), *aff'd*, 306 F.3d 17 (2d Cir. 2002).

In July 2000, a New Jersey-based website operator filed a class-action lawsuit charging that AOL/Netscape's "SmartDownload" software violated the ECPA and the CFAA. The suit alleged that AOL/Netscape secretly monitors file transfers between Internet sites and Internet users when users utilize the "SmartDownload" feature in the Netscape Communicator Web browser. The software at issue enables Netscape to track the name, type, and source of executable files a user downloads, along with cookie information that uniquely identifies the user. Netscape and AOL sought to compel arbitration and stay the proceedings, arguing that the dispute is subject to binding arbitration under a clause in the Netscape license agreement. The court held that the users of SmartDownload were not bound by the arbitration clause in the license agreement because they were not necessarily aware that they were entering a contract at the time of the download. (For discussion of this case in the context of enforceability of electronic agreements, *see* Chapter 6 at page 200). This litigation will therefore continue, though AOL has announced that it is dropping the consumer tracking feature from future versions of SmartDownload.

EF Cultural Travel v. Explorica, Inc., 274 F.3d 577 (1st Cir. 2001).

The plaintiff and the defendant compete in providing global tours for high-school students. The Court of Appeals for the First Circuit upheld a lower court injunction against the defendant's use of an electronic agent, which combed through the database of its competitor, the plaintiff, for pricing information. The court found that the plaintiffs would likely succeed on the merits of their CFAA claim.

➤ *United States v. McGuire*, Nos. 99-30165, 99-30166 (9th Cir. Oct. 11, 2002).

In the first known case addressing law-enforcement interception of fax transmissions, the issue before the court was whether federal law-enforcement agents were required to "minimize" the number of fax documents that they intercepted and stored that were unrelated to criminal activity, much as they are required to minimize phone tapping. The U.S. Court of Appeals for the Ninth Circuit ruled that police did not violate federal wiretap laws when they collected faxes while spying on a group convicted of bank fraud. To eavesdrop on the "Montana Freeman," the FBI obtained a court order permitting interception of voice conversations and faxes. The agents did not take steps to minimize the number of faxes they intercepted or the time during which they monitored fax transmissions.

State Laws and Proposals

Many states are considering proposals that address online privacy, and a few states have already passed such measures. For example, on December 19, 2001, New York Governor George Pataki signed into law a bill that requires state agencies to develop privacy policies. Minnesota has also passed a significant new piece of privacy legislation. The new law, effective March 1, 2003, requires Internet service providers either to obtain consent from consumers or to provide them with "conspicuous" notice and an opportunity to opt-out before disclosing personally identifiable information to third parties. By its terms, the law applies only to ISPs that provide consumers authenticated access to or presence on the Internet, and does not apply to online businesses in general.

Several states also are considering legislation specifically directed at preventing Internet companies from selling personal information obtained by tracking users' online movement. In addition, more than 20 states are considering legislation to address the privacy of health records stored in computer databases.

Online merchants have complained loudly, however, over the prospect of 50 different sets of rules governing the collection and use of information, arguing instead for uniformity. Proposed federal legislation would address the problem by expressly preempting state privacy laws.

Some privacy cases have already been brought under existing state consumer-protection laws and the common law of trespass. Summaries of a few notable cases are provided below:

In re RealNetworks, Inc. Privacy Litigation, 2000 U.S. Dist. LEXIS 6584 (N.D. Ill. May 11, 2000).

In November 1999, two class-action lawsuits were filed against RealNetworks, Inc. alleging that the company's software (which allows users to download compressed music files) also collected information, without disclosure, about user listening habits. Both lawsuits alleged violations of, among other things, state consumer-protection laws, because the RealNetworks privacy statement indicated that information was not being collected. In response to public criticism of its privacy practices, RealNetworks disclosed the use of identification numbers in its privacy statement and offered a patch to replace the identification codes in its products. The company also stated that it did not associate the identification code with user listening habits or personal information. The cases were consolidated in the federal court for the Northern District of Illinois. The court held that the plaintiffs were bound by the arbitration clause in the licensing agreement, because it was a written agreement and was not unconscionable. For more discussion of the enforceability of licensing agreements generally, *see* Chapter 6, pages 197-203.

In February 2000, two complaints seeking class-action certification were filed in the U.S. District Court for the Northern District of California against Alexa Internet, charging that the software company's program obtained information from users without disclosing the collection. The plaintiffs alleged that Alexa's program violated the ECPA, state deceptive-practices statutes, and the common law of trespass and invaded the privacy of users. Alexa settled the suit and agreed to make numerous changes to its data-collection practices, including requiring customers to opt-in to having their data collected before they can download the company's software. The FTC has stated that it will not take action against Alexa now that it has changed its stated privacy policy. The terms of the settlement can be found at http://www.alexa.com/settlement/.

The State of Texas brought suit against Living.com, an online furniture retailer that went out of business in August 2000, to enjoin the company from selling personal information it had obtained through its website. The case was settled. As part of the agreement, Living.com agreed to destroy any records of customer credit-card numbers, bank accounts, and Social Security numbers gathered through its website. Living.com will have the opportunity to sell the names and e-mail addresses of its customers, but only after the customers have been given the opportunity to opt-out of the sale of their information.

⚖ *Steinbeck v. Coremetrics, Inc.*, Case No. SCVSS 69202 (Cal. Super. Ct., July 28, 2000).

In July 2000, a class-action suit was filed in California alleging that Toys 'R Us violated California citizens' constitutional right of privacy, California's consumer-protection laws, and the common law of trespass by engaging a third-party marketing company to collect data from users of the toysrus.com and babiesrus.com websites without their knowledge. According to the complaint, the third-party marketer used "web bugs," data tags, and cookies to track consumer habits. After widespread consumer backlash, Toysrus.com announced that it would no longer use the services of the third-party marketing company.

Toysrus.com, Inc. has also entered into a consent decree with the New Jersey Division of Consumer Affairs. On December 26, 2001, Toysrus agreed to pay a fine of $50,000, covering costs and the development of programs to inform the public about issues related to Internet privacy. Toysrus will also maintain improvements to its privacy policy and ensure that any third parties who received personally identifiable information on New Jersey customers who used the Toysrus website will destroy or return the information.

⚖ In January 2001, e-Games, an online vendor of family-oriented game software, settled a suit brought by the Attorney General of Michigan. e-Games agreed to revise its software and to provide full disclosure of its data collection and use practices. The company is also offering software online that will remove the existing clear-gif collection software from existing installations of the games. The settlement was filed with the Ingham County Circuit Court.

Industry Self-Regulation

The FTC's Support for Self-Regulation

On July 27, 2000, the FTC announced its support of the self-regulation principles created by the Network Advertising Initiative (NAI). According to its website, NAI represents over 90 percent of companies that help provide online advertising based on consumer information gathered from the Internet, referred to by NAI as "Online Preference Marketing." The member companies include 24/7 Media, AdForce, AdKnowldege, Avenue A, Burst! Media, DoubleClick, Engage, L90, and MatchLogic.

As stated on the NAI website (http://www.networkadvertising.org), participants in the NAI program agree:

1. Not to use personally identifiable information about sensitive medical or financial matters, information of a sexual nature, or Social Security numbers for purposes of targeting online ads.

2. To mandate clear and conspicuous notice and an opportunity to opt-out on sites that collect information that is not personally identifying.

3. To mandate an opt-in for the merger of personally identifying information with previously collected information that is not personally identifying.

4. To mandate robust notice and choice before the collection of personally identifying information that will be merged with information that is not personally identifying collected on a going-forward basis.

Other Self-Regulation Efforts

- The Online Privacy Alliance, a coalition of industry groups, promulgated its Online Privacy Guidelines for members to follow when collecting personally identifiable information from online consumers. Members must indicate what information is being collected, how it is used, and what security measures are installed, and must provide consumers with adequate choices regarding data collection. The Guidelines are available at http://www.privacyalliance.org/resources/ppguidelines.shtml.

- TRUSTe is a nonprofit privacy organization that websites can join if they commit to TRUSTe's announced privacy principles and agree to comply with TRUSTe's oversight and dispute-resolution processes. TRUSTe's core principles—notice, choice, access, and security—correspond to those of the FTC. In addition, TRUSTe has articulated three primary principles for dealing with collecting personal information. These principles are: (1) mandatory third-party oversight of customer information; (2) consumer opt-in on the sharing of personally identifying information; and (3) corporate pledges to honor privacy agreements even after bankruptcy filings.

  Members receive a TRUSTe logo or seal for display on their websites. Information on the TRUSTe program can be found at http://www.truste.org. TRUSTe also offers an EU Safe Harbor seal indicating a site's compliance with the safe-harbor agreement between the United States and the European Union effective November 1, 2000. *See* pages 191-194, below, for a discussion of the EU Directive.

On October 25, 2000, TRUSTe filed a trademark infringement claim against American-Politics.com in U.S. District Court in Washington, D.C. The suit claims that American-Politics.com displayed the TRUSTe "seal of approval" without actually having received approval, and seeks at least $1 million in damages.

- BBBOnline, operated by the Better Business Bureau, offers a privacy program that awards seals to websites that meet BBB's guidelines. Its core principles also mirror those endorsed by the FTC: notice, choice, access, and security. Information on BBBOnline can be found at http://www.bbbonline.com.

- The McGraw-Hill Companies introduced a Customer Privacy Policy that the FTC hailed as an industry model. That policy conforms to the FTC's core principles of privacy protection. The policy comprises the following key principles: notice, choice, security, and review and correction of data. The McGraw-Hill privacy policy can be found at http://www.mcgraw-hill.com.

- Health on the Net (HON) is an international nonprofit organization focused on the use of the Internet for health and medicine. HON has issued a code of conduct to help provide some consistency in the quality of medical and health information available on the Internet and offers a seal to demonstrate that a member website follows the HON code principles. The code of conduct extends to matters beyond privacy, but includes a confidentiality principle pledging that confidentiality of personal data is respected, and that the website operators will follow or exceed applicable privacy laws.

Self-Protection

- The Anonymizer (http://www.anonymizer.com) allows individuals to surf the web anonymously.

- Cookie Central (http://www.cookiecentral.com) teaches individuals how to delete cookies from their computers. It also provides a comprehensive FAQ on cookies.

- Users can visit http://www.privacy.net/Analyze/ to obtain a free privacy analysis. The site automatically reports information they disclose to the sites they visit. This includes the user's IP address, the user's computer name, any cookies placed by the site on the user's system, the site from which the user linked, the user's operating system and browser type, the user's e-mail address, and the owner of the user's network.

- The World Wide Web Consortium has created the "platform for privacy preferences" or "P3P," an automated mechanism that allows users to specify how much personal information they will allow their computers to transmit to websites they visit. If the operator of a website expresses its privacy policy in a language that can be read by a P3P-enabled browser, the browser can compare the privacy preferences set by users with a "snapshot" of the website's privacy policy to see if the website meets the user's privacy requirements. Microsoft's most recent browser, Internet Explorer 6, implements the P3P standard, and its introduction has sparked a debate as to the feasibility of P3P technology. A machine-readable privacy policy cannot convey the nuances that often characterize website privacy policies. This raises concerns about unfair trade practices liability for misleading P3P programming, and loss of website traffic due to a poorly translated privacy policy. For more information on P3P visit the World Wide Web Consortium's P3P website at http://www.w3.org/P3P/.

- Microsoft has created "cookie alert" software that enables users to detect whether cookies have been placed on their computers and to indicate whether they wish to accept or reject them.

- Users can always simply opt not to disclose personal information when requested.

USA Patriot Act

On October 26, 2001, President Bush signed the USA PATRIOT Act into law. The Act (Uniting and Strengthening America by Providing Appropriate Tools Required to Intercept and Obstruct Terrorism) provides law enforcement with a variety of new tools and procedures to allow the monitoring of information that is transmitted by communications service providers. These changes will mostly affect the way that law-enforcement officials interact with the judiciary and the way that carriers and ISPs assist with investigations by providing information. Service providers can most likely expect that, because the government now has easier access to warrants and other authority to intercept communications of all kinds, new demands may be placed on their systems and their information processing and retrieval capabilities with respect to the customer information. Generally, the Act:

- Details a variety of new procedures available to law-enforcement authorities to allow better monitoring of international terrorist activities;

- Expands the definition of terrorist activities, expands government access to surveillance techniques, and amends banking procedures to better track financial resources that may support terrorist activities; and

- Amends several existing laws concerning government surveillance and privacy and, to a certain extent, seeks to harmonize disparate obligations among different types of communications service providers.

- The Act is of particular interest to Internet companies, Internet service providers, and telecommunications carriers, which have expanded obligations and immunities under the Act:

- The definition of a "trap and trace device" for purposes of the trap-and-trace statute (which governs the collection of non-content traffic information associated with communications, such as the phone numbers dialed from a particular telephone) has been significantly expanded to allow for access to routing and address information in any electronic communication, including Internet communications and e-mail;

- There is an obligation to respond to nationwide service of process so that a single court having jurisdiction over an offense can issue a nationwide search warrant for stored data, such as e-mail;

- Nothing in the Act creates any new requirements for technical assistance, such as design mandates;

- In several important areas, the Act expands service-provider protections (including immunities and good-faith defenses) for complying with new or existing surveillance authority;

- The Act expands the government's authority to conduct, at the request of service providers, wiretaps of hackers and other "trespassers" on service-provider networks;

- The Act amends and limits the Cable Act to make it clear that companies offering cable-based Internet or telephone service will be subject to the provisions of the Cable Act requiring notice to subscribers of government-surveillance requests only where detailed cable-viewing information is being sought; in all other instances, cable operators offering these services can respond to a government-surveillance request under ECPA, which does not require service providers to notify subscribers of requests for information.

The USA PATRIOT Act has come under heated criticism from advocates of civil liberties. For example, in addition to the nearly 25 lawsuits for civil liberties violations it has initiated since the attacks, the ACLU initiated a national campaign to challenge the government's anti-terror policies and the PATRIOT Act's provisions that expand government's authority to monitor citizens' activities.

International Response to Privacy Concerns—The EU Directive

The European Union's Directive on Data Protection (95/46/EC) became effective on October 24, 1998. The Directive requires member states to adopt national legislation meeting specified requirements for the collection and use of personal information.

The Directive requires that, subject to limited exceptions, personal data may be processed only if the data subject has unambiguously given his or her consent. Article 25 of the Directive prohibits the transfer of personally identifiable data to countries that do not provide an "adequate" level of privacy protection.

Safe Harbor

Because of the Directive's potential to lead to disputes that could seriously hamper U.S.-EU trade, the two sides have worked for years to devise a way for U.S. companies to comply with the EU Directive without unnecessarily harming online commerce. The U.S. and EU reached agreement on May 31, 2000 (the "Safe Harbor Agreement"), with the EU member states unanimously approving the U.S. "safe harbor" proposal. The proposal is a compromise between the two culturally divergent approaches to privacy, an attempt to accommodate both the U.S. self-regulatory framework and the EU's strict standards. As of February 2003, 300 companies had taken advantage of the safe harbor by registering with the Department of Commerce. A list of registered companies is available at www.export.gov/safeharbor.

The decision for companies to enter into the safe harbor is voluntary, and they may qualify for the safe harbor in different ways. For example, a company can join a self-regulatory privacy program that adheres to the principles, or it can develop its own self-regulatory privacy policies that conform to the principles. U.S. companies adhering to the agreement's principles will be viewed as providing adequate privacy protection, and would gain "safe harbor" from prosecution or lawsuits by EU governments. While European citizens do not lose their rights to sue U.S. companies directly, they are encouraged to follow a process whereby they first raise any complaints with the potential defendant and go through dispute resolution before proceeding with any suit.

To take advantage of the safe harbor, companies self-certify by providing an annual letter to the Department of Commerce or its designee, signed by a corporate officer, containing the information required by the Safe Harbor Agreement. The Department of Commerce or its designee maintains a list of all organizations that file such letters. Both the list and the self-certification letters submitted by the organizations are publicly available. All companies that self-certify for the safe harbor also have to state in their relevant published privacy policy statements that they adhere to the safe-harbor principles. Companies do not need to subject all personal information that they retain to the safe-harbor principles; rather, they would need to make sure that personal information received from the EU after they have joined the safe harbor is handled according to the principles. The Safe Harbor Agreement does not cover the financial services sector.

The Safe Harbor Agreement sets forth the following safe-harbor principles:

1. *Notice*. A company must notify consumers of the reasons for which it collects and uses personal information; how to contact the company with inquiries; the types of third parties with which it shares personal information; and the options consumers have to limit the use and disclosure of personal information. The notice must be clear and conspicuous and must be made when consumers are asked to provide information, or reasonably soon afterwards. Notice must be given before the company uses the information for something other than the original purpose for which it was collected, or before the company discloses the information to a third party for the first time.

2. *Choice*. For most information, a company must allow consumers to choose to opt-out of the use and disclosure of personal information. In most cases where sensitive personal information

(defined to include, among others, information about medical conditions, race, and political opinions) is involved, consumers must opt-in to disclosures to third parties or uses other than those for which the information was originally collected.

3. _Onward Transfer_. A company may disclose personal information to a third party only if it determines that the third party adheres to the safe-harbor principles.

4. _Security_. A company must take reasonable precautions to protect collected personal information.

5. _Data Integrity_. A company must not use personal information for purposes inconsistent with the original purpose for which the information was collected absent authorization from the consumer from whom the information was collected.

6. _Access_. Consumers must have reasonable access to personal information that has been collected about them so they can review and correct the information.

7. _Enforcement_. A company must agree to submit to enforcement mechanisms to address consumer complaints and investigate company practices, and must obligate itself to correct failures to adhere to safe-harbor principles. An enforcement mechanism will be deemed acceptable only if it includes "sufficiently rigorous" sanctions for failure to comply.

The Safe Harbor Agreement also contains a series of frequently asked questions that provide greater detail about the obligations of companies who choose to participate in the safe harbors. All documents can be accessed through http://www.ita.doc.gov/td/ecom/menu.html.

On July 26, 2000, the European Commission approved the Safe Harbor Agreement. The guidelines can be found in the _Federal Register_ at 65 Fed. Reg. 45,666 (July 24, 2000). The Safe Harbor Agreement took effect November 1, 2000.

Sanctions

Sanctions for non-compliance range in severity from publicity for findings of non-compliance to a requirement to delete data; from suspension and removal of a seal to compensation to individuals for losses incurred as a result of non-compliance. Injunctive orders are also available. Non-compliance with the safe harbor principles could also be subject to action under § 5 of the Federal Trade Commission Act prohibiting unfair and deceptive acts. Article 2 of the May 31, 2000, agreement provides that member state authorities may exercise their powers to suspend data flows to an organization if they have determined that there is a "substantial likelihood" that the safe-harbor principles are being violated; that there is a reason to believe that the enforcement mechanism in place is not taking or will not take adequate and timely steps to settle the case; that the continuing transfer would create an "imminent risk of grave harm to data subjects"; or that the competent authorities in the member state have made reasonable efforts to provide the organization with a notice and opportunity to respond. The suspension of data would cease as soon as compliance with the principles is assured and the proper EU authorities are notified.

ELECTRONIC CONTRACTS

Electronic Contract Basics

The term "electronic contracts" refers to agreements that are similar to traditional contracts, except that they are made online or using electronic media rather than on paper. An electronic contract involves the formation of an agreement between two or more people, just as a traditional contract, written on paper and signed in ink, does. Not surprisingly, courts have applied familiar principles of traditional contract law when deciding disputes involving electronic contracts.

Web Site Disclaimers and User Agreements. Web publishers often seek to reduce exposure to liability and to protect the integrity and proprietary value of their content by posting "visitor agreements" on their websites that contain various disclaimers of liability and notices concerning rights to content, restrictions on site use, and the like. Similarly, computer manufacturers and software publishers often include license agreements that are either printed on or included within a product's packaging materials. Case law indicates that these disclaimers and user agreements, which are often referred to as "shrinkwrap," "click-wrap," "click-through," "browse-wrap" or "browse-through" agreements, may constitute enforceable contracts.

Electronic Signatures (E-Signatures). An electronic signature has the same function as a traditional signature: to affirm the signer's intent to abide by the terms of the contract to which he or she affixes the signature. In the case of e-signatures, this affirmation takes place digitally instead of by the use of ink on paper. The federal government has passed legislation mandating that electronic signatures be given the same validity as ink signatures; all state-level governments in the United States have passed legislation to the same effect.

Web Site Disclaimers and User Agreements

Types of Disclaimers

Responsibility Statements

Websites often link to other websites. Disclaimers make clear that the original website is not responsible for the contents of the sites to which it links.

Liability Statements

Websites often disclaim liability for actions taken in reliance upon site content. This is common for sites that include medical advice, legal advice, and consumer recommendations. A "proceed at your own risk" disclaimer may help to absolve the site from legal liability.

Terms Relating to User-Supplied Content

User-Supplied Content: Controversial Content. Web publishers often note that chat rooms, bulletin boards, and similar areas within their sites contain user-supplied content that may not be regularly monitored, and could be considered controversial or offensive. Visitor agreements typically contain a disclaimer of responsibility for such content.

User-Supplied Content: Unlawful Content. Visitor agreements often warn users not to post any material that is defamatory, infringing, obscene, or otherwise unlawful, and will ask users to warrant that they have the rights to post any material that they supply. The site may stipulate that if any unlawful content is posted to the site, the result may be termination of the user's access to the site.

Visitor Agreements

Web publishers often use visitor agreements (sometimes referred to as "user agreements" or "terms of service") to establish the ground rules for access to the site or use of the contents provided within. Users who violate the visitor agreement may be denied access to the site in the future if the site is interactive or accepts user-supplied content.

Reservation of Rights

Visitor agreements often include reservation of rights language, allowing the publisher to remove any material posted by a user for any reason. Prompt removal of infringing material may help the publisher avoid liability for copyright infringement. (For discussion of limited liability for copyright infringement generally, *see* Chapter 3, pages 102-105.)

Intellectual Property Statements

Use of Publisher's Content. Web publishers typically include language granting users the right to use material on their websites only for the users' personal, non-commercial purposes. The visitor agreement may expressly prohibit reproduction and/or redistribution of website content.

Publisher's Use of User-Supplied Content. Many Web publishers include in the visitor agreement a grant of rights from users to the publisher, allowing the publisher to use, reproduce, transmit, store, and display any user-supplied content (such as bulletin-board postings) for any purpose. This could help negate any claim by a user that the website's use of the material exceeded the rights granted by the user, and protects the website owner's right to archive the material or republish it in a different format.

Restrictions On Linking and Framing. Some website owners include language in their visitor agreements addressing the right to link to their sites. These clauses typically state that linking to the site is permitted, but only in a manner that is not likely to cause confusion. However, there are some sites that object to linking without permission. For discussion of linking generally, *see* Chapter 2, pages 78-80, and Chapter 3, pages 95-98. Many Web publishers also include in their visitor agreements an explicit prohibition against framing the content of the website.

Enforceability of Electronic Contracts

A contract is formed when two or more parties, with notice of the terms of the contract, manifest their assent to those terms. Case law suggests that a reasonable contract of which a website user had notice may be enforceable even if the user never "signs" the agreement.

"Effective Notice": Was User Aware of Contract?

Whether an electronic contract is enforceable will likely depend in large part on whether the agreement is effectively brought to the attention of users. Courts generally seek to determine if the user had effective notice of the terms of the contract before any analysis of the validity of the terms themselves takes place. For publishers, three methods of bringing visitor agreements to the attention of users are most common:

1. Requiring users who wish to enter a website or an area of a website to click on a button to manifest assent to the agreement.

2. Including a link to the visitor agreement in a reasonably

noticeable location, such as a footer at the bottom of the home page, or, perhaps, each page of the site, often in proximity to copyright notices. The text accompanying the link may advise users that by using the website, they agree to be bound by the terms of the visitor agreement.

3. Posting a less obtrusive link to the visitor agreement, often in an area of the website that includes other information about the site. This alternative, however, may leave the agreement subject to challenge by users claiming insufficient notice of its terms.

General Enforceability of Contract Upheld

In *ProCD, Inc. v. Zeidenberg*, 86 F.3d 1447 (7th Cir. 1996), a "shrinkwrap" license was enforced against the purchaser of a CD-ROM product who uploaded data from the CD-ROM to a website in violation of the license. A shrinkwrap license is an unsigned license agreement included in the packaging of a product that states that the user accepts the terms of the license if he or she opens the packaging and proceeds to use or install the product. Although the terms of the license agreement were not printed on the outside of the package, the agreement permitted a buyer dissatisfied with terms of the agreement found inside to return the product for a full refund. By using the software, rather than returning it after reviewing the license agreement, the defendant manifested his consent to the terms of the license: "ProCD proposed a contract that a buyer would accept by using the software after having an opportunity to read the license at leisure. This Zeidenberg did. He had no choice, because the software splashed the license on the screen and would not let him proceed without indicating acceptance." 86 F.3d at 1452. *See also Moore v. Microsoft Corp.*, N.Y. Sup. Ct., App. Div., 2d Dept., Docket No. 2001-05569 (April 15, 2002) (holding a clickwrap agreement valid, noting that users were subjected to "prominent[ ] display" of contract terms and had to click on an "I Agree" button before downloading the software).

In *Hill v. Gateway 2000, Inc.*, 105 F.3d 1147 (7th Cir. 1997), *cert. denied*, 118 S. Ct. 47 (1997), the Court of Appeals for the Seventh Circuit enforced an arbitration clause included in the Terms & Conditions shipped with a computer. *See also Brower v. Gateway 2000, Inc.*, 676 N.Y.S.2d 569 (App. Div. 1998); *M.A. Mortensen Co. v. Timberline Software Corp., Inc.*, 998 P.2d 305 (Wash. 2000) (holding that a license agreement, which was printed on the outside of sealed diskette envelopes and the inside cover of a user manual, and referred to on a program's introductory screen, was enforceable despite the fact that its terms were not mentioned during negotiations); *but see Klocek v. Gateway, Inc.*, 104 F. Supp. 2d 1332 (D. Kan. 2000) (holding that the act of keeping a computer for more than five days was insufficient to show that the plaintiff expressly accepted the terms of a license, packaged with the computer, that included a five-day, review-and-return policy).

In *Pollstar v. Gigmania Ltd.*, 170 F. Supp. 2d 974 (E.D. Cal. 2000), the court held that a "browse-wrap" license agreement may be enforceable. The plaintiff's website provided time-sensitive concert information. The plaintiff placed a link to a license agreement on its home page, but the site could be accessed without the user specifically clicking, otherwise indicating acceptance of, or even viewing the actual text of the license agreement. The agreement limited use of the documents and information to non-commercial purposes. The defendant used the information to create its own commercial concert-information site. The court allowed the plaintiff to proceed with its claims for misappropriation, unfair competition, and breach of contract, holding that browse-wrap licenses are not invalid as a matter of law.

In *Hotmail Corp. v. Van$ Money Pie, Inc.*, 47 U.S.P.Q.2d 1020 (N.D. Cal. 1998), a federal trial court granted a preliminary injunction, finding, among other things, a likelihood that Hotmail would prevail on its breach of contract claim. The defendant had signed up for several accounts with Hotmail Corp., whose terms of service prohibit using the accounts to send spam and/or pornography. Although the court did not analyze the formation of the contract in any detail, the court noted that Hotmail had complied with all applicable conditions of the contract. The defendant, however, had breached the terms of service by facilitating the sending of spam and/or pornography.

In *i.LAN Sys., Inc. v. NetScoutServ.Level Corp.*, 183 F. Supp. 2d 328 (D. Mass. 2002), the United States District Court for the District of Massachusetts found that a clickwrap license agreement is an enforceable contract under Article 2 of the Uniform Commercial Code. The plaintiff, i.LAN, helps companies monitor their computer networks; the defendant, NetScout (formerly NextPoint Networks), sells sophisticated software that monitors networks. In 1998, the parties signed a Value Added Reseller agreement under which i.LAN agreed to resell NextPoint's software to customers. The dispute involved the interpretation of that agreement, the purchase order associated with the transaction, and the clickwrap agreement to which i.LAN agreed upon receipt of the software. The court relied on the fact that i.LAN specifically agreed to a limitation of liability provision when it clicked on the "I Agree" button. The court acknowledged that "Article 2 technically does not, and certainly will not, in the future, govern software licenses [alluding to the Uniform Computer Information Transactions Act ("UCITA") which specifically addresses software licenses], but for the time being, the Court will assume it does." 183 F. Supp. 2d at 332. (For discussion of UCITA generally, *see* Chapter 9, pages 274-276.).

In *Mathias v. America Online, Inc.*, 2002 WL 377159 (Ohio App. Ct., Feb. 28, 2002), the Ohio Court of Appeals affirmed summary judgment in favor of America Online, ruling that AOL did not breach its agreement with plaintiff users when they experienced access and connection problems. By clicking on a button to read the Internet service provider's terms, and subsequently not canceling their service, the plaintiffs were deemed to have acknowledged that the services would be provided on an as-available basis and that traffic congestion might occur.

General Enforceability of Contract Denied

In *Specht v. Netscape Communications Corp.*, 150 F. Supp. 2d 585 (S.D.N.Y. 2001), *aff'd*, 306 F.3d 17 (2d Cir. 2002), the U.S. Court of Appeals for the Second Circuit found that users of Netscape's "SmartDownload" Internet software download feature were not bound by an arbitration clause in the software-license agreement because they were not necessarily aware that they were entering a contract at the time they downloaded the "SmartDownload" software. The trial court noted that the user was not required to assent or even *view* the terms of the license agreement before downloading the software, though the site contained the admonition: "Please review and agree to the terms of the Netscape SmartDownload license agreement before downloading and using the software." The trial court found, however, that this language did not indicate "that a user *must* agree to the license terms before downloading and using the software." Rather, "this language reads as a mere invitation, not as a condition." *Specht*, 150 F. Supp. 2d at 596. The court of appeals agreed that users were not placed on sufficient notice of the agreement to be bound by the arbitration clause. In affirming, the court of appeals emphasized that though the button that users clicked to download the software was above the scroll on the users' computer screens, users would have had to scroll down below the fold to find any reference to the license agreement: "In circumstances such as these," the court of appeals wrote, "where consumers are urged to download free software at the immediate clicking of a button, a reference to the existence of license terms on a submerged screen is not sufficient to place consumers on inquiry or constructive notice of those terms." 306 F.3d at ___ (slip op. at 23).

Other courts have also found shrinkwrap licenses unenforceable under particular circumstances. *See Vault Corp. v. Quaid Software Ltd.*, 655 F. Supp. 750 (E.D. La. 1987), *aff'd*, 847 F.2d 255 (5th Cir. 1988); *Step-Saver Data Systems, Inc. v. Wyse Technology*, 939 F.2d 91 (3d Cir. 1991); *Arizona Retail Sys. v. Software Link*, 831 F. Supp. 759 (D. Ariz. 1993); *Novell, Inc. v. Network Trade Center, Inc.*, 25 F. Supp. 2d 1218 (D. Utah 1997).

Enforceability of Particular Provisions: Forum Selection and Arbitration Clauses

Not surprisingly, if a provision is usually found enforceable in a traditional paper contract, a court will ordinarily find it enforceable in an electronic contract.

In *Lieschke v. RealNetworks Inc.*, No. 99-C-7274 (N.D. Ill. Feb. 10, 2000), and *Simon v. RealNetworks Inc.*, No. 99-C-7380 (N.D. Ill. Feb. 10, 2000) (both cases combined and available at 2000 WL 198424), a federal trial court found enforceable an arbitration clause in a clickwrap agreement that had to be accepted before installation of a software package. *See also Stan McClain Inc. v. Smith-Gardner*, B149630 (Cal. Ct. App., 2d App. Dist April 22, 2002) (holding that where both disputants were sophisticated commercial entities, a forum selection clause in a contract to provide software was valid despite the fact the plaintiff alleged a tort claim rather than a breach-of-contract claim).

In *Caspi v. Microsoft Network*, 732 A.2d 528 (N.J. Super. Ct. App. Div. 1999), a forum-selection clause contained in a click-through online subscriber agreement was held enforceable. The plaintiffs sued Microsoft in a New Jersey court on various contract and fraud theories relating to membership-fee practices. Microsoft moved to dismiss on the grounds that the Microsoft Network membership agreement dictated that all disputes would be adjudicated in the courts of King County, Washington.

Before signing up for the Microsoft Network, users were given an opportunity to review the membership agreement online. To subscribe, they had to click on an "I Agree" button. The court found that the plaintiff subscribers must have known that they were entering a contract when they did so. The court also found that the plaintiffs had proper notice of the forum-selection clause, which was the first item in the last paragraph of the membership agreement. *See also Barnett v. Network Solutions, Inc.*, 38 S.W.3d 200 (Tex. Ct. App. 2001) (holding forum-selection clause requiring adjudication in Virginia to be valid); *Hughes v. America Online*, Civil Action No. 2001-10981-RBC (D. Mass. May 28, 2002) (upholding a forum-selection clause; it was undisputed that the plaintiff had agreed to AOL's terms of service when he became a customer).

➤ *Forrest v. Verizon Communications, Inc.*, 805 A.2d 1007 (D.C. 2002).

A District of Columbia court found the forum-selection clause in a clickwrap agreement for digital subscriber line service to be reasonable and enforceable against a subscriber. The court rejected the plaintiff's arguments that the provision should not be enforced because it was buried in a lengthy online agreement, it was viewable only in a small scroll box, and the agreement required consumers to waive their rights to bring class-action suits. The court found that the plaintiff had failed to demonstrate the forum-selection clause was fraudulent or overreaching, that it would "deprive the plaintiff of a remedy or of its day in court," or that its enforcement would be against public policy.

However, forum-selection clauses have not always been enforced:

➤ *Williams v. AOL*, 2001 WL 135825 (Mass. Dist. Ct. Feb. 8, 2001).

A Massachusetts judge ruled that the forum-selection clause in America Online's membership agreement, which requires all disputes to be resolved in Virginia, was not enforceable against the plaintiffs because they were already AOL members at the time that the forum-selection clause was added to the membership agreement and therefore had insufficient notice of the addition of the forum selection clause to the agreement. (*See* "Effective Notice," at page 197, above.)

➤ In *America Online, Inc. v. Superior Court of Alameda County*, 2001 WL 695166 (Cal. Super. Ct. June 21, 2001), an Alameda County, California, judge found the same AOL forum-selection clause to be unenforceable on two independent policy grounds. First, the court held that the unavailability of consumer-rights, class-action relief in Virginia represented a "material difference" in available remedies and thus violated the California public policy recognizing the importance of such actions. In addition, the court held that the forum-selection clause was unenforceable under the anti-waiver provision of the California Consumers Legal Remedies Act. In ruling against AOL, the court shifted the burden of proof on the enforceability of the forum-selection clause from the class-action plaintiffs to AOL. *See also Thompson v. Handa-Lopez, Inc.*, 998 F. Supp. 738 (W.D. Tex. Mar. 25, 1998) (finding unenforceable a provision in an online agreement governing use of the defendant's Internet casino that called for all disputes to be settled by arbitration in San Jose, California).

Comb v. PayPal, 218 F. Supp. 2d 1165 (N.D. Cal. 2002).

A federal trial court denied the defendant, PayPal's, motion to compel individual arbitration proceedings for each person who had joined a class-action suit against it. The court refused to uphold an arbitration clause in PayPal's clickwrap agreement, citing its unconscionability and questioning the notice provided to the plaintiffs. The court also indicated that the forum-selection provision in the clickwrap agreement was unreasonable.

Electronic And Digital Signatures

General

Online publishers, in their capacities as purchasers and vendors, may come to depend on the ability to make their e-commerce transactions secure by authenticating the signatures that accompany such transactions. Signature authentication has become the subject of extensive state, federal, and international legislative efforts, as well as activity by private organizations.

In the early days of e-commerce regulation, e-signatures were hailed as a new way to streamline the contracting process and the filing of government documents. The promises of new technology have not yet been fulfilled, as the combination of consumers' concerns over security and competing technological standards among companies marketing e-signature software have slowed the transition from ink to electrons. See Troy Wolverton, "Despite Law, Few People Use E-Signatures," CNET News.com (Apr. 17, 2002), available at http://news.com.com/2100-1017-884544.html.

Definitions

A signature is a mark made with the intent to authenticate a document, and an *electronic signature* is simply a signature transmitted through an electronic medium. An electronic signature is an electronic sound, symbol, or process attached to or logically associated with a contract or other record and executed or adopted by a person with the intent to sign the record. Electronic signatures can include typed signature notations; other typed notations, such as e-mail headers; and ink-on-paper signatures scanned electronically.

In contrast, a *digital signature*, properly defined, is a more specialized item. It is the result of encoding and decoding information through an encryption method, often a method known as public-key cryptography. Despite this distinction, many documents and legislative products use the term "digital signature" as simply a synonym for the broader, less-specialized "electronic signature."

Legislative Efforts

State Legislation

All 50 states and the District of Columbia have enacted legislation to require or encourage acceptance of some type of electronic signature. Most of these statutes apply to electronic signatures broadly defined. Many of these laws limit themselves to mandating acceptance of electronic or digital signatures by public agencies or require acceptance only in specific areas, such as medical records.

The National Conference of Commissioners on Uniform State Laws voted to approve the Uniform Electronic Transactions Act (UETA) on July 29, 1999. This model state legislation provides for acceptance of electronic signatures but does not require any specific type of electronic signature or method of authentication. As of October 15, 2002, 41 states had adopted UETA, and six other states had similar measures pending in their legislatures.

Federal Legislation

On June 30, 2000, President Clinton signed into law the Electronic Signatures in Global and National Commerce Act (E-SIGN). 15 U.S.C.A. § 7001 (2001). E-SIGN was enacted at the federal level to avoid wide variations in state law and to bolster the public's confidence in the legal validity of electronic contracts. This law makes electronic signatures legally binding, like "wet," or ink signatures, by prohibiting a rule of law from denying the legal effect of certain instruments of electronic commerce on the ground that (1) they are not in writing, if they are electronic records; or (2) they are not signed or affirmed by a signature, if they have been signed or affirmed by electronic signature.

The law further states that "[i]f a statute, regulation or other rule of law requires that a contract or other record relating to a transaction in or affecting interstate or foreign commerce be retained, that requirement is met by retaining an electronic record of the information in the contract." *See* 15 U.S.C.A. § 7001(d)(1). Under this provision, a record that accurately reflects the information set forth in the electronic contract and remains accessible to the parties for the period required by statute, law, or regulation will suffice as a record of the transaction under such statute, law, or regulation. *See id.*; *see also In re Real Networks, Inc.*, 2000 U.S. Dist. LEXIS 6584 (N.D. Ill. May 11, 2000) (decided before E-SIGN was enacted, this case involved an electronic agreement that was held to be an enforceable "writing" under the Federal Arbitration Act because it was easily printable and storable).

E-SIGN also preempts any state law addressing electronic signatures that gives greater legal status or effect to a particular technology. This technology-neutral approach allows merchants to decide which technology will best facilitate electronic commerce in their products. However, E-SIGN specifically provides that qualifying state versions of UETA are allowed to preempt E-SIGN.

International Efforts

. In November 1999, the European Commission approved a directive that is to be incorporated into member states' laws. The directive provides that all member states should accept electronic signatures considered valid by member states. The directive is technology-neutral and addresses acceptance of electronic signatures by countries outside the EU.

On September 29, 2000, the electronic commerce working group for The United Nations Commission on International Trade Law (UNCITRAL) adopted a model law on electronic signatures. The model law was presented to UNCITRAL in the summer of 2001. The draft is available at: http://www.uncitral.org/english/sessions/wg_ec/wp-84.pdf. The Working Group released a report on March 21, 2002 summarizing the Group's findings and recommendation that the UN prepare an international treaty dealing with electronic contracting issues. This report can be found at: http://www.uncitral.org/english/sessions/unc/unc-35/509e.pdf.

On October 10, 2002 the New Zealand Parliament passed the Electronic Transactions Bill, which includes language making electronic signatures valid on contracts, just like their paper-and-ink counterparts.

Case Law Developments: E-SIGN and E-Signatures

Although electronic signature technology and the E-SIGN legislation are relatively new, there have been a few cases that considered the validity of electronic signatures.

In *Sea-Land Service, Inc. v. Lozen International, LLC*, 285 F.3d 808 (9th Cir. 2002), the Court of Appeals for the Ninth Circuit found the presence of an electronic signature on a document sufficient proof that the document was authored by a party opponent and admissible as evidence under the applicable rules of evidence. 285 F.3d at 821.

On the state level, courts at opposite ends of the country have come to conflicting conclusions as to the validity of electronic signatures under the statute of frauds. (Though contracts do not ordinarily have to be in writing to be valid, the statute of frauds provides that certain categories of contracts—such as contracts for the sale of real estate and contracts that cannot be fully performed within a year of execution—are not enforceable unless memorialized in a signed written agreement.) A Massachusetts superior court held that typewritten names of the authors at the end of e-mail messages were equivalent to written signatures and thus fulfilled the requirements of the state's statute of frauds. *See Shattuck v. Klotzbach*, Civil Action No. 01-1109A (Mass. Super. Ct. Dec. 11, 2001). However, the Washington State Court of Appeals rejected the validity of some e-mail communications under that state's statute of frauds because they were written prior to acceptance of the offer. The court concluded that the e-mails were merely part of "continuing negotiations," and that even if the signatures were otherwise valid, the e-mail exchanges did not meet the writing requirement of Washington's statute of frauds. *See Hansen v. Transworld Wireless TV-Spokane, Inc.*, No. 99-2-03108-8 (Wash. Ct. App. April 25, 2002).

UNSOLICITED COMMERCIAL E-MAIL OR SPAM

General

"Spam" is common parlance for unsolicited (usually commercial) e-mail. From the sender's point of view, spam can be an effective means of sending bulk e-mail to variously targeted audiences. From the recipient's point of view, it is often considered the Internet equivalent of junk mail. According to a study by Brightmail, a San Francisco-based, anti-spam software maker, unsolicited messages accounted for 40 percent of all e-mail on the Internet in November 2002. A U.K. study, completed by Message Labs in February 2003, indicates that of the more than 100 million e-mails sampled, 25 percent were spam. Another report, by Ferris Research of San Francisco, projects that spam will cost American corporations more than $10 billion in 2003.

On December 18, 2002, the Federal Trade Commission (FTC) announced plans to establish a federal "do not call" registry to help consumers restrict telemarketing calls to their residential telephone lines. Many predict that one result of this program, not yet in effect, will be a marked increase in spam, as direct marketers look to e-mail addresses to replace the off-limits telephone numbers.

As the amount of spam grows, so do efforts to combat it. Perhaps the most comprehensive response has come from state legislatures: half the states have passed anti-spam laws within the past few years. The provisions of these state laws range from requiring consumer consent before commercial e-mail is sent to prohibiting the falsification of sender identification.

On the federal side, there are no laws that directly address the issue of spam. However, the FTC has stepped up efforts to stop commercial e-mails that are considered fraudulent or deceptive. Congress is also actively considering several new spam bills.

Telephone Consumer Protection Act of 1991

The Telephone Consumer Protection Act of 1991 (the TCPA), 47 U.S.C. § 227, could be viewed as the precursor to modern spam laws. The TCPA, among other things, makes it unlawful "to use any telephone facsimile machine, computer, or other device to send an unsolicited advertisement to a telephone facsimile machine." This "junk fax" statute allows anyone who receives such an unsolicited advertisement to sue for an injunction and/or for actual damages or $500 in statutory damages, whichever is greater. A court may award treble damages for willful violation of the statute.

First Amendment challenges to the TCPA have received mixed treatment in the courts. The Court of Appeals for the Ninth Circuit rejected such a challenge on the basis that "unsolicited fax advertisements shift significant costs to consumers." The Ninth Circuit found that the narrow language of the TCPA serves a specific purpose and directly advances consumers' significant interest in not paying the costs of receiving unsolicited advertisements by fax. *See Destination Ventures, Ltd. v. FCC*, 46 F.3d 54 (9th Cir. 1995). However, a federal trial court in Missouri recently declined to follow the Ninth Circuit's holding and instead held that the junk fax statute does violate the First Amendment. The Missouri court stated that there was no hard evidence proving that substantial costs are involved with receiving unsolicited faxes. The court also questioned whether the TCPA actually ameliorated the asserted harm. *Missouri v. American Blast Fax Inc.*, 196 F. Supp. 2d 920 (E.D. Mo. 2002).

Plaintiffs have not used the TCPA to combat spam, relying instead upon state consumer-protection statutes and those directly prohibiting unsolicited commercial e-mail. The U.S. Congress is considering a number of bills that address spam directly. Any new federal spam laws will probably also face First Amendment challenges, as evidenced by the challenges to state spam laws discussed below.

State Law

As of October 2002, 26 states had passed laws designed to regulate spam. Although there is no model statute, there seem to be some common approaches among states. The statutes generally provide for a private right of action against the senders of unsolicited commercial e-mail. In most states, the recipient of the e-mail or an Internet service provider that suffers any actual damages managing the e-mail may bring the claim. The plaintiffs often have the choice of recovering actual damages or a per e-mail statutory dollar amount, capped at a certain amount per day. However, a New York state court recently held that the bother of receiving junk mail and unwanted telephone solicitations did not constitute actual harm and therefore dismissed a class-action suit against a bank that had allegedly sold marketers information about its customers. For more discussion of this case, *Smith v. Chase Manhattan Bank*, 741 N.Y.S.2d 100 (N.Y. App. Div. 2002), *see* Chapter 5, page 180.

Prohibition of Fraud. Some states have sought to combat senders of bulk unsolicited e-mail who hide their identity or even fraudulently disguise themselves. Typically, states have prohibited falsifying the header information that accompanies an e-mail. Such states provide a cause of action not only for the recipient of forged e-mail, but also for any third party who may be fraudulently identified as the e-mail's sender.

Self-Identifying Disclosures. Other states require those who want to send unsolicited bulk commercial e-mail to supply self-identifying information, such as name and postal address, as well as a way to opt-out of receiving future e-mails. Some states require spammers to create a toll-free telephone number that recipients may call to stop receiving the e-mails.

Labels. Another method some states have adopted to combat spam is to require unsolicited e-mails to include in the subject line a label such as "ADV" for commercial e-mails, or even "ADV:ADLT" for commercial e-mails promoting adult content.

Technical Prohibitions. By prohibiting "trespass" upon a third-party computer server, some states prohibit a technique spammers use to bounce e-mails off of a third-party server in order to hide the actual sender's identity. States have also prohibited the intentional distribution of software that could be used to falsify e-mail header or routing information when that software has little use outside of such falsification.

The following states have enacted laws regulating spam:

- Arkansas. Ark. Code §§ 5-41-201, *et seq.* (2001).
- California. Cal. Bus. & Prof. Code §§ 17538.4, *et seq.* and Cal. Penal Code § 502 (West 2000).
- Colorado. Colo. Rev. Stat. §§ 6-2.5-101, *et seq.* (2000).
- Connecticut. Conn. Gen. Stat. § 53-451 (2001).
- Delaware. Del. Code. Ann. tit. 11, §§ 931, *et seq.* (1999).
- Idaho. Idaho Code § 48-603E (2000).
- Illinois. 815 Ill. Comp. Stat. 511/1-10 (West 2000).
- Iowa. Iowa Code Ann. § 714.E (West 2000).
- Kansas. 2002 Kan. Senate Bill 467 (2002).

- Louisiana. La. Rev. Stat. Ann. § 73.1-6 (West 2000).

- Maryland. Md. Laws 323 and 324 (2002).

- Minnesota. Minn. Laws 395 (2002), effective March 1, 2003.

- Missouri. Mo. Rev. Stat. §§ 407.020 *et seq.* (2000).

- Nevada. Nev. Rev. Stat. §§ 41.705, *et seq.* (1999).

- North Carolina. N.C. Gen. Stat. §§ 14-453, 14-458 (1999).

- Ohio. Ohio Rev. Code Ann. § 2307.64 (West 2002).

- Oklahoma. Okla. Stat. tit. 15, § 776 (2000).

- Pennsylvania. Pa. Cons. Stat. § 5903 (2000).

- Rhode Island. R.I. Gen. Laws §§ 6-47-1, *et seq.*, and §§ 11-52-1, *et seq.* (1999).

- South Dakota. S.D. Codified Laws § 37-24-6, and §§ 37-24-36, *et seq.* (2002).

- Tennessee. Tenn. Code Ann. §§ 47-18-2501, *et seq.* (1999).

- Utah. Utah Code §§ 13-34-101, *et seq.* (2002).

- Virginia. Va. Code Ann. § 18.2-152 (Michie 1999).

- Washington. Wash. Rev. Code § 19.190 (1999).

- West Virginia. W. Va. Code § 46A-6G (1999).

- Wisconsin. Wis. Stat. § 944.25 (2001).

Constitutionality and Application of State Spam Laws

State anti-spam laws have been challenged on constitutional grounds:

State v. Heckel, 24 P.3d 404 (Wash. 2001).

On October 29, 2001, the U.S. Supreme Court declined to hear an appeal of a challenge to Washington State's anti-spam law. The Washington Supreme Court had upheld the law on June 7, 2001, on an appeal from a ruling by a trial court that the law was unconstitutional. The trial court had held that the State of Washington could not successfully sue Jason Heckel of Salem, Oregon, under Washington's anti-spam law because the Commerce Clause of the U.S. Constitution gives Congress and the federal government the power to regulate interstate commerce and implies that states are limited in the ways that they can regulate businesses located in other states. The trial court noted that the anti-spam statute could subject a person to 50 standards of conduct and that this inconsistency could be problematic under the Commerce Clause. The State of Washington appealed directly to the state supreme court, which reversed the trial court's ruling and held that Washington's anti-spam law does not unduly burden interstate commerce. The court opined that the act applies equally to in-state and out-of-state spammers and serves the legitimate local interest of eliminating the cost shifting that occurs when deceptive spam is sent. The only requirement the Act places on spammers, the court held, is truthfulness in the subject lines of e-mail messages.

In September 2002, Heckel was found liable under the anti-spam statute. On October 18, 2002, the court ordered Heckel to pay fines of more than $98,000 for sending the misleading and unsolicited commercial e-mails. This marks the first time such a fine has been levied by a U.S. court against a defendant under an anti-spam statute. Heckel has indicated that he plans to appeal the judgment.

Ferguson v. Friendfinder Inc., 94 Cal. App. 4th 1255, 115 Cal. Rptr. 2d 258 (Cal. Ct. App. 2002).

The California Court of Appeal for the First District recently ruled that California's anti-spam statute is constitutional and valid. The appeals panel reasoned that the law did not discriminate against out-of-state actors, regulate commerce occurring wholly outside the state, conflict with other states' laws regulating spam, or unduly burden interstate commerce. Weighing the costs of unsolicited commercial e-mail to consumers and ISPs against the costs of complying with the law, the court concluded that the statute's affirmative-disclosure requirements did not "impose any appreciable burden" on senders of spam. The court rejected the defendant's claim that it was impossible to determine the residence of an e-mail recipient, and, therefore, impossible to determine when it was necessary to comply with the statute. Instead, the court held that a commercial e-mail sender's decision to comply with the law "all the time" in order to avoid the need for determining the recipient's physical location would amount to nothing more than "a business decision [that] simply does not establish" a constitutional violation. On April 10, 2002, the California Supreme Court denied the defendant's request for review of the appeals court decision.

People v. Willis, No. CV811428 (Cal. App. Dep't Super. Ct., filed Sept. 26, 2002).

On September 26, 2002, California's attorney general filed suit against PW Marketing, a California bulk-mail marketing company, that allegedly sent millions of unlawful unsolicited e-mails to California residents. The state seeks an injunction and civil penalties of at least $2 million.

Chart of State Statutes

The following chart outlines the provisions of the current state statutes relating to unsolicited commercial e-mail and lists the states that have enacted such restrictions:

Typical Provisions in State Unsolicited Commercial E-mail Statutes	Statutes Containing Such Provisions
DEFINITION OF "SPAM"	
Does not include commercial e-mail sent by a party who has a prior business or personal relationship with the recipient.	California, Colorado, Delaware, Illinois, Kansas, Minnesota, Nevada, North Carolina, Ohio, Rhode Island, Washington, West Virginia.
Prohibits any commercial e-mail sent without express consent or request from the recipient.	California, Colorado, Delaware, Illinois, Nevada, Rhode Island, Tennessee, Washington, West Virginia.
Exempts Internet service providers who merely transfer the unsolicited commercial e-mail via their networks.	Arkansas, California, Delaware, Idaho, Iowa, Maryland, Missouri, Nevada, Ohio, Rhode Island, Tennessee, Virginia, Washington, West Virginia.
Exempts organizations that send unsolicited commercial e-mail to their members.	Colorado, Connecticut, Delaware, Idaho, Iowa, Louisiana, Minnesota, North Carolina, Rhode Island, Virginia.

Typical Provisions in State Unsolicited Commercial E-mail Statutes	Statutes Containing Such Provisions
Exempts free e-mail service providers (such as Hotmail or Yahoo!) that require their members to consent to receiving unsolicited advertisements from certain authorized third parties as a condition of signing up a free e-mail account.	Idaho, Iowa, Maryland.
Exempts an employer sending e-mails to employees.	Colorado, Minnesota.
Exempts electronic mail advertisements voluntarily accessed by the recipient from an electronic bulletin board or other source.	Idaho, Iowa, Nevada.
REQUIRED DISCLOSURE	
Requires mailer to use specific language in an e-mail's subject line to disclose its commercial nature (*e.g.*, "ADV:," "ADV:ADLT," "ADVERTISEMENT," "COMMERCIAL E-MAIL," etc.).	California, Colorado, Kansas, Minnesota, Pennsylvania, South Dakota, Tennessee, Utah, Wisconsin.
Requires mailer to disclose the actual point of origin of the e-mail, so that the transmission information cannot be falsified or misrepresented.	Colorado, Idaho, Illinois, Iowa, Kansas, Oklahoma, Rhode Island, South Dakota, Utah, Virginia, West Virginia.
UNSUBSCRIBE PROVISIONS	
Requires mailer to provide a cost-free method for recipient to notify mailer not to send further e-mail. (Possible methods include a toll-free phone number, sender-operated e-mail, etc.)	California, Colorado, Idaho, Iowa, Kansas, Minnesota, Missouri, Nevada, Ohio, Rhode Island, Tennessee, Utah.
Requires mailer to inform recipients in a conspicuous manner of how to notify mailer not to send further e-mail.	California, Kansas, Minnesota, Ohio, Rhode Island, Tennessee, Utah.
Requires that the mailer stop sending e-mail to any recipient who so requests.	California, Colorado, Idaho, Iowa, Kansas, Ohio, Rhode Island, Tennessee, Utah.

Typical Provisions in State Unsolicited Commercial E-mail Statutes	Statutes Containing Such Provisions
ACCURATE SENDER, ROUTING, AND SUBJECT LINE INFORMATION	
Prohibits false or misleading information in the subject line.	Kansas, Maryland.
Prohibits falsification of transmission information or any other routing information.	Arkansas, Colorado, Connecticut, Delaware, Idaho, Illinois, Iowa, Kansas, Louisiana, Maryland, Minnesota, North Carolina, Ohio, Oklahoma, Pennsylvania, Rhode Island, Virginia, Washington, West Virginia.
Prohibits using a third party's name as the name of the sender without that third party's permission.	Arkansas, Colorado, Idaho, Illinois, Iowa, Kansas, Maryland, Minnesota, Rhode Island, Washington, West Virginia.
Requires e-mail to contain sender information (name, address, etc.)	Nevada, Ohio, Rhode Island, Utah, Washington, West Virginia.
Prohibits distribution of software that would enable falsification of e-mail transmission information.	Kansas, Oklahoma, Rhode Island, Tennessee, Virginia.
CONTENT RESTRICTION	
Prohibits sending of sexually explicit materials via unsolicited commercial e-mail.	Pennsylvania, Utah, West Virginia.
REMEDIES	
Classifies the first offense as a misdemeanor.	California, Connecticut, Delaware, Illinois, Louisiana, North Carolina, Pennsylvania, Utah, Virginia.

Typical Provisions in State Unsolicited Commercial E-mail Statutes	Statutes Containing Such Provisions
Escalates the offense to a felony under certain circumstances (such as recklessness, malice, actual damages above a certain monetary limit, multiple offenses).	Arkansas, California, Connecticut, Illinois, Louisiana, North Carolina, Pennsylvania, Rhode Island, Virginia.
Permits a recipient of unsolicited commercial e-mail to recover actual damages.	California, Colorado, Connecticut, Idaho, Illinois, Iowa, Kansas, Maryland, Minnesota, Missouri, Nevada, North Carolina, Oklahoma, Rhode Island, Tennessee, Virginia, Washington, West Virginia.
Permits a recipient of unsolicited commercial e-mail to recover, in lieu of actual damages, the lesser of either a fixed amount per e-mail (generally, $10) or per day (generally, $25,000).	Colorado, Connecticut, Illinois, Minnesota, Nevada, North Carolina, Oklahoma, Rhode Island, South Dakota, Tennessee, Utah, Virginia.
Permits a recipient of unsolicited commercial e-mail to recover, in lieu of actual damages, the greater of either a fixed amount per e-mail (generally, $10) or per day (generally, $1,000).	Idaho, Iowa, Missouri, Washington, West Virginia.
Permits an e-mail service provider to recover, in lieu of actual damages, the greater of either a fixed amount per e-mail (generally, $10) or per day (generally, $25,000).	California, Colorado, Connecticut, Illinois, Iowa, Maryland, Minnesota, Missouri, North Carolina, Ohio, Oklahoma, Rhode Island, Tennessee, Virginia, Washington, West Virginia.
Permits a recipient of unsolicited commercial e-mail to recover a fixed amount for each violation ($100), not to exceed a maximum amount ($50,000).	Ohio.

Additionally, some states are considering legislation to prohibit unsolicited text messages to mobile telephones. California Governor Davis signed such a bill in September 2002, to be effective January 2003. *See* Cal. Bus. & Prof. Code § 17538.41. The Arizona and New Jersey legislatures are considering similar bills.

Pending Federal Legislation

Currently, there is no federal law regulating spam. This is likely to change in the near future, however, given the volume of unsolicited commercial e-mail. The Direct Marketing Association announced in January 2003 that it advocates federal regulation of spam. The DMA had opposed most anti-spam bills, but now supports federal legislation as an alternative to an array of perhaps conflicting state anti-spam laws. Congress has considered various bills that would regulate spam:

CAN SPAM Act of 2001

The CAN SPAM (Controlling the Assault of Non-Solicited Pornography and Marketing) Act of 2001 (S. 630; related bill: Unsolicited Commercial Electronic Mail Act of 2001 (H.R. 95)) would make it illegal to send unsolicited, commercial e-mail messages containing false-sender information. The sender would also be required to include a valid return e-mail address and allow recipients to opt-out of receiving future e-mails. The bill would grant enforcement authority to the FTC. On May 17, 2002, the CAN SPAM Act was approved by the Senate Commerce Committee and ordered to be favorably reported to the Senate. On October 16, 2002, the committee submitted written report No. 107-318 and the bill was placed on the Legislative Calendar, No. 735.

Anti-Spamming Act of 2001

Introduced in March 2001, the Anti-Spamming Act of 2001 (H.R. 1017) would make it illegal to send unsolicited, bulk e-mail messages containing a false-sender address or header, as well as to distribute software designed to conceal the source of or routing information about e-mail messages. This bill was referred to committee and hearings were held in May 2001. No further activity has been reported.

Wireless Telephone Spam Protection Act

The Wireless Telephone Spam Protection Act (H.R. 113) was introduced in January 2001 and addresses the use of wireless messaging systems and cellular phones to send unsolicited advertisements. This bill has been referred to committee, with no further action reported since February 2001.

Unsolicited Commercial Electronic Mail Act of 2001

The Unsolicited Commercial Electronic Mail Act of 2001 (H.R. 718) would require network operators to contact every unwelcome marketer and ask them to stop sending messages before any legal action could be taken. The bill would also require that senders of bulk e-mail provide valid return e-mail (as well as physical mail) addresses to allow consumers to opt-out of receiving further electronic mailings. Once the consumer has opted-out, the sender would be prohibited from passing that consumer's e-mail address along to a third party. Under this bill, a consumer would have a private right of action against a sender that did not remove the consumer's name from a distribution list upon request, with penalties of $50 per violation, up to a maximum of $50,000. The bill includes explicit language declaring that the federal government has a substantial public interest in regulating spam; such language will likely be important if the bill is challenged on First Amendment commercial speech grounds in the future. H.R. 718 was introduced in February 2001 and was approved by the Energy and Commerce Committee in March 2001. On May 5, 2001, the bill was placed on the Union Calendar, No. 43.

Unsolicited Commercial Electronic Mail Act of 2001

The Unsolicited Commercial Electronic Mail Act of 2001 (H.R. 95) would require unsolicited commercial e-mail messages to be labeled and to include clear opt-out instructions. The use of false headers would be prohibited, as would using a provider's facilities to send such messages if the provider's policies against such use are clearly posted on its website. This bill was introduced in the House in January 2001 and is identical to amended H.R. 3113, passed in the House on July 18, 2000, by a vote of 427 to 1. This bill was referred to committee on February 12, 2001, with no further action reported.

FTC Enforcement Efforts

On February 12, 2002, the Federal Trade Commission announced a new three-point program designed to crack down on deceptive spam. Although no federal law expressly regulates the practice of sending unsolicited commercial e-mail, the FTC announced its intent to step up enforcement in this area under its general statutory mandate to prohibit false or deceptive trade practices. The announcement reported:

1. The settlement of charges against seven defendants accused of distributing a deceptive e-mail chain letter that promised returns of $46,000 on an investment of $5;

2. The issuance of warning letters to more than 2,000 individuals suspected of continuing to run this same e-mail chain letter scheme; and

3. The launch of a consumer-education effort, co-sponsored by

various ISP associations, to warn e-mail users about the dangers of illegal chain mail.

Although the current initiative focuses on e-mail chain letters and Internet pyramid schemes, Howard Beales, the Director of the FTC's Bureau of Consumer Protection, indicated that the Commission plans to "launch a systematic attack on fraudulent and deceptive spam." Speaking at the Second Annual Privacy & Data Security Summit on January 31, 2002, Beales told conference attendees that his bureau would work on cases involving false opt-out mechanisms and misleading unsubscribe links that only serve to verify and confirm the validity of a spam recipient's e-mail address. Anti-spam activists also expect the FTC to investigate the use of fraudulent return addresses in unsolicited commercial e-mail. The FTC's current commercial e-mail initiatives appear to target hardcore deceptive practices. Nonetheless, the step-up in enforcement could signal an FTC interest in more extensively regulating online marketing practices.

Self-Regulation

Sixteen companies, including some of the largest online marketers, founded a group called the Responsible Electronic Communications Alliance (RECA) to deal with the issue of spamming. The group (currently with 13 members) plans to propose standards and enforcement mechanisms for industry self-regulation. Both the members of RECA and the FTC favor self-regulation over legislative measures. On September 25, 2000, RECA issued draft privacy and enforcement principles aimed at ensuring that e-mails are only sent to willing recipients. The draft policy is available on the RECA website at http://www.responsibleemail.org.

Mail Abuse Prevention Systems, LLC (MAPS), maintains a real-time "Blackhole List" of entities it considers to be spammers, and distributes it to ISPs who use the list to block electronic mail from those listed. MAPS has faced numerous lawsuits from companies that objected to being listed on the Blackhole List. In January 2001, a federal district court in Massachusetts ruled that a plaintiff was unlikely to prevail in a defamation charge because of MAPS's truth defense. *Media3 Technologies LLC v. Mail Abuse Prevention System LLC*, No. 00-CV-12524-MEL, 2001 U.S. Dist. LEXIS 1310 (D. Mass. Jan. 2, 2001).

In August 2000, a federal trial court in New York similarly rejected a motion for preliminary injunction, finding that the plaintiff would suffer no irreparable harm from being listed by MAPS. *Harris Interactive Inc. v. Mail Abuse Prevention System, LLC*, No. 00-CV-6364L(F) (W.D.N.Y.

August 8, 2000). However, in November 2000, the U.S. District Court for the District of Colorado entered a temporary injunction preventing MAPS from listing Exactis.com (now Experian Emarketing, Inc.) on the Blackhole List, on the ground that Exactis.com was likely to be able to prove its claim that MAPS's listing unlawfully interfered with Exactis' business relationships. *Exactis.com, Inc. v. Mail Abuse Prevention System, LLC*, No 00-K-2250 (D. Colo. Nov. 20, 2000). MAPS settled the lawsuit by agreeing not to list the company again without first obtaining leave from the court.

Litigation

A number of cases have already addressed the legality of spam and the rights that consumers and businesses have with respect to spam. These cases have been brought under a number of legal theories, including, among other things, trespass, privacy, computer fraud, unfair competition, and breach of contract.

Cyber Promotions, Inc. v. America Online, Inc., 948 F. Supp. 436 (E.D. Pa. 1996).

Cyber Promotions, a business that sent millions of e-mails per day to AOL e-mail accounts, sued AOL because AOL had blocked Cyber Promotions e-mails from reaching AOL users. In the first major decision relating to spam, the court found that Cyber Promotions had no constitutional right to send spam. The judge later denied Cyber Promotions' claim that AOL was an "essential service" to which it had a right of access under antitrust law.

CompuServe, Inc. v. Cyber Promotions, Inc., 962 F. Supp. 1015 (S.D. Ohio 1997).

CompuServe, an Internet service provider, sued Cyber Promotions to stop it from sending spam to CompuServe users. Cyber Promotions had repeatedly ignored CompuServe's requests to stop spamming CompuServe customers, and CompuServe had been unable to block Cyber Promotions' spam through technical means. The judge issued a preliminary injunction to stop Cyber Promotions from spamming CompuServe users, finding that continued spamming constituted a trespass on CompuServe's computers. The parties subsequently settled their dispute.

🔨 *America Online, Inc. v. Netvision Audiotext, Inc. d/b/a Cyber Entertainment Network*, No. 99-CV-1186 (E.D. Va., amended complaint filed Dec. 22, 2000).

America Online sued Netvision Audiotext, an online adult-entertainment company, claiming that Netvision created "incentives" for its affiliated third-party Webmasters to send spam to AOL customers on Netvision's behalf. The lawsuit alleged violations of the Virginia Computer Crimes Act and federal Computer Fraud and Abuse Act, among other statutes. In April 2002, the parties settled pursuant to a court order requiring Netvision to pay an undisclosed amount of monetary damages to AOL and to discontinue soliciting Netvision affiliates to send spam.

🔨 *Classified Ventures, LLC v. Softcell Marketing, Inc.*, 109 F. Supp. 2d 898 (N.D. Ill. 2000).

Some spammers have tried to mask the source of their mass e-mail campaigns by using false return e-mail addresses. In this case, Softcell Marketing, a company that provides promotional services via spam e-mails, mounted a promotion of various pornographic sites using Classified Ventures' cars.com domain in the return address for their e-mails. Softcell was permanently enjoined from using the cars.com domain on the basis of service mark infringement, dilution, and unfair competition.

🔨 *Earthlink Inc. v. Doe*, No. 1:01cv02099 (N.D. Ga., complaint filed Aug. 7, 2001); *Earthlink Inc. v. Krantz*, No. 1:01cv02098 (N.D. Ga., complaint filed Aug. 7, 2001); *Earthlink Inc. v. Smith*, No. 1:01cv02099 (N.D. Ga., complaint filed Aug. 7, 2001).

On August 7, 2001, Internet service provider Earthlink filed suit against several defendants alleging that sending spam via Earthlink's systems violated the Electronic Communications Privacy Act, 18 U.S.C. §§ 2701, *et seq.*, the Computer Fraud and Abuse Act, 18 U.S.C. § 1030, the Lanham Act, and other federal and state laws. Earthlink maintained that the defendants used stolen credit-card numbers to purchase accounts from Internet service providers, used stolen passwords to obtain access to third parties' e-mail accounts, and used all of these stolen accounts to send spam. Earthlink sought damages, treble damages, punitive damages, attorney fees, and an injunction barring the defendants from sending spam to any Internet user; engaging in the theft or misuse of third-party credit-card numbers, passwords, or e-mail accounts; and using any computer or device to obtain Internet access.

➤ *Intel v. Hamidi*, 114 Cal. Rptr. 2d 244 (Cal. Ct. App. 2001), *review granted*, March 27, 2002

The California Court of Appeal, citing recent spam cases, ruled that the time employees spend reading and blocking electronic mail messages was enough to satisfy the injury requirements in a trespass to chattels claim. On six occasions, Hamidi, a disgruntled former Intel employee sent messages disparaging the company to between 8,000 and 35,000 Intel employees. The trial court had ruled that even though the messages did not damage the company's proprietary computer networks, the harm was sufficient to satisfy a trespass to chattels claim. On March 27, 2002, the California Supreme Court granted review of the court of appeal's decision.

➤ *Morrison & Foerster, LLP v. Etracks.com Inc.*, No. 40494 (Cal. Super. Ct., San Francisco, Cty., filed Feb. 6, 2002).

The plaintiff, Morrison & Foerster LLP, a California law firm, filed a complaint against Etracks, which sent Morrison & Foerster employees spam in violation of California's anti-spam law, Cal. Bus. & Prof. Code § 17538.45 and in violation of Morrison & Foerster's company policy. The law firm alleged that Etracks had actual notice of Morrison & Foerster's e-mail policy prohibiting unsolicited e-mail advertisements (based on the fact the firm sent the defendant an e-mail message to email-remove@response.etracks.com), and that the firm's e-mail equipment is located in California, as required to allege a violation of § 17538.45. The firm requested liquidated damages of $50 per unsolicited e-mail advertisement received, plus attorney fees and costs.

➤ *MonsterHut, Inc. v. PaeTec Communications, Inc.*, 294 A.2d 945 (N.Y. App. Div. 2002).

A New York State trial court issued a temporary restraining order prohibiting Internet service provider PaeTec from terminating the alleged spammer, MonsterHut, Inc., from its network. The ISP had received complaints that MonsterHut was sending unsolicited e-mails in violation of its contract, which represented it was a fully consensual, e-mail marketing service. MonsterHut argued that, under the parties' agreement, the spam restriction only would apply if more than 2 percent of the people who received MonsterHut's e-mails complained. An appeals court reversed the trial court ruling on May 3, 2002, stating that the parties' agreement prohibited MonsterHut from engaging in spamming. On May 8, 2002, PaeTec disconnected MonsterHut from its network.

On May 17, 2002, the State of New York filed suit against MonsterHut for fraudulently advertising that the company's e-mail marketing service was opt-in or "permission based." The suit alleged that many consumers who did not opt-in nonetheless received commercial e-mail. *New York v. Monsterhut Inc.*, No. 402140-02 (N.Y. Sup. Ct., complaint filed May 17, 2002).

Gillman v. Sprint Communications, No. 020406640 (Utah Dist. Ct., filed Aug. 1, 2002).

A class-action suit seeking to enforce Utah's anti-spam legislation was filed against Sprint. The suit sought damages of $10 per day for each unwanted e-mail, plus court costs. In a decision announced February 28, 2003, the court held "the email at issue in this case does not fit the statutory definition of an 'unsolicited commercial email' under the Utah statute" and granted Sprint's motion for summary judgment.

International Spam Laws

After two years of lobbying by consumer groups and Internet service providers, in May 2002, the European Parliament passed a strict anti-spam measure, called the Telecommunications Data Protection Directive. The Directive adopts an opt-in approach: companies may not send unsolicited e-mails to prospective customers unless they have previously agreed to receive them. This approach is quite different from the largely opt-out-based U.S. spam legislation. The Directive is now in the process of being ratified by the European Union's member states. Seven EU countries, Austria, Denmark, Finland, Germany, Greece, Italy, and Spain, ban spam (as well as unsolicited telemarketing and faxes). Britain does not bar spam. "Ofcom," Britain's recently created telecommunications and broadcasting regulatory agency, will not regulate the Internet or spam. In December 2002, Members of Parliament failed to win support for a bill that would have compelled Ofcom to ban some types of spam.

Australia is also considering proposals for legislation to combat spam. Australia's National Office for the Information Economy released its "Spam Interim Review Report" in late July 2002, summarizing its recommendations, including improving ISP support in combating spam, improving filtering systems, and passing legislation intended to protect consumers.

PERSONAL JURISDICTION

Personal Jurisdiction Basics

A defendant may be sued in the state in which he or she resides. When the defendant is not a resident of the place where the suit is brought, a court may require the defendant to stand trial only where the court properly exercises "personal jurisdiction" over the defendant. *World-Wide Volkswagen Corp. v. Woodson*, 444 U.S. 286, 291 (1980). Each state has a so-called "long-arm statute" that defines the circumstances under which the state's courts may exercise jurisdiction over out-of-state defendants. The reach of these long-arm statutes is circumscribed by the Due Process Clause of the United States Constitution.

Assuming the requirements of the forum state's long-arm statute are satisfied, a court may assert personal jurisdiction over a non-resident defendant either through the exercise of "general jurisdiction" or "specific jurisdiction." *Helicopteros Nacionales de Colombia, S.A. v. Hall*, 466 U.S. 408 (1984).

Specific Jurisdiction

When the litigation is related to or arises out of the defendant's contacts with the forum state, a court may properly assert jurisdiction over the defendant through the exercise of specific jurisdiction. *Helicopteros*, 466 U.S. at 414. Specific jurisdiction is properly exercised over a non-resident defendant via a state's long-arm statute when the defendant has "minimum contacts" with the forum such that maintenance of the suit does not offend "traditional notions of fair play and substantial justice," and the defendant would reasonably have been able to anticipate being hauled into court in the forum state. *World-Wide Volkswagen Corp.*, 444 U.S. at 291-92; *Int'l. Shoe Co.*, 326 U.S. at 316. If a non-resident defendant has "purposefully directed" his or her activities toward a state's residents or businesses and benefits from the protections provided by that state's laws, then the forum has specific jurisdiction over disputes arising from those contacts. *Burger King Corp. v. Rudzewicz*, 471 U.S. 462, 472 (1985).

General Jurisdiction

When the litigation does not relate to or arise out of the defendant's contacts with the forum state, a court may properly assert jurisdiction over the defendant only through the exercise of general jurisdiction. *International Shoe Co. v. Washington*, 326 U.S. 310, 318 (1945). General jurisdiction is properly exercised over a non-resident defendant only when the defendant is present in the forum state or maintains "continuous and systematic" contacts with the state. *Helicopteros Nacionales de Colombia, S.A.*, 466 U.S. at 414-16.

Personal Jurisdiction and the Internet

The existence of personal jurisdiction has traditionally been analyzed according to territorial concepts by which a non-resident defendant may understand that he or she is expected to abide by the forum state's legal rules. *See Digital Equip. Corp. v. AltaVista Tech., Inc.*, 960 F. Supp. 456, 462-63 (D. Mass. 1997). Commercial activities on the Internet, however, operate without traditional territorial boundaries. Though some magazines and a few newspapers have long enjoyed national distribution, the Internet permits immediate distribution to a national and international audience to an extent not available through other media. An online order form permits a retailer to complete sales without ever setting foot in a forum state, while a chat room may make defamatory comments available in every forum in the U.S. with minimal effort or planning on the part of the participants. Courts therefore must determine whether jurisdiction may attach over a non-resident defendant where the contacts involved are primarily, or even exclusively, electronic.

Although courts have generally analyzed cyberspace jurisdictional issues under the framework established for analyzing traditional jurisdictional issues, certain methods of analysis specific to cyberspace are developing. For example, courts analyzing personal jurisdiction in the Web publishing context factor electronic contacts, as well as traditional physical contacts, into their analyses to determine whether either specific or general jurisdiction may be properly exercised. *See EDIAS Software Int'l, L.L.C. v. BASIS Int'l Ltd.*, 947 F. Supp. 413 (D. Ariz. 1996). Courts also consider the nature of those electronic contacts; jurisdiction is more likely to be asserted in cases involving interactive websites than those involving passive websites. *See Zippo Mfg. Co. v. Zippo Dot Com, Inc.*, 952 F. Supp. 1119 (W.D. Pa. 1997).

In addition, many courts have used an "effects test" to analyze personal jurisdiction in tort cases, taking into consideration whether the forum state is the focal point of both the harmful activity and the harm created, or, similarly, whether the defendant intended to cause injury in, and knew injurious effects would be felt in, the forum state. *See Calder v. Jones*, 465 U.S. 783 (1984).

Finally, some courts have also adopted the *Keeton* test, which traditionally has been used in determining whether a court can properly exercise jurisdiction over a print publication. Under the *Keeton* test, continuous and deliberate circulation of a Web publication in a forum state can subject the publisher to personal jurisdiction in that state, regardless of whether the publication was targeted to a nationwide audience. *See Keeton v. Hustler Magazine, Inc.*, 465 U.S. 770 (1984); *Naxos Resources (U.S.A.) Ltd. v. Southam Inc.*, 24 Media L. Rep. 2265 (C.D. Cal. May 30, 1996). These methods of analysis, which are often used in conjunction with one another, are discussed below.

Totality of the Contacts

In determining whether a state may exercise personal jurisdiction over a non-resident defendant in the context of online communications, courts often use a "totality of the contacts" analysis, taking into account the defendant's electronic contacts, such as sales conducted via a website, as well as its physical contacts, such as attendance at a trade convention in the forum state. *See Telephone Audio Prod., Inc. v. Smith*, 1998 WL 159932 (N.D. Tex. 1998). Some examples of this analysis are described below.

Cases in Which the Totality of the Contacts Was Such That Exercise of Jurisdiction Was Found to Be Proper

EDIAS Software Int'l, L.L.C. v. BASIS Int'l Ltd., 947 F. Supp. 413 (D. Ariz. 1996).

EDIAS, an Arizona-based company, entered into a contract to distribute software for BASIS, a New Mexico-based company. BASIS subsequently became dissatisfied with EDIAS and terminated the contract. BASIS then posted a press release on its website and sent electronic mail messages to EDIAS customers stating that it had terminated the contract because EDIAS refused to guarantee customers a fair price and failed to provide technical support in selling BASIS software. EDIAS filed suit against BASIS in Arizona for, among other things, defamation and tortious interference with contract and prospective advantage.

The court found it appropriate to exercise specific jurisdiction over BASIS because BASIS had purposefully availed itself of the privilege of doing business in Arizona and therefore should have been able to predict that it would be subjected to jurisdiction in the state. In reaching this conclusion, the court not only focused on the fact that BASIS posted allegedly defamatory statements on its website and sent allegedly defamatory electronic messages into Arizona, but also noted, among other things, that BASIS had entered into a contract with, EDIAS, an Arizona corporation; had contacted EDIAS employees via telephone and facsimile in Arizona; had sold products to EDIAS for distribution; had sent invoices to EDIAS in Arizona; and had sent employees to visit Arizona.

See also Telephone Audio Prod., Inc. v. Smith, 1998 WL 159932, Case No. CIV A.3:97-CV-0863-P (N.D. Tex. 1998) (finding exercise of specific jurisdiction was proper because the defendant purposefully availed itself of the laws of Texas by traveling to Texas, selling products to Texas residents and targeting Texas residents in its marketing, which included operating a website that was accessible in Texas).

National Football League v. Miller, 2000 U.S. Dist. LEXIS 3929, 54 U.S.P.Q.2d 1575 (S.D.N.Y. 2000).

The defendant maintained a website, located at nfltoday.com, that was designed so that a visitor could click on a hyperlink and immediately connect to the official National Football League website, which was then framed by the defendant's nfltoday.com site. The defendant's website also contained banner ads for online gambling ventures. The plaintiff, the NFL, claimed that the defendant's website caused damage to the NFL in New York by linking the NFL's trademarks to gambling activities. In denying the defendant's motion to dismiss for lack of personal jurisdiction, the court noted that the defendant must have recognized that, because there were two NFL teams with a major New York presence, it was likely that this site "would ultimately appear on thousands of computer screens in New York." *Id.* The fact that the defendant earned substantial revenue from the website via advertising directed to New Yorkers was also a factor in the court's decision.

Metro-Goldwyn-Mayer Studios Inc. v. Grokster, Ltd., Case No. 01-08541 SVW (C.D. Cal., filed Oct. 2, 2001).

Record labels, film studios, and music publishers brought a copyright infringement action against distributors of software that allows file-sharing of digital works. The plaintiffs contend that KaZaA and other services violate copyright law by allowing their users to share protected works. (KaZaA already has more users than Napster did at its peak.) A Dutch court ruled that KaZaA was not responsible for the infringing activities of its users when Dutch copyright holders brought a similar action. *See Buma/Stemra v. Kazaa*, Amsterdam Court of Appeals (March 28, 2002), discussed in the Copyright section at page 116.

After U.S. plaintiffs had brought their action in a federal court in California, Sharman, Inc., purchased KaZaA's assets. Sharman is incorporated in the island nation of Vanuatu, with its principal place of business in Australia. Its computer servers operate from Denmark, and the source code for its software is alleged to be in Estonia. Sharman moved to dismiss the case for lack of personal jurisdiction. It argued that its only presence in California (and in the U.S.) is via its presence on the Internet, which by itself should not subject it to jurisdiction.

In January 2003, the District Court for the Central District of California rejected Sharman's contention and held that the court had personal jurisdiction over KaZaA. The KaZaA software has been downloaded an estimated 143 million times by Internet users in the United States. The court assumed that at least two million of those users are in California. Additionally, Sharman's distribution of the software is a commercial act. Because of Sharman's significant and commercial contact with California residents, there is a presumption that jurisdiction is proper. The court also noted that Sharman was well aware of the claims that its users infringe copyrights, and reasonably should have been aware that many music and video copyrights are owned by companies based in California. Accordingly, the court concluded that Sharman had purposely availed itself of the right to conduct commercial activity in California, with knowledge that its actions might impact the rights of California entities. Exercise of jurisdiction over KaZaA/Sharman, the court concluded, was appropriate.

On January 27, 2003, shortly after the court denied Sharman's motion to dismiss for lack of personal jurisdiction, Sharman filed suit against the copyright holder plaintiffs, alleging antitrust violations and seeking to enjoin them from enforcing their copyrights.

Cases in Which the Totality of the Contacts Was Such That Exercise of Jurisdiction Was Found Not to Be Proper

 Digital Control Inc. v. Boretronics Inc., et al., 161 F. Supp. 2d 1183 (W.D. Wash. 2001).

The defendants, Boretronics Inc. and Willie Lessard of Minnesota, designed and manufactured a transmitter for use in underground drilling. They advertised this transmitter in two industry journals, created a website offering the transmitter for sale, and maintained a toll-free number to handle customer inquiries and orders. The plaintiff, Digital Control Inc., brought suit in federal court in Washington alleging that the defendants had infringed its patents. The defendants sought dismissal of the plaintiff's claims for lack of personal jurisdiction. The court agreed.

The court found that "the defendants' limited contacts with the State of Washington [were] not such that they 'should reasonably anticipate being haled into court' [there]." 161 F. Supp. 2d at 1185. The court adopted the "website plus" rule, under which something more than nationwide advertising is needed to justify the exercise of personal jurisdiction. While the industry journals, website, and phone number by which the defendants advertised and sold their product were nationally distributed, the defendants did not receive any inquiries from or make any sales to residents of Washington. Therefore, because the defendants only used indiscriminate, nationwide forms of advertising, the court concluded that they had not availed themselves of the privilege of doing business in Washington.

Amberson Holdings v. Westside Story Newspaper, 110 F. Supp. 2d 332 (D.N.J. 2001).

The plaintiff, holder of the "West Side Story" trademark, sued in New Jersey claiming that the defendant's use of the mark in its newspaper title and domain name constituted infringement. The defendant operated its "Westside Story Newspaper" in Southern California and administered the content of its website there as well, but it assigned the website's "westsidestory.com" domain name to a host server owned and operated by a New Jersey corporation. Other than its contact with the host server, the defendant had never advertised, solicited, or conducted any business with New Jersey residents.

The court held that the defendant's contacts with New Jersey were not sufficient to support an exercise of personal jurisdiction because the written contract with the New Jersey corporation, in the absence of other contacts with the state, did not amount to the necessary "minimum contacts" with the forum. The court noted that the defendant had never made direct sales to New Jersey, solicited or advertised to sell its product there, made any shipment of merchandise directly into or through the state, maintained an office in the state, or owned any real or personal property there. The court found that the defendant's website constituted nothing more than a "passive advertisement"—it provided information about the defendant's company, displayed ads of outside vendors, and gave viewers the option to contact the company via e-mail.

The court also rejected the plaintiff's contention that the defendant's use of a New Jersey server provided sufficient additional contacts with the forum for the court to exercise personal jurisdiction.

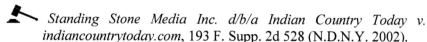

Standing Stone Media Inc. d/b/a Indian Country Today v. indiancountrytoday.com, 193 F. Supp. 2d 528 (N.D.N.Y. 2002).

Standing Stone owns *Indian Country Today*, a well-known, Native American newspaper, with an online version published at www.indiancountry.com. In January 2000, the newspaper's management decided to register additional domain names based on its trademark, "Indian Country Today." Two weeks after the decision to register the additional domain names (but before any action was taken), Miles Morrisseau, the newspaper's editor in chief, was fired. One week after he was fired, Morrisseau registered in his own name the domain names that Standing Stone had planned to register.

Standing Stone filed suit against Morrisseau in the Northern District of New York alleging cybersquatting. Morrisseau resided in Ontario, Canada, and had registered the name from there with Register.com, a domain-name registrar located in the Southern District of New York. The court determined that the controlling statute, the Anticybersquatting Consumer Protection Act (ACPA), did not provide jurisdiction over the defendant in a forum in which neither the domain-name registrar nor the defendant was located.

Nam Tai Electronics, Inc. v. Joe Titzer, 93 Cal. App. 4th 1301 (Cal. Ct. App. 2001).

A Colorado resident posted 246 messages on Yahoo!'s Internet message boards concerning Nam Tai, a consumer electronic-products manufacturer incorporated under the laws of the British Virgin Islands, based in Hong Kong, and traded on the NASDAQ exchange. To post to Yahoo! message boards, the defendant was required to register an alias, or Yahoo! ID, and to agree to Yahoo!'s terms of service, which state that California law governs the relationship between the person registering and Yahoo!. Nam Tai contended that at least three of the messages were false, misleading, or otherwise unlawful.

In the appellate court's view, "the determinative question is whether the websites themselves are of particular significance to California or Californians such that the user has reason to know the posting of a message will have significant impact on the state." The court found that Nam Tai failed to show sufficient contacts between the Colorado defendant and California to justify the court's exercise of personal jurisdiction. Specifically, there was no evidence that the defendant's messages or the message boards on which they were posted were directed at or disproportionately likely to be read by Californians. The court also rejected the plaintiff's argument that the Yahoo! Choice-of-law provision created jurisdiction over the defendant, finding that the Yahoo! terms of service only governed the relationship between Yahoo! and its users, not the relationship between Yahoo! and the libel plaintiff, Nam Tai.

Wildfire Communications, Inc. v. Grapevine, Inc., No. 00-CV-12004-GAO (D. Mass., Sept. 28, 2001).

Wildfire Communications, a Massachusetts-based company, was contacted via e-mail by Grapevine, Inc., an Illinois-based Internet service provider, in an effort to market Grapevine's online "business card" product, available for $14.95 a month. Through this contact, Wildfire learned of Grapevine's registration of the domain name "wildfire.net." Although Wildfire did not purchase Grapevine's product, it subsequently agreed to purchase Grapevine's "wildfire.net" domain name for $10,000. When the deal fell through, Wildfire sued Grapevine in federal court in Massachusetts, alleging trademark infringement and unfair competition.

The U.S. District Court in Massachusetts refused to assert personal jurisdiction based on the agreement to purchase the domain name. The court noted that "[t]he sum of defendant's contacts with Massachusetts include three web pages ... a contract with a Massachusetts corporation for the sale of a domain name ... and a one-time, unsuccessful solicitation." No. 00-CIV-12004-GAO at *7. The court found that these contacts with Massachusetts were not sufficient to satisfy the constitutional minimum-contacts test.

See also Hartcourt Cos. v. Hogue, Case No. 5D01-683 (Fla. Ct. App. June 7, 2002) (the defendant's maintenance of a website accessible in Florida, combined with a debt to be paid a Florida resident for finding investors, did not constitute sufficient minimum contacts).

Machulsky v. Hall, 210 F. Supp. 2d 531 (D.N.J. 2002).

The plaintiff, a New Jersey resident, bought and sold collectable coins on the eBay online auction site. She sued out-of-state customers for mail fraud, wire fraud, extortion, conspiracy, tortious interference with prospective economic advantage, and other related claims. The court determined it could not assert jurisdiction over the defendants. First, the defendants did not have sufficient minimum contacts with the state as a result of their transactions on eBay to allow the assertion of specific jurisdiction. In addition, the e-mail correspondence between the plaintiff and the defendants did not constitute purposeful availment by the defendants of the right to do business in New Jersey. Finally, the negative-feedback statements that the defendants posted on eBay about the plaintiff were considered "passive," analogous to the *Zippo* passivity standard (discussed below).

Nature of the Web Site (the Zippo Test)

In determining whether a non-resident defendant's website is sufficient to confer personal jurisdiction on the courts of a state in which the website is accessed, various courts have looked to the nature of the defendant's website to determine the appropriateness of exercising jurisdiction. To date, as a general rule, the more interactive the site, the more likely a court will exercise jurisdiction over the non-resident defendant. In determining whether a site is interactive, courts consider whether a site exchanges information with a user and is more commercial in nature (*e.g.*, sites that permit online product orders or allow users to exchange files with the server) or whether the site merely provides general information, much as a traditional print advertisement does.

The nature-of-the-website jurisdictional analysis was articulated in *Zippo Mfg. Co. v. Zippo Dot Com, Inc.*, 952 F. Supp. 1119 (W.D. Pa. 1997). In *Zippo*, the court stated that based on its review of the relevant case law, the likelihood that personal jurisdiction can be constitutionally exercised "is directly proportionate to the nature and quality of commercial activity that an entity conducts over the Internet." 952 F. Supp. at 1124. The court identified three categories of Internet activity:

1. The court noted that "[a]t one end of the spectrum are situations where a defendant clearly does business over the Internet. If the defendant enters into contracts with residents of a foreign jurisdiction that involve the knowing and repeated transmission of computer files over the Internet, personal jurisdiction is proper." (*citing CompuServe, Inc. v. Patterson*, 89 F.3d 1257 (6th Cir. 1996)).

    See, e.g., Quokka Sports, Inc. v. Cup Int'l, Ltd., 99 F. Supp. 2d 1105 (N.D. Cal. 1999) (specific jurisdiction in trademark infringement suit was proper where the court aggregated the foreign defendant's contacts with the U.S. and those contacts were interactive and involved commercial activity targeted at the U.S. market).

2. The "middle ground" along the spectrum "is occupied by

interactive websites where a user can exchange information with the host computer. In these cases, the exercise of jurisdiction is determined by examining the level of interactivity and commercial nature of the exchange of information that occurs on the website." (*citing Maritz, Inc. v. Cybergold, Inc.*, 947 F. Supp. 1328 (E.D. Mo. 1996)).

See also, e.g., People Solutions, Inc. v. People Solutions, Inc., 2000 U.S. Dist. LEXIS 10444, Civil Action No. 3:99-CV-2339-L (N.D. Tex. 2000) (the defendant's website could interact with, sell products to, and contract with residents of the forum, but there was no evidence that the website had done so; therefore, the court ruled there was no personal jurisdiction over the defendant); *Efford v. The Jockey Club*, Civ. No. 1621 EDA 2001, 2002 Pa. Super. 100 (Pa. Super. Ct., April 5, 2002) (the defendant's website provided general information about The Jockey Club and permitted users to register foals online, but the plaintiff failed to allege how many Pennsylvania foals had been registered on the website; therefore, the court ruled there was no personal jurisdiction over the defendant).

3.   The far end of the spectrum involves "situations where a defendant has simply posted information on an Internet website which is accessible to users in foreign jurisdictions. A passive website that does little more than make information available to those who are interested in it is not grounds for the exercise of personal jurisdiction." (*citing Bensusan Restaurant Corp. v. King*, 937 F. Supp. 295 (S.D.N.Y. 1996), *aff'd*, 126 F.3d 25 (2d Cir. 1997)).

See also, e.g., Mink v. AAAA Development, L.L.C., 190 F.3d 333 (5th Cir. 1999) (personal jurisdiction in copyright infringement suit was not proper where the defendant's website merely provided users with a printable, mail-in order form, a toll-free telephone number, a mailing address, and an e-mail address); *American Homecare Fed'n, Inc. v. Paragon Scientific Corp.*, 27 F. Supp. 2d 109 (D. Conn. 1998) (personal jurisdiction in trademark-infringement suit was not proper where the defendant's website merely provided a toll-free number and did not list any products for sale, provide any downloadable files, or contain any e-mail links); *Jewish Defense Org., Inc. v. Superior Court*, 85 Cal. Rptr. 611 (Cal. Ct. App. 1999) (personal jurisdiction in defamation suit was not proper, in part because the defendant merely contracted via computer with Internet service providers in the forum state and maintained a passive, informational website that did not seek to attract readers to site and did not capture or retrieve information from visitors).

Cases in Which the Nature of the Web Site Was Such That Exercise of Jurisdiction Was Found to Be Proper

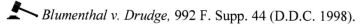 *Blumenthal v. Drudge,* 992 F. Supp. 44 (D.D.C. 1998).

White House aide and former journalist Sidney Blumenthal and his wife sued Matt Drudge, publisher of the "Drudge Report," and America Online for libel, invasion of privacy, and intentional infliction of emotional distress based on allegations appearing in the "Drudge Report." The plaintiffs were residents of the District of Columbia, the forum state. Drudge's base of operations for writing, publishing, and disseminating the Drudge Report was California, where he resided. Drudge moved to dismiss or to transfer for lack of personal jurisdiction.

In conducting its jurisdictional analysis, the court applied both the *Zippo* analysis and the "effects test" (discussed below at pages 245-260) and denied the defendant's motion to dismiss. The court focused primarily on the prong of the District of Columbia long-arm statute permitting jurisdiction to be exercised over a non-resident defendant who has "engage[d] in [a] ... persistent course of conduct [in the District of Columbia]." 992 F. Supp. at 53. The court found that Drudge had engaged in a persistent course of conduct in the District both because he operated "an interactive website that is accessible to and used by District of Columbia residents and, [because] ... he has had sufficient non-Internet related contacts with the District of Columbia," which included soliciting contributions from District residents. *Id.* at 56. The court further concluded that exercising jurisdiction over Drudge would not violate his constitutional rights because the District long-arm statute did "not reach the outer limits of due process. . . ." *Id.* at 58.

In analyzing the "level of interactivity" of the "Drudge Report," the court, relying on the *Zippo* framework, rejected Drudge's contention that his site was "passive." *Id.* at 56. Rather, the court concluded that "[t]he constant exchange of information and direct communication that District of Columbia Internet users are able to have with Drudge's host computer via his website is the epitome of website interactivity." *Id.* The court noted that users who access the website may request subscriptions to the "Drudge Report" by e-mailing their requests to Drudge's host computer and, in turn, as each new edition of the Report is created, it is sent to every e-mail address on Drudge's subscription mailing list.

For a discussion of this case in the context of service provider immunity under the Communications Decency Act of 1996, *see* Chapter 4, pages 137-138.

Ty, Inc. v. Baby Me, Inc., 2001 U.S. Dist. LEXIS 5761 (N.D. Ill. 2001).

The plaintiff, Ty, a Delaware corporation with its principal place of business in Illinois, sued the defendant, Baby Me, a Hawaii corporation, for copyright, trademark, and trade dress infringement. Ty owned numerous copyrights for "plush toys" marketed as "Beanie Babies" and also owned numerous federal trademark registrations, as well as common-law trademark and trade dress rights in a variety of marks associated with those toys. Baby Me manufactured and sold plush toy bears in Hawaii under the name "Baby Me Bears," and for seven months, the defendant also sold the bears online via its website, shipping the bears to customers' places of business or residences. The Baby Me website included an order form, pictures of the bears, and pricing information. Ty alleged that the "Baby Me Bears" infringed its copyrights and trade dress because they were confusingly and substantially similar to its "Beanie Babies" plush toys, and infringed its trademark rights by including the word "beanies" as a metatag on its website. (For discussion of trademark issues arising out of the use of metatags, *see* Chapter 2, pages 81-84.) According to Ty, an Illinois consumer purchased three "Baby Me Bears" from the website and had them shipped into the state.

Citing *Zippo*, the court found that the exercise of specific jurisdiction over Baby Me was proper because Baby Me's interactive website facilitated product ordering and shipping, indicating to the court that Baby Me intended to conduct business with consumers throughout the entire United States, including Illinois. Also important to the court was the sale of "Baby Me Bears" to at least one Illinois resident, which further indicated to the court that the company did business in Illinois over the Internet.

School Stuff, Inc. v. School Stuff, Inc., No. 00 C 5593, 2001 WL 558050 (N.D. Ill. May 21, 2001).

The plaintiff, School Stuff, Inc., an Indiana corporation and holder of the "School Stuff" trademark, sued the defendant, an Arizona corporation by the same name, in an Illinois court alleging trademark infringement and dilution based on the defendant's use of the "School Stuff" mark. Both parties sold educational and school supplies. The plaintiff alleged that personal jurisdiction in Illinois was proper because the defendant did business on the Internet totaling $8,748.61 in sales, of which $447.09 were made to Illinois residents.

After concluding that the defendant's sales in the state of Illinois were not "continuous and systematic" such that general jurisdiction could be asserted, the court applied the *Zippo* analysis and determined that specific jurisdiction was proper. The court concluded that the defendant had conducted business over the Internet with Illinois residents and therefore purposefully had availed itself of the privilege of doing business in the state. The court also noted that Illinois' interest in adjudicating injuries such as trademark infringement relating to companies located within its borders outweighed the burden on the defendant in having to appear before an Illinois court.

See also Park Inns Int'l, Inc. v. Pacific Plaza Hotels, Inc., 5 F. Supp. 2d 762 (D. Ariz. 1998) (finding personal jurisdiction proper where the defendants maintained websites through which hotel reservations could be made and through which seven reservations were solicited and completed by residents of the forum state); *Audi AG v. Izumi*, 204 F. Supp. 2d 1014 (E.D. Mich. 2002) (finding personal jurisdiction proper where the defendant's website enabled users in Michigan to place product orders and solicited business from Michigan residents).

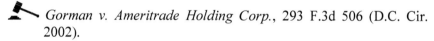 *Gorman v. Ameritrade Holding Corp.*, 293 F.3d 506 (D.C. Cir. 2002).

The plaintiff, David Gorman of Virginia, alleged Ameritrade.com breached a contract by removing a hyperlink to Gorman's website. The link had been posted on Freetrade.com, which Ameritrade purchased. Gorman alleged that his prior contract with Freetrade.com barred removal of the link by the new owner. The trial court found that Ameritrade, which had its principal place of business in Nebraska, was not subject to either specific or general jurisdiction in the District of Columbia, and dismissed the case before Gorman could discover the number of customers Ameritrade had in the forum.

The U.S. Court of Appeals for the District of Columbia Circuit disagreed, finding that Ameritrade's highly interactive website may provide sufficient "continuous and systematic" contacts to establish general jurisdiction in the forum. The court noted that Ameritrade's website allows customers to buy or sell stocks 24 hours a day, which would likely be sufficient to satisfy the requirement of D.C.'s long-arm statute that the defendants "do business" in the District. *Gorman*, 293 F.3d at 514. However, the court ultimately dismissed the case because Gorman had failed to properly serve the complaint on Ameritrade.

The court rejected Ameritrade's argument that its stock transactions took place in "cyberspace," rather than within the territorial boundaries of the forum. The court stated that "Ameritrade is quite wrong in treating 'cyberspace' as if it were a kingdom floating in the mysterious ether, immune from the jurisdiction of earthly courts." *Id.* at *25.

Computeruser.com, Inc. v. Technology Publications LLC, No. 02-832, 2002 U.S. Dist. LEXIS 13453 (D. Minn., July 20, 2002).

The interactive features of the "Sexiest Geek Alive" website were sufficient to permit assertion of personal jurisdiction over the site's operators. The plaintiff was Computeruser.com, a Minnesota company and publisher of the nationwide magazine *Computer User*. The defendant, Technology Publications, was a licensee, authorized to produce and distribute the plaintiff's magazine in Texas. Computeruser.com sued Technology Publications for trademark infringement for allegedly continuing to use computeruser.com's mark on its website without authorization after the termination of the license agreement. The defendant's site featured message boards, free e-mail, and regular communication with users, including the "Sexiest Geek Alive" contest. Over 18,000 applications to enter the contest were submitted via the website in two months' time, including, the court presumed, some from Minnesota residents.

In re Ski Train Fire in Kaprun, Austria on Nov. 11, 2000, No. 01-CIV-6554, 2002 U.S. Dist. LEXIS 14563 (S.D.N.Y., Aug. 6, 2002).

The accessibility and interactivity of a website were found sufficient to support assertion of jurisdiction over a foreign corporation that otherwise did not do business within the forum state in a suit that did not relate to website activities. In a lawsuit filed over a fatal accident, New York residents established jurisdiction over a Munich company based on the interactivity of its website. Other defendants in the case, who did not avail themselves of the right to do business in New York by operating an interactive website, successfully moved for dismissal based on lack of personal jurisdiction. *See Ski Train Fire*, No. 01-CIV-6554, 2002 U.S. Dist. LEXIS 17566 (S.D.N.Y., Sept. 19, 2002).

Cases in Which the Nature of the Web Site Was Such That Exercise of Jurisdiction Was Found Not to Be Proper

Cybersell, Inc. v. Cybersell, Inc., 130 F.3d 414 (9th Cir. 1997).

The plaintiff, Cybersell, Inc., an Arizona corporation and holder of the "Cybersell" service mark, sued the defendant, a Florida corporation by the same name, for service-mark infringement based on its use of the "Cybersell" mark on its website. The plaintiff, which provided Internet advertising, marketing, and consulting services, had no website and had not yet been granted a registration for the "Cybersell" mark when the defendant decided to offer Web page construction and consulting services under the Cybersell name. The district court granted the defendant's motion to dismiss for lack of personal jurisdiction, and the plaintiff appealed. The plaintiff conceded that the Arizona court did not have general jurisdiction over the defendant, but alleged that specific jurisdiction could be properly exercised.

The court held that the exercise of specific jurisdiction was not proper because the defendant's use of the "Cybersell" mark on its website was passive and the defendant conducted no commercial activity in Arizona. The defendant's website merely displayed information about the defendant's services and included an e-mail link for inquiries related to those services. No Arizona resident could contract with the defendant via the website, and there was no evidence that the defendant had entered into any contract or conducted any business with any resident of Arizona. Additionally, with the exception of an e-mail from the plaintiff, there was no evidence of any online communication between the defendant and Arizona residents. Therefore, the court concluded that the defendant had not taken any action or consummated any transaction by which it purposefully availed itself of the privilege of conducting business in Arizona.

Copperfield v. Cogedipresse, 26 Media L. Rep. (BNA) 1185 (C.D. Cal. 1997).

Magician David Copperfield brought a libel action against the author, publisher, and distributors of *Paris Match* magazine. Copperfield alleged that a story published in *Paris Match* contained false and defamatory information about his relationship with model Claudia Schiffer. Copperfield argued, among other things, that the existence of a *Paris Match* website established general jurisdiction over the defendant in California. The court, although concluding that the website was sufficiently interactive and commercial in nature to fall within the second ("middle ground") category identified in *Zippo*, declined to find personal jurisdiction on that basis, noting, among other things, that the "interactivity [was] limited" and the commercial aspect of the site "consist[ed] almost entirely of advertising." 26 Media L. Rep. at 1188. The court also declined to assert specific jurisdiction under the "effects test" (discussed below at pages 245-260). The court did not state whether the allegedly defamatory statements at issue were available on the *Paris Match* website.

Mallinckrodt Medical, Inc. v. Sonus Pharmaceuticals, Inc., 989 F. Supp. 265 (D.D.C. 1998).

The defendant, in Seattle, posted an allegedly defamatory message on an AOL bulletin board that resided on a Web server located in Virginia. Pointing to that message, the plaintiff claimed that a District of Columbia court had jurisdiction since approximately 200,000 District of Columbia residents are subscribers to AOL with potential access to the posting. In rejecting this argument, the court relied on the long-arm statute of the District of Columbia, which, in relevant part, required that the non-resident defendant "transact ... business" in the District of Columbia. 989 F. Supp. at 270. The court concluded that the defendant's conduct failed to satisfy this requirement because "[t]he [allegedly defamatory] message was not sent to or from the District of Columbia, the subject matter of the message had nothing to do with the District of Columbia, and neither plaintiffs nor [defendant] reside in, have their headquarters in or are incorporated in the District." *Id.* at 272. The court further noted that the act of merely posting a message on an electronic bulletin board, which users may or may not choose to access, is not sufficient to confer personal jurisdiction over a non-resident defendant.

Barrett v. Catacombs Press, 44 F. Supp. 2d 717 (E.D. Pa. 1999).

The defendant, an Oregon resident, allegedly defamed the plaintiff, a Pennsylvania resident who ran a well-known website called "Quackwatch," by allegedly posting statements on two websites. In addition, the defendant allegedly posted messages regarding the plaintiff on various national listservs and USENET discussion groups with links back to the defendant's websites. The defendant moved to dismiss the plaintiff's lawsuit for lack of personal jurisdiction.

The court, following the analysis used by the court in *Zippo,* examined the nature and quality of the defendant's contacts over the Internet. The court concluded that the defendant's websites were entirely passive, and that such sites were insufficient to trigger jurisdiction in the forum state absent evidence that the defendant was targeting

Pennsylvania residents. In addition, the court stated that although the defendant's posting of messages to listservs and USENET discussion groups differed from passive websites because such "messages [were] actively disseminated to those who participate[d] in such groups," such contacts nevertheless also were insufficient to establish personal jurisdiction over the defendant in Pennsylvania. 44 F. Supp. 2d at 728. The court based its ruling on the fact that the listserv and USENET postings "were accessible around the world and never targeted nor solicited Pennsylvania residents." *Id.*

Desktop Technologies, Inc. v. Colorworks Reproduction & Design, Inc., No. 98-5029, 1999 U.S. Dist. LEXIS 1934 (E.D. Pa. Feb. 25, 1999).

The plaintiff, a Pennsylvania corporation and owner of the U.S. trademark "Colorworks," brought suit against the defendant, a Canadian company that owned the Canadian registration for the same mark, for trademark infringement and unfair competition resulting from the defendant's use of the mark in its domain name. The defendant operated its business exclusively in British Columbia and had never transacted business with residents of Pennsylvania. However, the defendant maintained a website, accessible to all Internet users, including those in Pennsylvania, that displayed general information about the company, advertisements for the company, and a listing of employment opportunities with company. The site listed local telephone and fax numbers and specifically stated that the defendant serviced clients in the local area. The defendant moved to dismiss the lawsuit for lack of personal jurisdiction.

The court granted the defendant's motion, holding that personal jurisdiction could not be asserted because the defendant's website was merely a passive advertisement. The court first rejected the plaintiff's argument for general jurisdiction, reasoning that the website's e-mail links, which were its only interactive element, were "the electronic equivalents of advertisements' response cards," the use of which is insufficient by itself to establish general jurisdiction. 1999 U.S. Dist. LEXIS 1934 at *9, *quoting Grutkowski*, 1998 WL 962042 at *5. The court then rejected the plaintiff's argument for specific jurisdiction because the level of interactivity on the defendant's website was such that it could be considered passive under the *Zippo* analysis. The court noted that the defendant's had never transacted business in Pennsylvania and its website did not exist for the purpose of attracting or entering into contracts with consumers outside of Canada.

➤ *Mid City Bowling Lanes & Sports Palace, Inc. v. Ivercrest, Inc.*, 35 F. Supp. 2d 507 (E.D. La. 1999), aff'd without opinion, 208 F.3d 1006 (5th Cir. 2000).

The plaintiff, Mid City Bowling Lanes operated a bowling alley in New Orleans, Louisiana, where patrons could bowl while listening to live musical entertainment. Mid City coined the phrase "Rock 'N' Bowl" to advertise this entertainment combination and subsequently was granted a federal registration for the "Rock 'N' Bowl" trademark. The defendant, Ivercrest, used the "Rock 'N' Bowl" mark in association with the Diversey River Bowl, a bowling alley it owned and operated in Chicago, Illinois. Ivercrest used the "Rock 'N' Bowl" mark in Diversey's local advertising campaign, on Diversey's website, and in its domain name. After becoming aware of Ivercrest's use of the mark on the Diversey website, Mid City sued Ivercrest alleging trademark infringement and unfair trade practices. The defendant moved to dismiss the suit for lack of personal jurisdiction.

After noting the local nature of the bowling services being sold by each entity, the court held that the defendant's use of the plaintiff's mark on an Internet website that was available to anyone who had Internet access was an insufficient basis for the exercise of personal jurisdiction. The website merely contained the mailing address and local phone number of the defendant's facility and other information concerning entertainment options at the bowling alley. There was no evidence that the defendant had any contact with Louisiana other than by making the website available to Louisiana residents. Internet users could not make any purchases or engage in any direct communication with the defendant through the website. Therefore, the court found that the plaintiff had failed to establish "minimum contacts" sufficient to support either specific or general jurisdiction.

➤ *Callaway Golf Corp. v. Royal Canadian Golf Assn.*, 125 F. Supp. 2d 1194 (C.D. Cal. 2000).

The defendant, the Royal Canadian Golf Association (RCGA), announced publicly through its website and other media that it would not permit the use of certain golf clubs in its regulation tournaments. Callaway, a California manufacturer of one of the prohibited clubs, brought several claims in federal court in California, including defamation, based on the announcement. RCGA filed a motion to dismiss for lack of personal jurisdiction. The plaintiff replied that jurisdiction in California could be established on the basis of the RCGA website, which was accessible in California.

The court held that RCGA had not purposefully availed itself of the privileges and protections of California law through the maintenance of its website. The decision noted that the site was both passive, as it displayed general information about golf and the Association, and interactive, as it allowed users to purchase tickets to RCGA-sponsored golf tournaments and other items. Few Californians had taken advantage of the commercial aspects of the site, and the revenue from the commercial activity as a whole comprised less than 1 percent of the defendant's sales. The court maintained that even if the site were more interactive, personal jurisdiction still could not be exercised over the defendant. It reasoned that the operation of the website had no relationship to the claims of the plaintiff. Because the press release itself was more like an advertisement (*i.e.*, passive in nature) and not directed specifically at the forum, the court dismissed the suit for lack of personal jurisdiction over the Canadian defendant.

Lofton v. Turbine Design, Inc., 100 F. Supp. 2d 404 (N.D. Miss. 2000).

The plaintiffs, a Mississippi-based, aircraft-conversion company that designed and developed engine applications and several of its shareholders, sued a Florida-based competitor (TDI), for posting allegedly defamatory statements to its website about one of the plaintiff's aircraft designs. The defendant moved to dismiss for lack of personal jurisdiction.

The plaintiff argued that the accessibility of the defendant's website to Mississippi residents was sufficient to establish personal jurisdiction. Using a *Zippo* analysis, the court noted that TDI's website was used solely to advertise its services and was purely passive in nature. The court dismissed the case for lack of personal jurisdiction because "[t]he website [did] not contain a price list for services, contract for engagement of services, or order form."

Bailey v. Turbine Design, Inc., et al., 86 F. Supp. 2d 790 (W.D. Tenn. 2000).

The plaintiff, a resident of Tennessee, brought suit in Tennessee for libel, tortious interference with contract, and conspiracy, based on a website produced by the defendants that contained, among other things, allegations of technical problems associated with the plaintiff's work and the plaintiff's criminal history, and a reference to the plaintiff's company as a group of "con artists." The defendants, a Florida corporation and a Florida resident, moved to dismiss for lack of personal jurisdiction. In granting the defendants' motion to dismiss for lack of personal jurisdiction, the court applied both the *Zippo* analysis and the "effects test" (discussed below at pages 245-260).

In holding that there was no personal jurisdiction under the criteria set forth in *Zippo*, the court stated that "[h]ere, there is no indication whatsoever that the website is anything other than wholly passive" and that "the allegedly defamatory statements were merely posted on the website to be viewed by whomever cared to do so." 86 F. Supp. 2d at 795. The court further noted that there was "no evidence to suggest that any effort was made to reach out to Tennessee residents any more than to persons residing elsewhere," and, in fact, there was no indication that any Tennessee resident except for the plaintiff ever visited the website. *Id.*

Amazon.com, Inc. v. Kalaydjian, 2001 U.S. Dist. LEXIS 4924 (W.D. Wash. Feb. 20, 2001).

The plaintiff, whose principal place of business was in Washington, alleged that the defendant, Kalaydjian, infringed and diluted its trademark through the marketing of his sun-tanning products in California. The defendant marketed his products on a website bearing the domain name, AmazonTan.com. On the website, customers could receive information about his products, but they could not exchange information with the defendant or purchase his products.

After deciding that general jurisdiction over the defendant was lacking, the court dismissed the action for want of specific jurisdiction. Though the defendant's registered domain name was similar to the plaintiff's trademark, the posting of a website bearing that name was not sufficient to indicate that the defendant had taken advantage of the privilege of conducting business in Washington. Similarly, the shipment of a single bottle of suntan lotion to a Washington resident in response to a request from the resident did not constitute purposeful availment of the benefits of Washington. The website was not sufficiently interactive to confer jurisdiction because, in the court's eyes, it did little more than provide information available to those who were interested in it. Finally, communications between the two parties concerning the alleged trademark infringement did not establish a basis for jurisdiction in Washington.

Remick v. Manfredy, 52 F. Supp. 2d 452 (E.D. Pa. 1999), *aff'd*, 238 F. 3d 248 (3d Cir. 2001).

The plaintiff, a Pennsylvania attorney, sued a former client (a boxer), the client's advisers, and an Illinois law firm representing his former client for, among other things, libel. The alleged libel arose out of a letter to the plaintiff (copied to one of the other defendants) from the Illinois law firm, which alleged that the plaintiff had engaged in certain misconduct. The defendants, none of whom resided in the forum state of Pennsylvania, moved to dismiss the lawsuit for lack of personal jurisdiction.

The plaintiff argued that the court could exercise general jurisdiction over the defendant boxer and the Illinois law firm, because they maintained websites that purportedly solicited business in Pennsylvania. The court disagreed, granting the defendants' motion to dismiss. Using the *Zippo* analysis, the court concluded that both websites were "passive" in nature and that "there [was] no evidence that they [were] interactive or offer[ed] anything other than general information and advertising." "Advertising on the Internet has been held to fall under the same rubric as advertising in a national magazine and it is well settled law in [the Third] Circuit that advertising in a national publication does not constitute the 'continuous and substantial contacts with the forum state' required to give rise to a finding of general jurisdiction."

The Court of Appeals for the Third Circuit affirmed. *See also Resnick v. Manfredy*, 52 F. Supp. 2d 462 (E.D. Pa. 1999) (concerning companion action, where court issued an opinion virtually identical to *Remick*).

 Robbins v. Yutopian Enterprises Inc., Civ. No. CCB-01-3096 (D. Md. May 15, 2002).

The plaintiff, Charles Robbins of Pennsylvania, sued the California-based defendant Yutopian Enterprises for copyright infringement in federal court in Maryland. The defendant allegedly placed an unauthorized copy of the plaintiff's software, which allows users to play an online version of the ancient board game "Go," on the defendant's website, Yutopia.com.

The federal district court found that it lacked personal jurisdiction over the defendant, though Yutopia.com had completed 46 sales to Maryland residents over 10½ months via the website and telephone orders. The court found those contacts did not provide the "continuous and systematic" presence required for general jurisdiction. The court also concluded that the plaintiff's copyright claim did not arise out of those Maryland contacts, and so could not give rise to specific jurisdiction.

ALS Scan, Inc. v. Digital Service Consultants, Inc., 293 F.3d 707, No. 01-1812 (D.C. Cir. 2002), *cert. denied*, No. 02-463 (U.S. Jan. 13, 2003).

The Maryland-based plaintiff ALS Scan, a company that creates and markets adult photographs of female models, alleged that the defendant, a Georgia-based Internet service provider, infringed its copyright rights by allowing one of its website customers to copy hundreds of the plaintiff's photographs and place them on his website. The defendant ISP argued that it had no contracts with persons or businesses in the forum state of Maryland, conducted no business in Maryland, had no offices in Maryland, and did not advertise in Maryland other than through its website, which was equally accessible to Internet users everywhere.

The federal trial court in Maryland found that it had no general or specific jurisdiction over the defendant, and the Court of Appeals for the Fourth Circuit agreed. The court of appeals adapted a version of the *Zippo* test specifically for websites that target or direct activity at a forum state: "[A] State may, consistent with due process, exercise judicial power over a person outside of the State when that person (1) directs electronic activity into the State, (2) with the manifested intent of engaging in business or other interactions in the State, and (3) that activity creates ... a potential cause of action cognizable in the State's courts." *Id.* at *11. Under this modified test, non-residents who operate "passive" websites remain immune from personal jurisdiction in foreign states. *Id.* Applying this test, the court concluded that the defendant's activity was, at most, passive activity and did not subject it to the jurisdiction of the Maryland court.

The U.S. Supreme Court is to decide if it will review the Fourth Circuit's decision.

See also Newspaper Association of America v. Mancusi, Civ. Action No. 01-1635-A (E.D. Va. May 8, 2002) (the defendant's website, which served as a portal to newspaper websites from across the nation, did not seek any information from users and did not offer sale of any goods or services, so it did not meet the due-process requirement for minimum contacts).

Donmar, Inc. v. Swanky Partners, Inc., No. 02-C-1482, 2002 U.S. Dist. LEXIS 15308 (N.D. Ill., Aug. 19, 2002).

An out-of-state nightclub's website that allowed users to sign up for a mailing list and receive local driving directions did not have sufficient minimum contacts with the forum to support jurisdiction. The court also considered favorably the defendant's attempts to limit the area in which it conducted business by editing its mail list and only providing directions from within its home state. Such acts suggested to the court that the website was not targeting out-of-staters. Accordingly, the defendant nightclub should not be subject to the court's jurisdiction.

Nexgen Solutions, Inc. v. Nexgen Solutions Corp., No. AW-02-736 (D. Md., Aug. 28, 2002).

The plaintiff, Nexgen Solutions, Inc., held a federal trademark registration for NEXGEN SOLUTIONS INC. Nexgen Solutions, Inc. sued the defendant over its use of the trademark in Nexgen Solutions, Corp.'s domain name. The court determined that use of a trademark in a domain name is insufficient to establish jurisdiction. The court relied on *Zippo* in characterizing the defendant's site as passive, and therefore not sufficient to subject the defendant to personal jurisdiction in the forum.

Aero Prods Int'l, Inc. v. Intex Corp., No. 02 C 2590 (N.D. Ill., Sept. 20, 2002).

In a patent infringement suit over the design of an air mattress, the U.S. District Court for the Northern District of Illinois ruled that an operator of a website that merely advertised the mattress was not subject to specific jurisdiction. The court found that the defendant did not specifically direct its advertising to forum residents because the site involved only a moderate degree of interactivity (under the *Zippo* analysis), did not allow sales, and did not exchange information with its users.

Accuweather, Inc. v. Total Weather, Inc., No. 4-CV-02-006, 2002 U.S. Dist. LEXIS 18576 (M.D. Pa., Oct. 2, 2002).

The plaintiff alleged that the defendant improperly registered domain names that included the plaintiff's trademark. The court granted the defendant's motion to dismiss based on lack of jurisdiction because the court found that the defendant lacked minimum contacts necessary to subject it to jurisdiction in the forum. The court transferred the action from Pennsylvania to the Western District of Oklahoma, where the defendants resided and where all its Internet activities originated.

Effects Test

Many courts looking to decide whether a publisher may be sued in a foreign jurisdiction have used an "effects test" to determine whether the forum state "is the focal point both of the story and the harm suffered." *Calder v. Jones*, 465 U.S. 783, 788 (1984). When confronted with online distribution of a publication, some courts have similarly examined whether the defendant intended to cause injury in the forum state and whether the non-resident defendant knew that the "effects" of such injury would be felt in the forum state.

The courts often place emphasis on whether the forum state was the target or focus of the defendant's activities. For example, in libel cases, the defendant's comments must have been directed against the individual in his local capacity, not against his national persona. *See Blumenthal v. Drudge*, 992 F. Supp. 44 (D.D.C. 1998). Similarly, some courts have reasoned that the "effects test" is less applicable to international and national corporations, as such companies are not confined to a particular geographic location. *See Conseco, Inc. v. Hickerson*, 698 N.E. 2d 816 (Ind. Ct. App. 1998). Also, in domain-name disputes, the mere posting of a website with a domain name that contains another corporation's trademark will not be enough to subject the publisher to jurisdiction in a particular forum absent some purposeful targeting of the forum or knowledge of the plaintiff's whereabouts prior to posting. *See American Info. Corp. v. American Infometrics, Inc.*, 139 F. Supp. 2d 696 (D. Md. 2001). However, purposeful targeting of the forum state is not dispositive, and some courts exercise personal jurisdiction even in the absence of targeted activity if the harm itself occurs in the forum state. *See Peregrine Financial Group, Inc. v. Green*, 2001 U.S. Dist. LEXIS 14317 (N.D. Ill. Aug. 28, 2001).

Cases in Which the "Effects Test" Was Applied and Assertion of Jurisdiction Was Found to Be Proper

California Software, Inc. v. Reliability Research, Inc., 631 F. Supp. 1356 (C.D. Cal. 1986).

Reliability Research operated an Internet bulletin-board service that allowed users to post or view messages. The plaintiffs alleged that Reliability Research had made false and defamatory statements to users residing outside of California about the plaintiffs' right to market certain software.

Citing *Calder*, the court noted that personal jurisdiction may be exercised where the defendant's intentional, out-of-state conduct is directed at the forum state. The court concluded that Reliability Research was subject to personal jurisdiction in California because it had intentionally directed communications over its online service to third parties outside of California with the intent to cause harm in California. "Because defendants intentionally influenced third parties to injure the California plaintiffs, defendants should have foreseen answering for the veracity of their statements and the propriety of their conduct in California." 631 F. Supp. at 1362.

EDIAS Software Int'l, L.L.C. v. BASIS Int'l Ltd., 947 F. Supp. 413 (D. Ariz. 1996).

In addition to finding specific jurisdiction on grounds that BASIS had purposefully availed itself of the laws of Arizona (in the *Cybersell* case discussion above at page 237), the court found that "BASIS' e-mail messages to Arizona and ... website which reaches Arizona customers ... confer jurisdiction in Arizona under the 'effects test.'" 947 F. Supp. at 420. The court determined that "BASIS directed the e-mail, Web page, and forum message at Arizona because Arizona is EDIAS' principal place of business." *Id.* Although the court did not mention the number of e-mail messages sent to Arizona or whether evidence showed that any Arizona user had in fact accessed the BASIS website, it nevertheless ruled that exercising personal jurisdiction over BASIS was appropriate because BASIS could have foreseen that its actions might cause a loss of potential customers to EDIAS in Arizona. *Id.* at 422.

Blumenthal v. Drudge, 992 F. Supp. 44 (D.D.C. 1998).

The court, in addition to exercising personal jurisdiction over Drudge because of the interactivity of his website (discussed above at page 233) and because of his non-Internet related contacts with the District, also determined that jurisdiction was appropriate under an "effects test." The court noted that "[b]y targeting the Blumenthals who work in the White House and live in the District of Columbia, Drudge knew that 'the primary and most devastating effects of the [statements he made] would be felt' in the District of Columbia." 992 F. Supp. at 57 (citation omitted). Thus, Drudge "should have had no illusions that he was immune from suit here." *Id.*

Panavision Int'l, L.P. v. Toeppen, 141 F.3d 1316 (9th Cir. 1998).

In *Panavision*, the court of appeals affirmed the trial court's decision to exercise personal jurisdiction over an out-of-state defendant who registered "panavision.com" as an Internet domain name and thereby prevented Panavision International, a California-based business, from using its own trademark as a domain name. The court noted that the defendant had engaged in a scheme to register Panavision's trademark "for the purpose of extorting money from Panavision." Because the defendant's conduct "had the effect of injuring Panavision in California where Panavision has its principal place of business and where the movie and television industry is centered," the "effects test" was satisfied.

For a discussion of this case in the cybersquatting context, *see* Chapter 2, page 49.

Blakey v. Continental Airlines, Inc., 730 A.2d 854 (N.J. Super. Ct. 1999), *rev'd and remanded*, 751 A.2d 538 (N.J. 2000).

The plaintiff, a pilot with Continental Airlines, alleged that she was libeled by certain online postings made by the defendants on the Continental Crew Management System, which provides Continental crew members, pilots, and flight attendants with flight information, schedules, and a bulletin board on which to exchange information and opinions. The plaintiff alleged that the defendants, who were Continental pilots, had posted on the Crew Management System bulletin board certain defamatory statements relating to the plaintiff's skills as a pilot and the motives behind a lawsuit that she had filed against Continental. All but one of the defendants resided outside of New Jersey, as did the plaintiff. Nevertheless, the plaintiff asserted that the New Jersey court could exercise jurisdiction over the defendants because the alleged defamatory comments were published in the forum state via the bulletin board.

The Supreme Court of New Jersey held that "defendants who published defamatory electronic messages, with knowledge that the messages would be published in New Jersey and could influence a claimant's efforts to seek a remedy under New Jersey's Law Against Discrimination, may be properly subject to the State's jurisdiction." The court said that "traditional principles of jurisdictional analysis" should be applied "irrespective of the medium through which the injury was inflicted." Thus, the "minimum contacts" test was applied. The court ruled that if the allegedly defamatory statements were published with the knowledge or purpose of causing harm to the plaintiff in pursuit of her civil rights within New Jersey, then the minimum-contacts test would be satisfied and personal jurisdiction would exist. The court stated that it could not determine from the record whether the defendants knew of the plaintiff's other lawsuit at the time of their allegedly libelous statements, so it remanded the case to the trial court for further proceedings.

Amway Corp. v. Procter & Gamble Co., No. 1:98-CV-726, 2000 U.S. Dist. LEXIS 372 (W.D. Mich. Jan. 6, 2000).

The defendant, an Oregon resident, operated a passive website entitled "Amway: the Untold Story," on which he posted anecdotal information about individuals' negative experiences with Amway Corporation, a mail-order company located in Michigan. Amway joined the defendant to a suit it had initiated against Procter & Gamble in

Michigan federal court for tortious interference with contract, among other claims, based on allegations that Procter & Gamble had facilitated the development of the defendant's website. Amway alleged that the defendant caused harm to Amway in Michigan by publishing on his website defamatory statements about the company and its officers.

The defendant asserted that his website was "passive" and therefore, under *Zippo*, the court could not exercise personal jurisdiction over him. The court acknowledged that for personal jurisdiction to exist there must be "something more" than merely a passive site. The court, however, determined that "'something more' may be satisfied under the 'effects doctrine.'"

Thus, the court analyzed the case under *Calder* and concluded that the plaintiff must show the following to establish jurisdiction over an out-of-state defendant: "(1) The defendant committed an intentional tort; (2) The plaintiff felt the brunt of the harm in the forum such that the forum can be said to be the focal point of the harm suffered by the plaintiff as a result of that tort; (3) The defendant expressly aimed his tortious conduct at the forum such that the forum can be said to be the focal point of the tortious activity." 2000 U.S. Dist. LEXIS 372 at *11. Applying these factors, first, the court determined that Amway had alleged that the defendant committed an intentional tort. Second, the court concluded that Amway suffered the brunt of the harm in Michigan, its principal place of business. Third, the court concluded that the defendant had an "insider's knowledge" of Amway and specifically targeted his website at the company and its officers in Michigan. *Id.* at *15. Accordingly, the focal point of the harm was in Michigan. Based on these factors, the court determined that it could exercise personal jurisdiction over the defendant.

Peregrine Financial Group, Inc., et al. v. Green, 2001 U.S. Dist. LEXIS 14317 (N.D. Ill. Aug. 28, 2001).

The plaintiffs, Peregrine Financial Group, Inc., an Illinois corporation, and Utrade.com, a Georgia corporation, filed suit in federal court in Illinois against the defendant, David Green, a resident of Arizona, alleging defamation, tortious interference with business expectancy, commercial disparagement, and unfair competition arising from e-mails sent by the defendant to Utrade.com customers.

The defendant and his company, CTCN, had entered into a contract with Utrade.com to provide a trading system that would take and fill the plaintiffs' trade orders. Within two weeks of signing the contract, the plaintiffs became concerned about the validity of Green's trading system, "the integrity of [d]efendant as one of the purported system developers, and the aggressive advertising utilized by [d]efendant." 2001 U.S. Dist. LEXIS 14317 at *3. As a result of those concerns, the plaintiffs terminated their contract with the defendant. The plaintiffs alleged that the defendant then "began a campaign of defamation against Utrade . . ." in the form of e-mail messages sent to the plaintiffs' customers and "other persons" containing defamatory remarks about the plaintiffs. *Id.* However, none of the approximately 30 customers who received the defendant's e-mails was a resident of Illinois, and the content of the e-mails appeared to be targeted not at Peregrine, the only Illinois plaintiff, but at a past partner of Peregrine, and at Utrade.com. Further, all of the defendant's actions were taken in Arizona and all of his contacts with Peregrine were through Utrade.com in Georgia. The defendant moved to dismiss the suit for lack of personal jurisdiction and improper venue.

The court found the exercise of jurisdiction proper. The court relied on *Janmark Inc. v. Reidy*, 132 F.3d 1200 (7th Cir. 1997), which applied the "effects test" to the Illinois long-arm statute. The *Janmark* court held that "'there can be no serious doubt' after the Supreme Court's decision in *Calder v. Jones* that 'the state in which the victim of a tort suffers injury may entertain a suit against the accused tortfeasor.'" 2001 U.S. Dist. LEXIS 14317 at *7, quoting *Janmark*, 132 F.3d at 1202. According to *Janmark*, this principle holds true "even though the actions taken by the defendant constituting the alleged tort may have occurred wholly outside the borders of Illinois." *Id.* However, the court granted the defendant's motion to dismiss because it found that Illinois was not the proper venue for the case.

In reaching its decision on jurisdiction, the court expressed concern about the defendant's connection with Illinois, stating, "[the] plaintiffs run dangerously close to forcing [the] defendant to defend a suit because of his 'random, fortuitous, or attenuated contacts' with Illinois, or because of the 'unilateral activity of another party or third person.'" 2001 U.S. Dist. LEXIS 14317 at 10, *quoting Burger King Corp. v. Rudzewicz*, 471 U.S. 462, 475 (1985).

Bird v. Parsons, No. 00-4556, 2002 U.S. App. LEXIS 9543 (6th Cir. May 21, 2002).

The plaintiff, Darrell Bird, an Ohio resident, brought an action for trademark infringement against the co-defendants, Marshall Parsons and Dotster.com, a national domain-name registrar. Bird owned the trademark for his computer software company "Financia." The defendant, Marshall Parsons, registered "efinancia.com" through the co-defendant, Dotster.com.

Dotster.com argued the court lacked personal jurisdiction because Dotster.com is not based in Ohio and does not have its servers there. In an attempt to show Dotster.com had sufficient contacts, the plaintiff simply divided the total number of Dotster.com's clients by 50 states, estimating Dotster.com had registered nearly 5,000 websites in Ohio. The court found that 5,000 figure was sufficient to confer specific jurisdiction over Dotster.com, because it showed Dotster had an interactive website and an intent to do business with Ohio residents, although there was no evidence of the true number of Dotster.com clients in Ohio. "[T]he proffered evidence that Dotster regularly chooses to do business with Ohio residents is sufficient to constitute purposeful availment." *Id.* at *12.

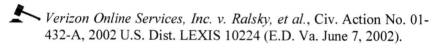 *Verizon Online Services, Inc. v. Ralsky, et al.*, Civ. Action No. 01-432-A, 2002 U.S. Dist. LEXIS 10224 (E.D. Va. June 7, 2002).

The defendants, who were Michigan residents, sent millions of unsolicited bulk e-mails, which allegedly overloaded the servers of the plaintiff's network, causing system delays and customer complaints. Applying the effects test, the court found the defendants knew or should have known that the brunt of the harm from the spamming would fall on Verizon's servers in Virginia. The court found the defendants purposefully availed themselves of the privilege of doing business in Virginia because sending unsolicited e-mails was a deliberate act to solicit business from Verizon's subscribers for financial gain. *Id.* at *26. As such, the court concluded that the unsolicited e-mails constituted sufficient minimum contacts with Virginia, and personal jurisdiction over the defendants was therefore proper. At the end of October 2002, Verizon settled the case with Ralsky.

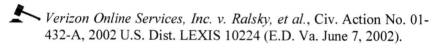 *Northwest Healthcare Alliance, Inc. v. Healthgrades.com, Inc.*, No. 01-35648 (9th Cir., Oct. 7, 2002) (not for publication).

The plaintiff, a Washington State company, is a provider of home health-care services. The defendant, a Colorado company, operated a website that rated the quality of home health-care providers. The plaintiff sued in federal court in Washington, alleging libel and violations of Washington's consumer-protection statutes. The trial court dismissed the case for lack of personal jurisdiction, applying the "sliding scale" *Zippo* test. The U.S. Court of Appeals for the Ninth Circuit reversed, stating that the appropriate test was *Calder*'s "effects test"; the defendant had "purposely interjected" itself into the Washington forum, and most of the harm occurred in Washington.

Cases in Which the "Effects Test" Was Applied and Assertion of Jurisdiction Was Found Not to Be Proper

➤ *Naxos Resources (U.S.A.) Ltd. v. Southam Inc.*, 24 Media L. Rep. (BNA) 2265 (C.D. Cal. 1996).

Naxos Resources, a wholly owned California subsidiary of a Canadian corporation, sued the Canadian publisher of the *Vancouver Sun* in California over an allegedly libelous article published in the *Sun*. Approximately 500 hard copies of the *Sun* were routinely distributed in California and the article was available to readers on the Internet and through LEXIS and WESTLAW.

The court noted that under the "effects test," personal jurisdiction did not exist unless the plaintiff showed: (1) that the defendant's article was "calculated" to cause injury in the forum state; and (2) that the defendant "knew or intended" that the "brunt" of the injury would be felt in the forum state. *Id*. at 2267.

The court held that the plaintiff failed to meet either prong of the test. First, the article was distributed and read primarily in Canada and therefore did not appear directed at California in particular. *Id*. at 2267-68. Second, it was far from clear that the article's reference to "Naxos Resources Ltd." was intended to refer to the plaintiff, Naxos Resources (U.S.A.), rather than to its parent corporation, Naxos Resources (Canada). *Id*. Consequently, the court concluded that due process prohibited it from exercising personal jurisdiction over the defendant. *Id*. at 2269.

➤ *Copperfield v. Cogedipresse*, 26 Media L. Rep. (BNA) 1185 (C.D. Cal. 1997).

In addition to rejecting the plaintiff's argument that general jurisdiction was established over the defendant (discussed above at pages 237-238), the court, employing the "effects test," also declined to exercise specific jurisdiction over the defendant. The court found that the alleged defamation was not "primarily directed at plaintiffs in California" and that the defendants did not "kn[o]w or intend[] that the brunt of the injury caused by the defamation would be felt in California." 26 Media L. Rep. at 1189. The court noted, among other things, that "[t]he alleged defamation was contained in an article published in France in a French magazine, written in the French language, investigated by

French reporters, and with a circulation primarily to readers in France."
Id.

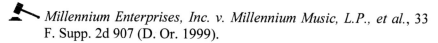 *Millennium Enterprises, Inc. v. Millennium Music, L.P., et al.*, 33 F. Supp. 2d 907 (D. Or. 1999).

The plaintiff, an Oregon corporation that owned retail outlets named "Music Millennium," filed suit against the defendants, Millennium Music, Inc. and Millennium Music, L.P., both South Carolina companies, alleging trademark infringement and dilution, and unfair competition. Both parties sold music through retail stores and the Internet, but the majority of the defendants' business was conducted through its retail stores in South Carolina. The defendants' contacts with the forum consisted of a website available to consumers in Oregon, the sale of a single compact disc to an Oregon resident via the website, which was orchestrated by the plaintiff through an acquaintance of counsel, and limited purchases from an Oregon manufacturer. The defendants filed a motion to dismiss for lack of personal jurisdiction.

The court held that the defendants' one commercial sale in Oregon and their limited purchases from an Oregon manufacturer did not establish the requisite minimum contacts. The court then rejected the plaintiff's argument that the defendants should be subject to jurisdiction under the *Calder* "effects test" because the effects of the infringing activities caused harm in Oregon. The court found there was no evidence that the defendants intentionally directed their activities at Oregon knowing that the plaintiff would be harmed. Finally, the court undertook a *Zippo* analysis and held that although the defendants' website was interactive and had the potential for sales and contacts with all Internet users, "deliberate action" within the forum state was lacking and therefore personal jurisdiction was not proper. 33 F. Supp. 2d at 921. The court stated that the fact that someone who accesses the defendants' website can purchase a compact disc does not render the defendants' actions purposefully directed at the forum.

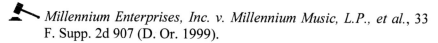 *Search Force, Inc. v. Dataforce Int'l, Inc.*, 112 F. Supp. 2d 771 (S.D. Ind. 2000).

The plaintiff, Search Force, Inc., owner of the trademark "Data Force," brought an action against the defendant, Dataforce International, Inc., alleging unfair competition and trademark infringement. The defendant moved to dismiss the suit for lack of personal jurisdiction. Search Force maintained its principal place of business in Indiana, while Dataforce conducted business in Florida. Both corporations provided employment services, including personnel recruitment and placement, in the area of information technology. Both companies also used Internet postings, national advertising, and toll-free numbers to reach prospective recruits and employers. They both paid fees to post job openings on two interactive, online-recruiting websites owned and operated by third parties. However, Dataforce only advertised one job position located in Indiana, and the majority of its placements were for positions located in Florida. It did not have any employees, agents, contractors, or offices in Indiana, nor did it circulate any hard-copy advertisements in that state.

The court stated that "something more" than mere Internet presence was required to establish personal jurisdiction over the defendant. In the context of trademark infringement claims in which the mark is used in connection with the defendant's Internet activity, the "something more" is provided by a particularized injury suffered in the forum state. In other words, the court stated, the mere fact that the forum state is the principal place of business for the plaintiff does not form the basis of personal jurisdiction. The court observed that recent precedent had diverged from an earlier trend that presumed personal jurisdiction where a defendant used an interactive website and did not purposefully avoid the forum state. More recent cases supported the conclusion that the defendant must avail itself of the forum state in a manner that is more purposeful than simply including an allegedly infringing mark on an interactive website.

The court found that Dataforce had not entered into or maintained any continuing relationship with any Indiana resident or entity. The injury to Search Force was not concentrated in Indiana beyond the extent that the plaintiff's main operations were conducted in that state. Dataforce's Internet activity was not specifically directed to Indiana, and the single listing of an Indiana position placed several years before the suit did not create any marketplace confusion that was particularized to Indiana. Therefore, the court dismissed the suit for lack of personal jurisdiction over the defendant.

CoStar Group, Inc., et al. v. LoopNet, Inc., 106 F. Supp. 2d (D. Md. 2000).

CoStar Group, Inc. and CoStar Realty Information, Inc. (collectively "CoStar"), both Delaware corporations with their principal place of business in Maryland, created, produced, and distributed databases containing photographs and descriptions of real estate. The defendant, LoopNet, a California corporation, provided a Web hosting service for users who wanted to advertise real estate over the Internet. Users of the LoopNet service could post information and photographs on the site, which could then be searched by others. Before the photographs were posted, they were reviewed to ensure that the pictures were related to real estate and did not bear any copyright notice. Only after review were the photographs posted, and then they were posted by a LoopNet employee, not the users. The LoopNet site was available to Maryland residents and contained listings of Maryland properties. CoStar filed suit alleging direct and contributory copyright infringement by LoopNet based on its posting of several photographs from CoStar databases. In response, LoopNet filed a motion to dismiss the suit for lack of personal jurisdiction.

CoStar asserted that the court could exercise personal jurisdiction over LoopNet based on the "effects" test. The court disagreed, stating that "[t]he mere fact that a nonresident defendant's act causes an effect in the forum state, or even that such effect was foreseeable, is not enough by itself to support jurisdiction. ... [c]ourts have carefully limited the application of the effects test to cases where the nonresident defendant commits an intentional tort knowing the conduct will cause harm to the plaintiff in the forum state." 106 F. Supp. 2d at 785. The court stated that there was no evidence that LoopNet had knowingly posted infringing photographs on its website. At best, the court postulated, the procedure by which the photographs were reviewed before their posting was negligent. The court explained that although the distinction between an intentional and negligent tort is irrelevant for purposes of copyright infringement liability, it is dispositive in the *Calder* "effects" analysis. Because CoStar failed to show intentional infringement on the part of the defendant, personal jurisdiction was not proper.

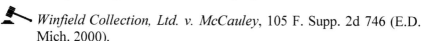 *Winfield Collection, Ltd. v. McCauley*, 105 F. Supp. 2d 746 (E.D. Mich. 2000).

The plaintiff, Winfield Collection, Ltd., was a Michigan manufacturer and seller of home-craft patterns. The defendant, McCauley, was a citizen of Texas who purchased craft patterns from the plaintiff by mail. McCauley made crafts based upon the plaintiff's patterns and sold almost all of these crafts in the Houston area. However, two customers in Michigan purchased the defendant's crafts on eBay, an online auction. The plaintiff sued for copyright infringement based on McCauley's commercial use of the patterns. The plaintiff claimed that the court had personal jurisdiction over the defendant based on the defendant's sales to the two Michigan residents and the interactive nature of the defendant's website.

The court granted the defendant's motion to dismiss for lack of personal jurisdiction. The court found that the defendant's contacts with Michigan were "random" and "attenuated"; the function of an eBay sale is to award the product to the highest bidder, and the defendant had no control over who that bidder would be. Therefore, she never purposefully availed herself of the privilege of doing business in Michigan. The court also rejected the plaintiff's argument that personal jurisdiction was proper due to the interactive nature of the defendant's website. The court countered that the real inquiry was whether the defendant had sufficient minimum contacts with the forum, and the mere presence of an interactive website is not sufficient. "The manner of establishing or maintaining those contacts, and the technological mechanisms used in so doing, are mere accessories to the central inquiry." 105 F. Supp. 2d at 750. The plaintiff failed to present any evidence that the defendant targeted Michigan customers through her website. Further, the court applied the "effects test" and found that the defendant's conduct was not aimed at the forum state, nor did it have an effect there. The defendant's contacts with the forum state were therefore "fortuitous and de minimus" and beyond the defendant's control. *Id.* at 751.

See also Metcalf v. Lawson, No. 2001-138 (N.H. June 25, 2002) (finding that the sale of an excavator through eBay by a seller in New Jersey to a purchaser in New Hampshire was not sufficient to create minimum contacts in New Hampshire).

➤ *Bailey v. Turbine Design, Inc.*, 86 F. Supp. 2d 790 (W.D. Tenn. 2000).

In addition to ruling that personal jurisdiction could not be asserted under the *Zippo* test, discussed above at page 188, the court held that personal jurisdiction likewise could not be asserted under the "effects test." The court stated that the "[p]laintiff was not attacked as a Tennessee businessman. Indeed, the alleged defamatory comments had nothing to do with plaintiff's state of residence. Thus, it cannot be said that the defamatory statements constitute actions 'expressly aimed' at Tennessee." 86 F. Supp. 2d at 796. Given these circumstances, the court refused to exercise personal jurisdiction based solely on the fact that "some of the harm caused by alleged tortious conduct occurred in Tennessee." *Id.*

➤ *Oasis Corp. v. Judd, et al.*, 132 F. Supp. 2d 612 (S.D. Ohio 2001).

The plaintiffs, the Oasis Corporation and several of its employees, were located in Ohio; the defendants were residents of Oklahoma. Oasis produced and distributed water coolers. The defendants, tenants of a Oklahoma building that had burned down, sought compensation from plaintiffs, whose product they believed to be responsible for the fire. After they were unsuccessful in their attempts to recover from the plaintiffs, the defendants launched a "gripe site" on the Internet. The gripe site voiced complaints about Oasis and provided the e-mail addresses and phone numbers of several Oasis employees. The site was never used for commercial gain. Oasis and the employees filed suit, claiming that Oasis's trademarks had been damaged, and that the employees had been libeled and their privacy invaded. The defendants responded by filing a motion to dismiss the suit for lack of personal jurisdiction.

Three significant factors contributed to the court's decision to grant the motion to dismiss for lack of personal jurisdiction over the defendants: (1) the alleged wrongs arose solely from the content of the defendants' website; (2) the site was non-commercial in nature; and (3) neither the defendants nor the website had any inherent connection to Ohio. The first factor was important to the court's determination that several calls, faxes, and e-mail messages from the defendants to the plaintiffs were unrelated to the libel claims of the plaintiffs. The court then turned to the substance and function of the defendants' website. The non-commercial nature of the site lead the court to believe that the *Zippo* interactivity analysis did not apply. Finally, the court determined that the website had no connection to Ohio. The computers hosting the site were not located in Ohio, nor had there been meaningful interaction between the site and a significant number of Ohio residents. Applying the "effects test," the court also concluded that Ohio was not the "focal point" of the website's accusations.

Revell v. Lidov, 2001 WL 285253 (N.D. Tex. Mar. 20, 2001), *aff'd,* No. 01-10521, 2002 U.S. App. LEXIS 27200, *1 (5th Cir. Dec. 31, 2002).

The defendant published an article on a Columbia University website implicating the plaintiff in an alleged conspiracy involving the bombing of PanAm Flight 103. The plaintiff, a resident of Texas, sued the defendant for libel in federal court in Texas. The defendant, Lidov, moved to dismiss the complaint for lack of personal jurisdiction, claiming he had never solicited or engaged in any business or entered into any contract with any Texas resident. The defendant also claimed he was unaware that the plaintiff resided in Texas, and that he did not have a commercial purpose in disseminating the article. Though items could be purchased through the website, both parties stipulated that the article itself could not be purchased and could only be viewed by those who chose to access the site.

The trial court held that the plaintiff had failed to establish the minimum contacts necessary to proceed in Texas court. The opinion concluded that the website was passive under the *Zippo* analysis. The mere ability of users to post documents on the portion of the site where articles were displayed did not make the site interactive in the court's eyes. The court reached this conclusion even though other portions of the site were more interactive. It also rejected application of the "effects" test, noting that, in this case, the material was not intentionally circulated in such a manner that the defendant would have known his defamatory statements would have reached the forum state. Additionally, the court stated that the article did not address the plaintiff's role as a resident of Texas, but instead criticized his national persona, further indicating that the defendant did not knowingly direct the Internet posting to the forum state.

The U.S. Court of Appeals for the Fifth Circuit affirmed. The court viewed the *Zippo* analysis as ill suited to the general jurisdiction inquiry, "because even repeated contacts with a forum residents by a foreign defendant may not constitute the requisite substantial, continuous and systematic contacts required for a finding of general jurisdiction." But the court had no trouble disposing of the question of general jurisdiction: the defendants' contacts with Texas, even if continuous, were not "substantial."

As to specific jurisdiction, the court considered both the *Zippo* interactivity analysis and the *Calder* effects tests, ultimately concluding exercise of jurisdiction by the trial court would have been "unfair," and therefore would have violated the defendants' due process rights: "This inquiry into fairness captures the reasonableness of hauling a defendant from his home state before the courts of a sister state; in the main a pragmatic account of reasonable expectations—if you are going to pick a fight in Texas, it is reasonable to expect that it be settled there." The court looked to "the geographic focus of article," found that it was not Texas, and affirmed the trial court's dismissal for lack of personal jurisdiction over the defendants.

See also Jewish Defense Org., Inc. v. Superior Court, 85 Cal. Rptr. 611 (Cal. Ct. App. 1999) (personal jurisdiction in libel suit was not proper, in part because the plaintiff, a New York resident, failed to provide evidence that California was his principal place of business, or that the alleged libel was targeted at California or would cause the brunt of any harm there).

English Sports Betting Inc. v. Tostigan, et al., Civ. No. 01-2202, 2002 U.S. Dist. LEXIS 4985 (E.D. Pa. March 15, 2002).

The plaintiff, Dennis Atiyeh, a Pennsylvania resident and owner of a Jamaica-based, online gambling enterprise, alleged that the defendant author and website owners libeled him by publishing articles about the plaintiff's legal problems. The plaintiff argued personal jurisdiction over the defendants was proper under the "effects test" because the defendants "purposely targeted a Pennsylvania resident with defamatory comments." *Id.* at *7. The court rejected this argument, ruling that it did not have jurisdiction over the defendants. The court stated that the defendant's audience was targeted based upon a shared interest in off-shore sports gambling, rather than a geographic location. *Id.* at *9.

 *Griffis v. Luban*, 646 N.W.2d 527 (Minn. 2002).

A Minnesota resident posted a message on the Internet challenging an Alabama teacher's credentials, and accusing the teacher of obtaining her degree "from a box of Cracker Jack." The teacher sued in an Alabama court for defamation, and obtained an injunction prohibiting the Minnesota resident from continuing to make such allegations. The teacher filed the Alabama judgment with a Minnesota court and sought to enforce the injunction. A Minnesota trial court found that the Alabama court had personal jurisdiction over the defendant, and the defendant appealed. To determine whether the Minnesota court could enforce the Alabama judgment against the Minnesota defendant, the Minnesota Supreme Court applied the *Calder* effects test. The Minnesota Supreme Court held that the plaintiff teacher had not satisfied the third prong of the effects test: the plaintiff did not show that the defendant had expressly aimed her tortious conduct at the Alabama forum such that Alabama was the focal point of the defamation. That the defendant knew that the teacher lived and worked in Alabama was not sufficient to warrant exercise of personal jurisdiction in Alabama over the defendant. The Minnesota Supreme Court vacated the decision of the Minnesota trial court enforcing the Alabama judgment.

Pavlovich v. Superior Court of Santa Clara County, No. S100809, 58 P.3d 2 (Cal. Nov. 25, 2002).

The defendant, Pavlovich, a resident of Texas, knowingly posted to the Internet computer code that could be used to decrypt DVD copy protection controls. The DVD Copy Control Association, Inc. (DVD CCA, the party in interest in the case) sued him in California, seeking an injunction requiring removal of the code from the Internet. The plaintiffs argued that California jurisdiction was proper because the industry most harmed by the defendant's conduct, the film industry, is primarily situated in California. The California Supreme Court rejected that argument. Applying the effects test, the court held that the mere knowledge that an intentional act might have an adverse affect on an industry connected to the California-based plaintiffs was not sufficient to establish that the act was expressly targeted to California. The only contact Pavlovich had with California was via the Internet; he owned no property, had no telephone, and conducted no business in California. His knowledge that his actions might harm a company located in California did not, in the court's view, warrant exercise of personal jurisdiction by a California court.

The DVD CCA requested a stay of the ruling by the U.S. Supreme Court, which granted its request on December 26, 2002. But on January 3, 2003, the Supreme Court vacated the stay, ending DVD CCA's efforts to keep the California Supreme Court's ruling from taking effect.

Keeton Test

In *Keeton v. Hustler Magazine, Inc.*, 465 U.S. 770 (1984), the Supreme Court decided that a non-resident defendant not physically present in the forum state, but who "continuously and deliberately" circulates its publications in such forum, should reasonably foresee answering for the truth of its content in that state. 465 U.S. at 781. In *Keeton*, the publisher produced a national magazine targeted to a nationwide audience, yet with only a small percentage of its overall circulation aimed at the forum state. In the court's mind, however, there was "no unfairness in calling it to answer for the contents of that publication wherever a substantial number of copies are regularly sold and distributed." *Id*. Therefore, under the *Keeton* test, a court might choose to exercise jurisdiction over a non-resident defendant who has posted a libelous publication on the Internet, depending on whether such posting was continuously and deliberately available to a wide audience, including residents of the forum state. The standard for what constitutes a "substantial number of copies" has been subject to various interpretations.

Naxos Resources (U.S.A.) Ltd. v. Southam Inc., 24 Media L. Rep. (BNA) 2265 (C.D. Cal. 1996).

After failing to find a basis for jurisdiction based on the "effects test" (discussed above at page 245-260), the court found that neither the newspaper's print circulation of 500 copies per week in California nor the newspaper's availability online in California constituted systematic and continuous activity sufficient to allow exercise of general jurisdiction over the defendants. Citing to *Keeton*, the court concluded that electronic contacts caused by mere presence on the Web could not give rise to general jurisdiction because, if they could, online publishers could be subject to suit in any state for activities unrelated to the state.

Telco Communications Group, Inc. v. An Apple A Day, Inc., et al., 977 F. Supp. 404 (E.D. Va. 1997).

The plaintiff, a Virginia corporation, alleged that a Missouri corporation posted multiple press releases on the Internet that libeled the plaintiff and depressed its stock price. The plaintiff claimed that jurisdiction attached under Virginia's long-arm statute, which permits jurisdiction over a defendant that causes injury within the state if the defendant regularly conducts business in the state.

The court found that exercising jurisdiction over the non-resident defendants was proper pursuant both to the Virginia long-arm statute and the Due Process Clause. The court noted that, in posting the press releases in question, the defendants were advertising their firm and soliciting investment-banking assistance, and that this advertising and solicitation was available to Virginia residents 24 hours a day. The court ruled that these activities "constitute[d] a persistent course of conduct, and that the two or three press releases rise to the level of regularly doing or soliciting business [in Virginia]." *Telco Communications Group,* 977 F. Supp. at 407. The court emphasized that its ruling did not offend the Due Process Clause because the defendants reasonably should have known that allegedly libelous information posted on the Internet would be circulated or distributed in Virginia and that plaintiff was based in Virginia. Thus, "their activities were sufficient to serve as an analogue for physical presence." *Id.*

 Young v. The New Haven Advocate, et al., 184 F. Supp. 2d 498 (W.D. Va. 2001), *rev'd* No. 01-2340, 2002 U.S. App. LEXIS 25535, *1 (4th Cir. Dec. 13, 2002).

The plaintiff, a warden of a Virginia prison, sued Connecticut-based newspapers *The New Haven Advocate* and *The Hartford Courant* for libel allegedly stemming from articles written about the prison's treatment of Connecticut inmates. The defendants argued that they had a miniscule number of subscriptions in Virginia and that none of the writing, reporting, or editing took place in Virginia, although the reporters performed telephone interviews with Virginia sources and the articles were posted on the newspapers' websites. The plaintiff countered he had never been to Connecticut, but he was able to view the allegedly defamatory articles in Virginia via the Internet.

The federal district court first applied the "effects test" and found that the harm to the warden's reputation, if any, occurred in Virginia. Then, applying the *Keeton* test, the court concluded that an article regarding Virginia prisons and available in Virginia via the Internet was sufficient to allow personal jurisdiction over the defendant newspapers. *Id.* at 508. On December 13, 2003, the U.S. Court of Appeals for the Fourth Circuit reversed the lower court's ruling. The court held that a newspaper's presence on the Internet, by itself, was not sufficient to subject the newspaper to personal jurisdiction in every state in which its website was accessible. The court found that the newspaper's content was aimed at a Connecticut audience and that it did not target Virginia readers simply by making its content available online. Therefore, the newspaper did not have sufficient contacts with Virginia to warrant exercise of personal jurisdiction. A Virginia court could properly exercise jurisdiction over defendant newspapers only if they had "manifest[ed] an intent to target and focus on" a Virginia audience. *See Young*, at *17.

Nicosia v. Rooy, 72 F. Supp. 2d 1093 (N.D. Cal. 1999).

The plaintiff, a California resident, brought an action against the defendant, a Washington State resident, for slander and libel in connection with statements the defendant published on her website. The court determined that a non-resident's maintenance of a website is not sufficient by itself to establish jurisdiction. Rather, the court maintained that a non-resident defendant must do "something more" to direct its activities to the forum state.

The court determined that "something more" existed in this case because the defendant "sent at least eleven e-mails, out of a total 100, to California addresses, inviting the recipients to view the articles on her website." The court rejected the defendant's contention that personal jurisdiction could not be exercised because the e-mails she sent merely invited people to view her website, and thus did not deliver the defamatory material into the forum state. The court deemed the defendant's argument "a distinction without a difference" because the "e-mail invitations target California residents in a way similar to sending the defamatory materials." 72 F. Supp. 2d at 1095.

Lawsuits Brought in Foreign Jurisdictions

Potential liability in defamation suits brought in foreign courts is particularly troubling to U.S. publishing companies that maintain substantial assets abroad. But it also presents a broader societal risk. No legal system in the world is as protective of speech as the U.S. system. If U.S. publishers subject themselves to suit throughout the world every time they publish on the Web, financial self-interest will necessarily make them more timid, less willing to take on difficult issues and powerful foreign interests.

For discussion of international defamation issues generally, *see* Chapter 4, pages 146-152.

🔨 A recent case involving the government of Zimbabwe illustrates the potential danger. Zimbabwe employs intelligence officers to surf the Internet looking for criticisms of the country. When officers found an allegedly false criticism of the government on Guardian Unlimited, the website for London-based newspaper *The Guardian*, prosecutors charged Guardian journalist Andrew Meldrum with criminal charges for "false publication." Prosecutors argue that the statute allows punishment of anyone who publishes an article that is subsequently proven false, no matter how credible the information in the report appeared at the time of publication. A Zimbabwe court must determine whether the article was "published" in London, where it was uploaded to the Guardian Unlimited Web server, or in Harare, Zimbabwe, where it was downloaded at the Central Intelligence Organization. If convicted, Meldrum and anyone else responsible for publication of the article could be punished by up to two years in prison. The court has heard opening arguments, but has yet to issue a ruling on the jurisdictional issue. *See* Geoffrey Robertson, "Mugabe Versus the Internet," *The Guardian* (June 17, 2002), *available at* http://www.guardian.co.uk/internetnews/story/0,7369,739026,00.html.

For a discussion of this case in the context of defamation, *see* Chapter 4, page 148.

🔨 *Dow Jones & Co. v. Gutnick*, [2002] HCA 56 (Dec. 10, 2002).

On December 10, 2002, Australia's highest court rejected the efforts of Dow Jones & Company to have a libel suit against it transferred from Australia to a U.S. court. The case involved an allegedly libelous article about Australian mining magnate Joseph Gutnick, who lives and works in Victoria, Australia. Gutnick claimed to have been libeled by a February 2000 Barron's article that appeared on WSJ.com, the online edition of the *Wall Street Journal*. The court found that Australian courts have jurisdiction to hear a libel claim based on the article, even though few print copies of the article circulated in Australia and the online version of the article was likely accessed by a few hundred readers, at most, in Australia. Dow Jones sought to have the case transferred to a U.S. court, arguing that the online version of the article was "published" in New Jersey where Dow Jones' Web servers are located, and, therefore, a U.S. court, not an Australian court, should hear any challenge to the article. Dow Jones contended that subjecting a Web publisher to suit in every nation in the world from which its website could be accessed would severely curtail freedom of speech on the Web. The High Court of Australia, however, disagreed, finding that "the spectre which Dow Jones sought to conjure up in the present appeal, of a publisher forced to consider every article it publishes on the World Wide Web against the defamation laws of every country from Afghanistan to Zimbabwe is seen to be unreal when it is recalled that in all except the most unusual of cases, identifying the person about whom material is published will readily identify the defamation law to which that person may resort."

For discussion of the defamation aspects of this case, *see* Chapter 4, page 151.

Limiting Recourse to Foreign Courts

The discussion below focuses on potential bars to suits brought in foreign jurisdictions. Because the United Kingdom and Canada, as English-speaking countries lacking the speech protections afforded under the U.S. Constitution, are attractive forums for defamation suits brought against U.S. publishers, those jurisdictions will be the focal point of this discussion.

Jurisdiction and Service of Process

United Kingdom

If an electronic publication is accessed in the United Kingdom, personal jurisdiction over the publisher is presumed, subject to service of process according to the relevant rules. Mark Stephens, *Cyberspace: The Latest Developments in England*, Media Defense in the Twenty-First Century, Libel Defense Resource Center Conference (1997), at 1. If an ISP is named as a defendant publisher, personal jurisdiction may be asserted even if the terms and conditions of use of the ISP's services indicate a specific choice of law.

Where an action has been commenced against a U.S. defendant, a court in the United Kingdom is competent to hear the case: (1) if the defendant is present within the United Kingdom; (2) if the defendant consents to the court's jurisdiction; or (3) if there has been proper service on the U.S. defendant outside the jurisdiction in accordance with the British Conflict of Law Rules. *See* P.M. North & J.J. Fawcett, *Cershire and North's Private International Law* 179, 191 (12th ed. 1992).

Several years ago, the High Court in London gave permission for service of process over the Internet in a case concerning anonymous e-mail messages that were being transmitted into the United Kingdom from another part of Europe. *Anonymous v. Anonymous* [1996] (unreported).

The European Union's E-Commerce Directive mandates that proper choice of law is in the "country of origin" (*i.e.*, where the originator of the allegedly defamatory statements is domiciled) for its member states; however, the "country of origin" rule does not apply to countries outside the E.U, such as the United States. U.S. entities posting potentially defamatory materials on a website accessed within the EU may well be subject to a foreign nation's laws, even if the expression would otherwise be protected in the U.S. *See* Directive 2000/31/EC of the European Parliament and of the Council of 8 June 2000, available at http://europa.eu.int/comm/internal_market/en/ecommerce/2k-442.htm, on certain legal aspects of information society services, in particular electronic commerce, in the Internal Market, OJ L 178, 17.7.2000, p. 1; Thomas C. Vinje & Ann-Charlotte Hogberg, *Whose Law Governs in EU?*, N.Y.L.J., Apr. 30, 2001, p. 3.

Canada

In Canada, the general rule is that personal service will confer personal jurisdiction on the court. Steven M. Siros, "Borders, Barriers, and Other Obstacles to a Holistic Environment," 13 N. Ill. U. L. Rev. 633, 646 (1993). Personal jurisdiction can be asserted over foreign defendants by service if there are consequences from the defendant's actions in the forum province, even if the damage was caused by activities abroad. *Id.* at 647.

Forum Non Conveniens

If a defendant is properly served and subject to a court's jurisdiction, the action may still be subject to stay under the doctrine of *forum non conveniens*. In either the United Kingdom or Canada, if the foreign defendant is served inside the forum country, the burden is on the defendant to show that another forum is more appropriate. If, however, the defendant is served outside the forum country, the burden is on the plaintiff to demonstrate that the United Kingdom or Canada is the appropriate forum. Mark Stephens, *Cyberspace: The Latest Developments in England*, Media Defense in the Twenty-First Century, at 2; *Frymer v. Brettschneider* [1994] 19 O.R. 3d 60, 84-85.

The United Kingdom

English courts have recently developed a list of factors to consider in conducting a *forum non conveniens* analysis in the defamation context.

▲ *Chada and Osciom Technologies Ltd. v. Dow Jones & Co. Inc.,* The Times (C.A. May 18, 1999).

The plaintiffs sued defendants for defamation over statements published in defendants' magazine. The Court of Appeal affirmed the lower court's stay of the proceedings on grounds of *forum non conveniens*. The key facts the court relied on in deciding that the United States would be the more appropriate forum were: (1) only 1,257 copies of the magazine were sold in the United Kingdom as opposed to 283,520 copies sold in the United States; (2) the content of the magazine, including articles, advertising, and quotations from stock markets related to the United States; (3) the plaintiff only had a business relationship in the U.K. for four months; and (4) there was no evidence showing that plaintiff's reputation in the United Kingdom was harmed by the article. The court also listed eight factors that should be considered when analyzing *forum non conveniens* cases: (1) the personal status of the plaintiff; (2) the business status of the plaintiff; (3) the plaintiff's connections to the U.K.; (4) the status of the defendants; (5) the extent of the publication; (6) the nature of the publication; (7) the meanings which the plaintiff attaches to the article; and (8) the juridical advantages and disadvantages of the case being heard in the U.K. as opposed to the U.S.

▲ *Berezovsky and Another v. Forbes Inc.*, The Times (C.A. Nov. 27, 1998).

The Court of Appeal overruled a trial court decision holding that the United Kingdom was not the appropriate forum for a libel action based on an article published in *Forbes* magazine. The court applied the fact-intensive *Spiliada* test (*see Spiliada Maritime Corp. v. Cansulex Ltd.* [1987] 1 AC 460, [1986] 3 All ER 843), which calls for the court to identify the jurisdiction in which the case may be tried most suitably for the interests of all the parties and for the ends of justice.

The trial court found that Russia would be the most appropriate forum because the plaintiffs were from Russia, witnesses were in Russia, and the plaintiffs' connections to England were tenuous. The Court of Appeal disagreed, finding that the plaintiff (a leading Russian businessman who also served as Deputy Secretary of the Security Council of the Russian Federation) had cultivated a reputation in England through years of effort and, as a result, the article accusing him of involvement in organized crime damaged his reputation in England. It further found that the magazine's content was international in scope and noted that the magazine published worldwide on the Internet. Finally, it found that *Forbes* had about 6,000 readers in England, not including Internet readers. Thus, trying the case in the United Kingdom met the standards of *Spiliada.*

Canada

In *Olde v. Capital Publishing Ltd. Partnership*, 64 A.C.W.S. 3d 1138 (July 26, 1996), *appeal dismissed*, 77 A.C.W.S. 3d 970 (Jan. 22, 1998), the Ontario Court of Justice permanently stayed a libel suit against New York-based *Worth* magazine. Where all parties were U.S. citizens, 99 percent of the magazine's distribution was in the United States, the article focused primarily on business operations in the United States, and the bulk of the plaintiffs' injury, if any, occurred in the United States, the Court determined that "all of the relevant factors ... point overwhelmingly to the U.S.A. as the appropriate jurisdiction." Ontario Ct. of App. Decision, at 1.

International Choice of Law

Even though a defamation suit is filed in a foreign court, that country's choice-of-law rules may require the court to apply the laws of another jurisdiction. If a foreign court determines, for example, that U.S. law has a more significant relationship to the action, it may apply the laws of the United States, rather than the laws of the forum. *Cf. Desai v. Hersh*, 719 F. Supp. 670 (N.D. Ill. 1989) (suggesting that a United States court would apply Indian law, rather than United States Constitutional law, where statements published in India were not matters of public concern in the United States or where defendant intentionally and directly exploited the Indian market), *aff'd*, 954 F.2d 1408 (7th Cir.), *cert. denied*, 506 U.S. 865 (1992). If a foreign court applies United States law with its First Amendment protections, the advantages won by the plaintiff's forum shopping are lost.

In *Ellis v. Time, Inc.*, 26 Media L. Rep. 1225 (D.D.C. 1997), the plaintiff, in addition to his American libel law claims, argued that the court should apply English libel law based on the publication in Britain of the allegedly defamatory statements. The court rejected this contention because application of English libel standards would violate the First Amendment's protection of free speech.

Recognition and Enforcement of Foreign Judgments

The states in this country have traditionally relied on principles of "comity" in recognizing and giving effect to judgments obtained in foreign countries. *See Hilton v. Guyot*, 159 U.S. 113, 164 (1895). More recently, many states have codified the rule of comity by enacting the Uniform Foreign-Money Judgments Recognition Act (UFMJRA) available at http://www.law.upenn.edu/bll/ulc/fnact99/1920_69/ufmjra62.pdf. Craig A. Stern, "Foreign Judgments and the Freedom of Speech: Look Who's Talking," 60 Brook. L. Rev. 999, 1020-21 (1994).

While the applicable law will vary slightly from state to state, generally, under the UFMJRA, other state statutes, or the common-law rule of comity, a state is precluded from enforcing a foreign judgment if the judgment was rendered in a proceeding incompatible with due process and can decline to enforce a judgment where enforcing the judgment would be repugnant to the public policy of the state. *See Uniform Foreign Money-Judgments Recognition Act* § 4, 13 U.L.A. 268 (1986). *See also* Jeremy Maltby, Note, "Juggling Comity and Self-Government: The Enforcement of Foreign Libel Judgments in U.S. Courts," 94 Colum. L. Rev. 1978, 1986-87 (1994). Some U.S. courts have refused to enforce British libel judgments on public policy grounds because the standards of British defamation law are antithetical to protections afforded the press by the U.S. Constitution. *Bachchan v. India Abroad Publications, Inc.*, 585 N.Y.S.2d 661, 664 (N.Y. Sup. Ct. 1992); *Telnikoff v. Matusevitch*, 702 A.2d 230, 239 (1997). Indeed, in *Bachchan*, the court suggested that where the public policy to which the foreign judgment is repugnant is embodied by the First Amendment, the refusal to recognize the judgment is "constitutionally mandated." 585 N.Y.S.2d at 663. *But see Desai*, 719 F. Supp. at 679-81 (suggesting that the First Amendment can protect speech published in a foreign country only where the speech is a matter of public concern in the United States, and that a defendant may shed his or her First Amendment protections if the defendant intentionally and directly exploits a foreign market).

However, at least one court has enforced a foreign judgment despite the UFMJRA. In *Reading & Bates Constr. Co. v. Baker Energy Resources Corp.*, 976 S.W.2d 703 (Tex. Ct. App. 1998), the appeals court overruled a trial court decision refusing to enforce a Canadian patent infringement judgment on the grounds that it violated the public policy of the United States. *Reading & Bates*, 976 S.W.2d at 704. The appeals court ruled that the applicable public policy under the UFMJRA is state policy, not national policy. *Id.* at 709. Because federal courts have exclusive jurisdiction in patent and trademark actions, the court held that the measure of damages in patent infringement cases does not have an impact on the public policy of Texas. *Id.* at 708-09. The court also held that the judgment should not be denied on reciprocity grounds because it is not clear that Canada would automatically refuse to enforce a similar judgment rendered in Texas. *Id.* at 709-10.

In November 2000, a French court ordered Yahoo! to stop French users from accessing Yahoo! sites over which Nazi memorabilia were sold. Under French law, it is illegal to exhibit or sell objects with racist overtones. Yahoo! France barred the sale of Nazi memorabilia, but French users could still access Yahoo.com, where such items were listed for sale. Yahoo! subsequently prohibited the sale of Nazi merchandise on its auction sites, but asked a U.S. court for a declaratory judgment that it is not bound to filter out French users or face the $13,000-per-day fine for failure to do so threatened under French law. In 2001, the U.S. District Court in California ruled in *Yahoo!, Inc. v. La Ligue Contre Le Racime et L'Antisemitisme*, 169 F. Supp. 1181, that U.S. law, not French law, governs Yahoo!'s right with respect to content on U.S.-based servers. An appeal is pending. On February 26, 2002, a French criminal court said it will try Yahoo! and its former CEO, Tim Koogle, for allegedly condoning war crimes by allowing the sale of Nazi memorabilia. The criminal hearing was set for January 2003.

For discussion of the free speech implications of this case, *see* Chapter 1, page 28.

MISCELLANEOUS

Unauthorized Access to Web Sites

Traditional protections against wiretapping and trespass have been applied in recent years to prohibit unauthorized access to websites.

Application of Wiretapping Law

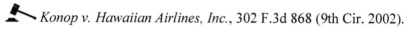 *Konop v. Hawaiian Airlines, Inc.*, 302 F.3d 868 (9th Cir. 2002).

The U.S. Court of Appeals for the Ninth Circuit held that gaining unauthorized access to a password-protected website does not violate the Wiretap Act. Accessing a website does not constitute the sort of "interception" of a communication necessary to establish a violation of the Act. The ruling established that an unlawful interception occurs only with respect to contemporaneous transmissions, not files in temporary or permanent storage, such as the pages of a website.

Konop, a pilot for Hawaiian Airlines, created a website where he posted criticisms of the Airline, its executives, and its employees' union. Access to the site was limited to users with passwords. Konop asserted that the Airline violated the Wiretap Act when it obtained a password and used it to access the site without Konop's permission or knowledge. The court rejected his Wiretap Act claim on the ground that accessing stored files (the pages of a website) was not the interception of a communication.

Application of Trespass Law

Courts have recently upheld the application of the law of trespass in the context of computer systems. However, different courts have come to different conclusions about the degree of interference the trespass must have caused to the plaintiff's computer system to be actionable.

eBay, Inc. v. Bidder's Edge, Inc., 100 F. Supp. 2d. 1058 (N.D. Cal. 2000).

Bidder's Edge is an auction aggregation site that conducts automated searches of more than 100 other websites and consolidates items being auctioned. eBay sued Bidder's Edge, alleging that its use of search robots (commonly referred to as "bots") to search the eBay site constituted trespass on eBay's website. According to eBay, the automated searches being conducted by Bidder's Edge took up an estimated 1.11 to 1.53 percent of eBay's server capacity, resulting in irreparable harm to eBay. A federal court in California found the concept of trespass applicable to computer systems and held that the defendant's unauthorized searches intentionally interfered with the plaintiff's possessory interest in the computer system, proximately causing damage to the plaintiff. The court enjoined Bidder's Edge from using bots to search the eBay site for listings, reasoning that if many other aggregators did the same thing, eBay's servers would be overwhelmed.

⚖ *Ticketmaster Corp. v. Tickets.Com, Inc.*, No. CV99-7654, 2000 U.S. Dist. LEXIS 12987 (C.D. Cal. August 10, 2000).

A federal court in California denied the plaintiff, Ticketmaster's, motion for a preliminary injunction prohibiting the defendant, Tickets.Com, from deep-linking to the plaintiff's website. Ticketmaster, an online entertainment-events booking agent, filed a motion to prohibit Tickets.com, an online events-referral agent, from routing its customers directly to Ticketmaster's interior Web pages, bypassing Ticketmaster's home page, and leaving less advertising revenue for Ticketmaster. Ticketmaster alleged that this deep-linking constituted a trespass and copyright infringement, as well as false advertising and passing-off.

The court recognized the application of the law of trespass to the computer medium following *eBay v. Bidder's Edge*; however, the court held that there was no trespass in this case: "A basic element of trespass to chattels must be physical harm to the chattel (not present here) or some obstruction of its basic function (in the court's opinion not sufficiently shown here)." 2000 U.S. Dist. LEXIS 12987 at *3. In addition, the court held that there was no copyright infringement. as Tickets.com used a Web crawling spider to collect mere factual information regarding events. (Facts themselves, as opposed to the expression of facts, are not subject to copyright protection.)

For discussion of this case (and of deep-linking in general) in the context of copyright and trademark infringement, *see* Chapters 2 at page 79, and Chapter 3 at page 98.

⚖ *Register.com, Inc. v. Verio, Inc.*, 126 F. Supp. 2d 238 (S.D.N.Y. 2000).

A federal court in New York granted the plaintiff's motion for a preliminary injunction prohibiting the defendant's search engine from accessing registrant contact information contained in the plaintiff's database and from using that information for mass marketing. The plaintiff, Register.com, a domain-name registration service, brought a trespass suit against Verio, an Internet service provider, seeking to enjoin it from marketing its services to individuals who had recently registered domain names through Register.com. Verio had been using search robots to search Register.com's database of individuals who had recently registered domain names, and used this information to solicit business from the individuals by telemarketing and e-mail. The court found that the plaintiff was entitled to the injunction, as it had demonstrated a likelihood of success on the merits and irreparable harm on its trespass and other claims. The court followed the *eBay v. Bidder's Edge* rationale and held that Verio's search bots had presented and would continue to present an unwelcome interference with Register.com's computer system. The court also expressed the concern that if the court denied the injunction, other companies would be encouraged to deploy search bots and further diminish Register.com's server capacity.

Oyster Software, Inc. v. Forms Processing, Inc, No. C-00-0724 JCS, 2001 WL 1736382 (N.D. Cal. Dec. 6, 2001).

The plaintiff, Oyster Software, is a California company that develops forms-processing software for companies. The defendant, Forms Processing, Inc. (FPI), is a Florida company offering document management services. FPI hired a Web design company, Top-Ten, to create and promote its company website. Using data-scraping robots, Top-Ten designers appropriated metatags from Oyster's site and incorporated them into the FPI site. Oyster sued FPI in federal court in California, arguing that FPI's scraping of Oyster's metatags constituted a trespass.

The court refused to dismiss FPI's trespass claim, even though Oyster could show only a "negligible" load placed on its computer systems by Top-Ten's robot. The concept of trespass, the court held, does not require anything greater than *use* of the complaining party's property. 2001 WL 1736382 at *13.

On April 25, 2002, Homestore.com, an online real-estate services company, filed suit in federal court in Los Angeles against Bargain Network, an online classified service, claiming that Bargain Network was unlawfully scraping listings off the Homestore website and that the site had been deep-linking to Homestore's real-estate listings without consent. The complaint alleges trespass, breach of contract, and tort claims. *See* "Linking, A Fundamental Premise of the Web, is Challenged," Siliconvalley.com (June 9, 2002), *available at* http://www.siliconvalley.com/mld/siliconvalley/news/editorial/

3435606.htm. For discussion of this case in the context of deep-linking, *see* Chapter 2, page 97.

➤ *EF Cultural Travel v. Explorica, Inc.*, U.S. Ct. of App. No. 01-2000 (December 17, 2001).

The plaintiff and the defendant companies compete in the field of providing global tours for high-school students. The Court of Appeals for the First Circuit upheld a lower-court injunction against the defendant's use of an electronic agent that combed through the plaintiff's database for pricing information. The court found that the plaintiff would likely succeed on the merits of its claim under the Computer Fraud and Abuse Act (CFAA). In particular, the court found that the plaintiff could make out a claim under the CFAA even if the unauthorized intrusion did not in and of itself cause damage to the system, because the alleged $21,000 that the plaintiff said it had spent assessing the effect of the defendant's data scraper on its Web server was sufficient to meet the minimum threshold set by the statute.

UCITA—A Commercial Code for Computer Information Transactions

General

The National Conference of Commissioners on Uniform State Laws (NCCUSL) voted to approve the Uniform Computer Information Transactions Act (UCITA) on July 29, 1999. Just as the Uniform Commercial Code (UCC) was designed to govern the sale of tangible goods, UCITA is a commercial code that applies to computer information transactions—transactions in which the subject matter includes information that can be processed by or received by a computer. *See generally* Mary Jo Howard Dively, "The New Laws that Will Enable Electronic Contracting: Survey of Electronic Contracting Rules in the UETA and the UCITA," Practicing Law Institute (Mar. 2001), 38 Duq. L. Rev. 209 (extensive discussion of UCITA). Like the UCC, UCITA provides the default rules for transactions while allowing contracting parties to opt out of these rules.

Application of UCITA: Examples

UCITA is a broad statute that addresses a variety of commercial issues within computer information transactions, including warranties, perfect tender, manifesting assent to a contract, mass market licenses, choice of law and forum, and shrinkwrap licenses.

UCITA only governs transactions that include an agreement to create, modify, transfer, or license computer information. If a contract involves both computer information and another product, UCITA applies only to the part of the deal that involves computer information. For example, if an individual buys a computer, the sale of the computer falls under Article 2 of the UCC because the computer is a good; however, licenses to the software pre-loaded on the computer would be governed by UCITA. *See, e.g., M. A. Mortenson Co. v. Timberline Software Corp.*, 998 P.2d 305 (Wash. 2000); *but see Advent Systems Ltd. v. Unisys Corp.*, 925 F.2d 670, (3d Cir. 1990) (pre-UCITA holding that software is a "good" according to the UCC). The Official Comments to UCITA emphasize that the distinguishing factor between computer information transactions and sales of goods is whether the primary subject matter of the transaction, about which the purchaser or licensee has the most interest, is a tangible good. For example, in a computer information transaction, the information exchanged may be contained on a CD-ROM or some other physical medium, but the licensee "has little interest" in the CD itself once the information on that CD is transferred to the buyer's computer.

Examples of contracts covered by UCITA: Contracts to create or develop computer information; contracts for Internet access; agreements to create or distribute multimedia works; contracts for data processing or analysis of computer information; contracts involving distribution of computer programs; and contracts involving the grant of rights to use computer programs.

Examples of contracts not covered by UCITA: Contracts that do not significantly involve computer information; contracts for the sale of computers, televisions, DVD players, and the like; contracts for print media; contracts for sound recordings; contracts for motion pictures, or for broadcast or cable programming; contracts for airline transportation, even if they involve electronic ticketing; contracts to create and publish print books, even where the author delivers the manuscript in electronic form; contracts for digital-signature certificates (the product is identification services, not computer information); and personal services (except contracts for computer information development or support).

Recent Developments

In August 2002, the National Conference of Commissioners on Uniform State Laws approved 38 new amendments to UCITA in response to criticism leveled at the statute by the American Bar Association.

The Committee report that resulted in the amendments is available at http://www.nccusl.org/nccusl/ucita/UCITA_Standby_Comm.htm. The amendments are largely designed to clarify the language of certain UCITA provisions. Substantive changes will allow consumers to criticize software companies without the risk that their licenses could be revoked and to reverse-engineer some software.

Status of UCITA in State Legislatures

As of November 1, 2002, Maryland and Virginia are the only states to have passed UCITA (with some amendments). The Maryland statute took effect in October 2000; the Virginia statute took effect in July 2001. Versions of UCITA have been introduced in at least eleven other states, namely Arizona, Delaware, Hawaii, Illinois, Louisiana, Maine, New Hampshire, New Jersey, Oklahoma, Oregon, and Texas, as well as the District of Columbia and the U.S. Virgin Islands. Iowa has not only rejected UCITA, but has enacted legislation to protect Iowa residents and businesses from its effects. If a contract signed by an Iowa resident or business contains "a choice of law" provision stating that the contract is to be interpreted under the law of any state that has enacted UCITA, the choice-of-law provision will be voidable and the contract will, instead, be interpreted under Iowa law. The FTC has voiced reservations concerning the Act, and, according to one report, overall support for UCITA seems to be waning. Menn, Joseph, "Support for Software Law Eroding," *L.A. Times*, Nov. 20, 2000.

Detailed information related to UCITA is available on the NCCUSL website, www.nccusl.org.

Internet Taxation

In states that impose a sales tax, buyers are obligated to pay the tax and sellers that operate within the state are obligated to collect the tax and remit it to the government. There has been much debate about whether states should be allowed to force out-of-state companies to collect taxes on their behalf for online purchases. For example, when a customer from North Dakota buys a sweater online from L.L. Bean in Maine, should L.L. Bean apply the appropriate North Dakota sales tax to the purchase and remit the tax to North Dakota? State governments want the transaction taxed because a purchase online instead of at a local store means less tax revenue for the government. Traditional retailers do not think it is fair that their goods are taxed while those sold online are not.

Internet Tax Moratorium

Enacted in 1998, the current Internet tax moratorium has been extended through October 31, 2003. The moratorium covers Internet access fees, as well as multiple or so-called discriminatory taxes on electronic commerce, such as a state taxing a transaction already taxed by another state, or taxing electronic sales differently than other sales. Included in the original moratorium was a grandfather clause that permitted some states to retain existing taxes on Internet access.

Under the moratorium, states remain free to collect sales taxes or "use" taxes, which are the equivalent of sales taxes owed on sales by out-of-state merchants. Any purchases made from a catalog, out-of-state or over the Internet, may be subject to Internet sales or use taxes.

Although consumers owe the tax, the Supreme Court has declared that states cannot compel remote merchants to collect the tax. *Quill Co. v. North Dakota*, 504 U.S. 298 (1992). Several states have begun education campaigns to inform citizens about their tax obligations, and some states, such as California, Washington, Iowa and Wisconsin, have begun sending tax bills to residents who do not pay a sales or use tax on out-of-state purchases. These notices, however, have been limited primarily to online sales of tobacco where states have had moderate success in obtaining the customer lists of online tobacco sellers via the federal Jenkins Act. For other online sales, the states may not have an effective means of discovering which of their citizens are making online purchases and in what amounts, making tax collection difficult.

On January 7, 2003, members of each House of Congress introduced bills that would extend indefinitely the Internet tax moratorium, currently set to expire on October 31, 2003. Senator Wyden (D-Or.) and Congressman Cox (R-Cal.) introduced identical bills (S. 52 and H.R. 49) that are intended to prohibit states from imposing new taxes.

State Laws Enacted During Tax Moratorium to Protect Sales Tax Interest

Under a New York law that took effect in November 2000, tobacco can only be shipped to authorized dealers. This law effectively prevents online retailers of tobacco products from selling in New York, indirectly protecting the State of New York's tax interest in tobacco sales. The law is currently being challenged in court by Brown & Williamson Tobacco Corp. The challenge is said to be based on Commerce Clause grounds similar to the arguments made in *American Library Association v. Pataki*, discussed earlier, in Chapter 1 at pages 10-11. Several state laws banning the sale of wine over the Internet are also being challenged throughout the country.

In March of 2001, Arkansas passed a law requiring an online seller to collect taxes on sales made to customers in Arkansas if the seller is affiliated with a brick-and-mortar retailer in the state. The law is predicated on the unitary theory of sales tax nexus—a theory rejected by the courts in its application to mail-order companies. *See, e.g., SFA Collections, Inc. v. Bannon*, 217 Conn. 220 (1991), 585 A.2d 666; *Quill Corp. v. North Dakota*, 504 U.S. 298 (1992) (holding that physical presence of company or its agent is required to collect use tax).

In April 2002, the New York State Department of Taxation and Finance expressed the opinion that the sale of a gift certificate by an Internet merchant resulted in income to that merchant, taxable in New York, when the customer who purchased the gift certificate accessed the merchant's website from a location in New York. According to the department's Advisory Opinion, the sale would result in taxable income in New York regardless of where the website was located. See NY State Dep't of Taxation and Finance, Office of Tax Policy Analysis Technical Services Division, Advisory Opinion TSB-A-02(3)C (Apr. 18, 2002), available at http://www.tax.state.ny.us/pdf/Advisory_Opinions/Corpora tion/A02_3c.pdf.

On November 12, 2002, 30 of 35 states, plus the District of Columbia, approved the Streamlined Sales and Use Tax Agreement. The agreement lays the groundwork for voluntary sales-tax collection by vendors lacking physical presence in a given jurisdiction — the so-called remote vendors, typically retailers conducting business transactions through the Internet or by mail. The agreement will be effective no earlier than July 1, 2003, and requires conforming legislation in at least ten states representing at least 20 percent of the total population of all sales tax states. (Forty-five states and the District of Columbia impose sales tax.) Under the agreement, states would establish uniform definitions of taxable goods and services, and maintain a single tax rate statewide for each product or service.

In January 2003, the Massachusetts Revenue Commissioner announced that its state income tax forms will include a new line item, asking taxpayers to estimate and pay sales tax on items they purchased out of state, including items purchases over the Internet. The sales tax itself is not new; it has been required since 1967, but the Commonwealth, like most states, has done little to enforce it. Now that Internet sales are increasingly depriving states of tax revenue, states such as Massachusetts are taking steps to minimize the losses.

In California, Governor Gray Davis recently indicated he would support an Internet sales tax. The tax would require retail outlets that conduct catalog or Internet business, but have physical presence in the state, to collect sales taxes on all of its sales to California consumers. California has not joined the Streamlined Sales and Use Tax Agreement, nor has it participated in proceedings that led to this agreement.

Nexus for State Tax Purposes

In July 2002, the Court of Appeals of Tennessee reversed a trial court's grant of summary judgment in favor of America Online on the tax commissioner's claim that AOL's activities in Tennessee provide a sufficient nexus to subject it to state taxes. The court found that a reasonable finder of fact could conclude that AOL has a nexus with the state by virtue of the many in-state businesses, including network service providers, that help make AOL services available to Tennessee residents. *See America Online, Inc. v. Johnson*, No. M2001-00927-COA-R3-CV (Tenn. Ct. App., July 30, 2002).

Proposed Federal Legislation

The Jurisdictional Certainty Over Digital Commerce Act (H.R. 2421 IH), sponsored by Rep. Cliff Stearns (R-Fla.), "would reserve to Congress the right to regulate 'commercial transactions of digital goods and services conducted through the Internet' [and] ... would cover purely digital items such as downloaded software, e-books and music files." Margaret Kane, "Digital Commerce Sparks Tax Tango" (July 20, 2001), *available at* http://news.cnet.com/news/0-1007-200-6614719.html. The bill was referred to the Subcommittee on Commercial and Administrative law on July 16, 2001.

State Internet Taxation Decisions

In re Borders Online Inc., Cal. State Bd. of Equalization, No. SC OHA 97-638364 (September 26, 2001).

Borders.com's policy of giving its customers the option of returning items for cash refunds at Borders retail stores made Borders (the corporation that operated the retail stores) the authorized representative of Borders.com (the separately incorporated website) and thus demonstrated that Borders.com was doing business in California. Consequently, Borders.com was required to collect tax on sales made in California, even though Borders.com, unlike Borders (the retail store) had no physical presence in California. This case is available at http://www.boe.ca.gov/legal/pdf/borders.pdf.

International Taxation Efforts

On May 7, 2002, the European Union approved a plan to begin requiring payment of the European VAT (Value Added Tax) by U.S. firms selling products over the Internet to European consumers. European companies selling to non-European consumers will not have to pay the VAT. *See* "EU Taxes U.S. E-Commerce," *Wired* (May 6, 2002), available   at http://www.wired.com/news/business/0,1367,52325,00.html. The plan is seen by some Europeans as necessary to level the playing field between U.S. and European competitors. *See* Owen Gibson, "EU Clamps Down On Tax Loophole," *The Guardian* (UK) (May 7, 2002) available at http://media.guardian.co.uk/Print/0,3858,4408610,00.htm   (discussing the European perspective). U.S. industries, however, complain that the VAT is an attempt to add barriers to trade and will ultimately be impossible to enforce. *See* Joanna Glasner, "U.S. Not Happy About EU Tax," *Wired* (May 8, 2002), *available at* http://www.wired.com/news/business/0,1367,52378,00.html (describing U.S. industry reaction to the tax measures).

On the other hand, a British businessman named Nigel Payne is reportedly petitioning the United States government to *allow* him to pay taxes to the IRS on his online gambling business. Payne is lobbying Congress to allow Internet gambling companies to operate in the United States by attempting to point out the direct financial benefits the U.S. government could reap by allowing (and taxing) an online gambling industry. See "Let Me Pay £7.5m Tax, Begs Chief," *The Guardian* (UK) (May 14, 2002).

The Americans With Disabilities Act (ADA)

The Americans With Disabilities Act (ADA), 42 U.S.C. §§ 12101, *et seq.*, was passed in 1990 to provide "a clear and comprehensive national mandate for the elimination of discrimination against individuals with disabilities." The statute prohibits discrimination "on the basis of disability in the full and equal enjoyment of the goods, services, privileges, advantages, or accommodations of any place of public accommodation by any person who owns, leases, or operates a place of public accommodation." 42 U.S.C. § 12182(a).

Places of Public Accommodation

Places of public accommodation typically include physical locations, such as inns, restaurants, theaters, schools, parks, retail stores, and recreational facilities. Whether the ADA applies to non-physical entities is a subject of debate.

 Carparts Distribution Center, Inc. v. Automotive Wholesalers Assn. of New England, 37 F.3d 12 (1st Cir. 1994).

The U.S. Court of Appeals for the First Circuit found that the ADA applied to non-physical structures when it held that an AIDS patient's employer-provided health plan could be a public accommodation under the ADA.

See also Doe v. Mutual of Omaha Ins. Co., 179 F.3d 557, 559 (7th Cir. 1999) (recognizing that websites and other "electronic space[s]" might be deemed public accommodations for purposes of the ADA); *Morgan v. Joint Administration Board*, 268 F.3d 456, 459 (7th Cir. 2001) (indicating that the ADA would apply to a health plan if it were sold over the Internet).

 Rendon v. Valleycrest Prod., 294 F.3d 1279 (11th Cir. 2002).

The U.S. Court of Appeals for the Eleventh Circuit determined that the automatic "fast finger" device used to advance contestants on the television game show *Who Wants To Be A Millionaire?* was within the scope of the ADA, but only because of its relation to the physical space of the game-show studio.

Web Sites as Places of Public Accommodation

Because the Internet is not a physical place, there has been considerable debate about whether the ADA applies to websites, and if so, to what extent.

Both Congress and various courts have been asked to decide whether a website is a place of public accommodation subject to ADA compliance. In 2000, the House of Representatives held a hearing on whether the ADA should apply to private Internet sites, but to date Congress has not sought to amend the Act to address the issue.

In 1999, the National Federation of the Blind sued America Online, claiming that AOL violated the ADA by failing to make its service accessible to blind persons. The Federation dropped its suit when AOL agreed to offer software that makes its system compatible with devices used by visually impaired computer users. *See National Federation of the Blind v. America Online, Inc.*, No. 99-CV 12303EFH (D. Mass., filed Nov. 4, 1999). National Federation of the Blind/ America Online Accessibility Agreement is available at http://www.nfb.org/Tech/accessibility.htm.

➤ *Access Now, Inc. v. Southwest Airlines, Co.*, No. 02-21734-CIV, 2002 U.S. Dist. LEXIS 19795 (S.D. Fla. 2002).

On October 18, 2002, the U.S. District Court for the Southern District of Florida ruled that the ADA does not apply to commercial websites.

The plaintiff, Access Now, sued Southwest Airlines, alleging that its website, which offers special rates and convenience, violated the ADA because it did not allow for access by blind persons using screen-reader technology. Without the technology, blind Internet users are unable to access many of the site's functions. Southwest Airlines contended that a website is not a public accommodation, and therefore not subject to the ADA.

The plaintiff argued that the website was a place of public accommodation, characterizing it as a "place of exhibition," like theaters, movie houses, and stadiums; as a "display," like museums, libraries and galleries; and as a "sales establishment," like bricks-and-mortar retail stores.

The court determined that the ADA applies to physical structures only. "To expand the ADA to cover 'virtual' spaces would be to create new rights without well-defined standards." 2002 U.S. Dist. LEXIS 19795 at *14.

Access Now has filed other complaints alleging that various websites violate the ADA. Barnes & Noble, the retail bookseller that operates a website at www.bn.com, reportedly settled a suit with Access Now. *See* "Web Site Held Not 'Public Accommodation' Under 1990 Americans With Disabilities Act," *Electronic Commerce & Law*, Vol. 7, No. 42, Oct. 30, 2002, at 1077. This article is available at http://www.cla.org/bna7_42.htm.

Access Now also sued American Airlines, asserting that the airline's website violates the ADA because it does not operate with screen-reader technology that would allow blind persons to use the website. The airline's motion to dismiss the case was pending as of October 15, 2002. *Access Now v. American Airlines*, No. 02-CV-22076 (S.D. Fla., filed July 12, 2002).

➤ *Martin v. Metropolitan Atlanta Rapid Transit Auth.*, 225 F. Supp. 2d 1362 (N.D. Ga. 2002).

The plaintiffs, a group of disabled individuals, sued Atlanta's metropolitan transit authority (MARTA) under the ADA and moved for a preliminary injunction. As part of their complaint, the plaintiffs alleged that MARTA's website was not equally accessible to able and disabled persons. On October 7, 2002, a federal trial court granted the plaintiffs' motion for a preliminary injunction, in part, and directed the parties to confer in good faith toward agreeing on appropriate remedies for the ADA violations. MARTA officials had already been working toward making the website more accessible, including schedules available in Braille output, and content that is easily detectable by plain-text reading software for visually impaired users.

Hooks v. Okbridge, No. 99-50891, 2000 U.S. App. LEXIS 23035 (5th Cir. Aug. 24, 2000).

In an unpublished opinion, the U.S. Court of Appeals for the Fifth Circuit affirmed the trial court's ruling that a commercial website was not a place of public accommodation subject to the ADA.

Even if Congress were to legislate, or a court were to rule, that a website is a public accommodation, website operators may not be required to alter the content of their sites to provide access to disabled persons. The regulations implementing the ADA indicate that a public accommodation is not required "to alter its inventory to include accessible or special goods that are designed for, or facilitate use by, individuals with disabilities." 28 C.F.R. § 36.307(a). Cases in which courts have suggested that a website might be deemed a public accommodation have not gone so far as to say that a website must therefore provide access to its contents to disabled persons. For example, in *Doe v. Mutual of Omaha Insurance Co.*, although the court suggested that a website could be considered a public accommodation, it stated that the ADA "does not regulate the content of the products or services sold." 179 F.3d at 564. Likewise, *McNeil v. Time Ins. Co.*, 205 F.3d 179, stated that a place of public accommodation, which includes a health insurance plan, a non-physical entity, "need not modify or alter the goods and services that it offers in order to avoid violating [the ADA]." 205 F.3d at 188.

Self-Regulation Initiatives

The World Wide Web Consortium (W3C) has been promoting Web accessibility through its Web Accessibility Initiative (WAI), which it started in 1997. The W3C encourages voluntary compliance with ADA provisions and provides guidelines and recommendations for software and Web content providers and publishers.

On December 17, 2002, W3C issued its User Agent Accessibility Guidelines, representing consensus among developers and the disability community on accessibility features needed in browsers and multimedia players used to allow disabled users to access the Web. The guidelines urge designers to make websites more accessible to disabled users. For example, designers are encouraged to provide commands that operate through the keyboard as well as a mouse, and to design applications with screen readers or refreshable Braille output.

To comply with the Web Accessibility Initiative, a website must include:

- text equivalent for every non-text element in a site;

- auditory descriptions of the important information in visual content;

- tables that identify row and column headers;

- if all else fails, a link to an alternative website that has adopted the WAI recommended technologies.

Information about the WAI is available at http://www.w3.org/WAI/.

Index

References are to page numbers.

licensing/royalty systems, 126-
127
Effects test
jurisdiction found, 247-254
jurisdiction not found, 254-262
Keeton test compared, 227, 262-
264
nature of, 226, 247
Electronic Communications
Privacy Act (ECPA), 167,
182-186
Electronic contracts
arbitration provisions, 203-205
browse-wrap license, 197, 201
clickwrap license agreements,
197, 200-201
defined, 197
effective notice, 199-200
e-signatures. *See* E-signatures
forum selection provisions, 203-
205
intellectual property agreements,
199
liability statements, 198
linking and framing, 199
publisher content agreements,
199
reservation of rights agreements,
198
responsibility statements, 198
shrinkwrap licenses, 200, 202-
203
Uniform Computer Information
Transactions Act, 201-
202, 276-278
user-supplied content, 198
visitor agreements, 198
web site disclaimers and user
agreements, 197
Electronic signatures. *See* E-
signatures
Electronic Signatures in Global and
National Commerce Act (E-
SIGN), 206-207
E-mail, unsolicited. *See* Spam
E-signatures
case law, 207-208

concerns, 205
definitions, 205-206
Electronic Signatures in Global
and National Commerce
Act, 206-207
federal legislation, 206-207
function, 197
international legislation, 207
need for, 205
state legislation, 206
EU Directive on Data Protection
enactment, 193
safe harbor, 193-195
sanctions, 195-196
Evidence
identities of anonymous Internet
users, 21
lack of legitimate right or
interest in domain name,
64-66

~ F ~

Famous trademarks, 30
Fax transmissions, 186, 210
Federal Agency Protection of
Privacy Act, 174
Federal Trade Commission Act,
168
"Fighting" words, 3
Financial services information,
173, 179, 180-182
First Amendment. *See* Freedom of
speech and the First
Amendment
Foreign judgments, 270-271
Forum shopping
defamation, 148-150
electronic contract provisions,
203-205
foreign jurisdictions, 264-266
Uniform Computer Information
Transactions Act, 276-
278
Fourteenth Amendment, 3
Framing
copyright issues, 100-101
electronic contracts, 199

~ L ~

Labels
  archival material, 163spam, 211
Liability statements, 198
Libraries
  Children's Internet Protection
      Act, 9
  defamation, 140
  Internet access restrictions, 11,
      19
Limited purpose public figures, 155
Linking
  Better Business Bureau, 80
  Children's Online Privacy
      Protection Act of 1998,
      167
  copyrights, 97-100
  deep linking, 79, 98
  electronic contracts, 199
  patent disputes, 80
  trademark cases and issues, 79
Local governments
  criticism of local officials, 147
  immunity under CDA, 138
  sovereign immunity, 145
Long-arm statutes, 225

~ M ~

Medical information privacy, 179-
    180
Message boards
  community standards, 16-17
  copyright infringement, 102-103
  defamation. *See* Defamation
  identities of anonymous Internet
      users, 20-25
  personal jurisdiction tests, 231,
      240, 248
  public figures. *See* Public
      figures
  retraction statutes, 158
Metatags, 81-84
Minors. *See* Children and minors

Motion to dismiss on the pleadings
    in defamation actions, 145-
    146
MP3 file distribution, 115-122
Municipal corporations
  criticism of local officials, 147
  immunity under CDA, 138
  sovereign immunity, 145
Music
  file swapping. *See* Music
      technology
  licensing, 123-125
  technology. *See* Music
      technology
  webcasting. *See* Webcasting
Music technology
  encryption, 122
  government involvement, 123
  MP3 files, 115-122
  popularity, 115
  Secure Digital Music Initiative,
      122-123
  watermarking, 122

~ N ~

NAI, 188
".name" domain names, 35
Names
  domains. *See* Domain names
  personal and geographic name
      protection, 71-73
Napster
  Internet music licensing, 123
  "legal Napsters," 124
  peer-to-peer MP3 file swapping,
      115
Nature of Web site test
  categories of Internet activity,
      233-235
  jurisdiction found, 235-238
  jurisdiction not found, 239-247
  requirements, 233-235
Network Advertising Initiative
    (NAI), 188
Network Solutions, Inc. (NSI)
  domain name dispute resolution,
      60

ABOUT BRADFORD PUBLISHING

Founded in 1881, Bradford Publishing Company is Colorado's oldest and most trusted publisher of legal forms and information. Today Bradford Publishing has an inventory of more than 800 legal forms and books specific to Colorado law. Our forms are accurate and up-to-date because we consult with attorneys and state agencies to keep them that way. All of our products are available on our website and many of our forms can be downloaded and completed on-screen. Bradford forms are accepted by the Colorado courts.

Visit the books section of our website to see our growing list of legal publications. If you live or work in the Denver Metro area, you can find all our books, forms and supplies at our store in lower downtown.

BRADFORD PUBLISHING COMPANY

1743 Wazee Street

Denver, Colorado 80202

800-446-2831

303-292-2590

303-298-4014 Fax

For quantity discounts on *Law of the Web*, please give us a call.

www.bradfordpublishing.com

UPDATE SERVICE!

Law of the Web will be published annually so that you can be assured of staying current with all of the important legal developments—court cases and legislation—that impact Internet publishing.

As a special offer, Bradford Publishing will also provide online PDF updates available six months after each publication.

If you would like to be informed when the online updates will be available, or when the new edition of *Law of the Web* will be published, please e-mail marketing@bradfordpublishing.com, enter "*Law of the Web* Update" in the subject line, and provide a mailing address where we can send information letting you know when forthcoming new editions will be available. We will e-mail you with a link to the PDF online update site when it is available.

We do not rent or sell the personal information you provide. This includes, but is not limited to, mailing addresses, telephone or fax numbers, and e-mail addresses.